# THE
# CELEBRITY
# BOOK
# OF LISTS

Also by Ed Lucaire:

*Celebrity Trivia*
*Joan Embery's Collection of*
    *Amazing Animal Facts* (with Joan Embery)

# THE CELEBRITY BOOK OF LISTS

**Fascinating Facts
about
Famous People**

## Ed Lucaire

STEIN AND DAY/Publishers/New York

Third printing 1984
Second printing 1984
**First published in 1984**
Copyright © 1983 by Edward Lucaire
All rights reserved, Stein and Day, Incorporated
Designed by Louis A. Ditizio
Printed in the United States of America
STEIN AND DAY/*Publishers*
Scarborough House
Briarcliff Manor, N.Y. 10510

**Library of Congress Cataloging in Publication Data**

Lucaire, Ed.
 The celebrity book of lists.

 Includes index.
 1. Biography—20th century.   I. Title.
CT105.L79     1984          920'.009'.04          83-61721
ISBN 0-8128-2935-2

## Dedication

To my wife, Lewise, daughter, Laurin, and son, Eddie, who tolerate my eccentricities and remain in good spirit

## Acknowledgments

I wish to thank the following people and institutions for their ideas and contributions:

Benton Arnovitz, Mr. Blackwell, Jacques de Spoelberch, Dr. and Mrs. Dale C. Hager, Charles Hamilton, the Hollywood Women's Press Club, Alice and William Lucaire, Elvira and Maynard Hess, Marketing Evaluations/TV Q Inc., *People* Magazine, *Time* Magazine, *TV Guide*, Steve and Valerie Strauss, Georgette Ulrich, Morris Wattenberg, Gary Gold, John Gabriel, Rod Landau, *The World Almanac*, and the New York Public Library system.

# CONTENTS

# INTRODUCTION

In my first book, *Celebrity Trivia,* I revealed thousands of little-known facts about well-known people. I continued to collect more bits of interesting information and realized that many of them lent themselves to the list format that so many people enjoy.

Since the original Wallace/Wallechinsky *Book of Lists* was published, dozens of similarly motivated books have appeared—sports lists, rock lists, TV lists, movie lists, and the like, but none has dealt exclusively with famous people and, more specifically, contemporary celebrities. Given the public's fascination with celebrities (*People* magazine has 20 million readers per week!), *The Celebrity Book of Lists* seemed like a book idea that would have a wide audience and also would be a fun project.

I pored through biographies, autobiographies, *Who's Who,* and thousands of other nonfiction books. Lists started developing: celebrities who were born on the same day, famous people who changed their names, stars who had plastic surgery, leading men who wear toupees, successful people who were high school dropouts—even famous people who were buried in the same cemeteries! The potential lists seemed endless.

Many authors agonize over the research required to write a book, but I actually enjoyed every hour of it. I hope that you have as much fun reading *The Celebrity Book of Lists* as I had compiling it.

Ed Lucaire
New York City

# The Stars Are Born | 1.

## FOREIGN-BORN
### People Born Where You Might Not Have Expected

| | Place of Birth |
|---|---|
| Dawn Addams | Suffolk, England |
| Ann-Margret | Valsjobyn, Sweden |
| Theodore Bikel | Vienna, Austria |
| Mae Busch | Melbourne, Australia |
| Irving Berlin | Tenum, Russia |
| Susan Blakely | Germany |
| Ray Bloch | Alsace-Lorraine |
| George Brent | Dublin, Ireland |
| Raymond Burr | New Westminster, B.C., Canada |
| Frank Capra | Palermo, Italy |
| Claudia Cardinale | Tunis, Tunisia |
| Charlie Chaplin | London, England |
| Julie Christie | Chukur, India |
| Colin Clive | St. Malo, France |
| Claudette Colbert | Paris, France |
| Dorothy Collins | Windsor, Ont., Canada |
| Michael Collins | Rome, Italy |
| Linda Cristal | Argentina |
| John Daly | Johannesburg, South Africa |
| Yvonne De Carlo | Vancouver, B.C., Canada |
| Olivia De Havilland | Tokyo, Japan |
| Colleen Dewhurst | Montreal, Canada |
| Marie Dressler | Ontario, Canada |
| Jinx Falkenburg | Barcelona, Spain |
| José Ferrer | Santurce, Puerto Rico |

| | |
|---|---|
| Errol Flynn | Hobart, Tasmania |
| Joan Fontaine | Tokyo, Japan |
| Glenn Ford | Quebec, Canada |
| Sam Goldwyn | Warsaw, Poland |
| Bernard Gorcey | Switzerland |
| Lorne Greene | Ottawa, Canada |
| Monty Hall | Winnipeg, Man., Canada |
| June Havoc | Vancouver, B.C., Canada |
| Audrey Hepburn | Brussels, Belgium |
| Bob Hope | London, England |
| Engelbert Humperdinck | Madras, India |
| Olivia Hussey | Buenos Aires, Argentina |
| Walter Huston | Toronto, Canada |
| John Ireland | Vancouver, B.C., Canada |
| Lou Jacobi | Toronto, Canada |
| Al Jolson | St. Petersburg, Russia |
| Katy Jurado | Guadalajara, Mexico |
| Ruby Keeler | Halifax, Nova Scotia, Canada |
| Margot Kidder | Yellow Knife, B.C., Canada |
| Stan Laurel | Ulverston, England |
| Art Linkletter | Saskatchewan, Canada |
| Rich Little | Ottawa, Canada |
| Peter Lorre | Rosenberg, Hungary |
| Sheila MacRae | London, England |
| John McEnroe | Wiesbaden, Germany |
| Audrey Meadows | Wu Chang, China |
| Jayne Meadows | Wu Chang, China |
| David Merrick | Hong Kong |
| Toshiro Mifune | Tsing Tao, China |
| Yves Montand | Monsummano, Italy |
| Rita Moreno | Humacao, Puerto Rico |
| Paul Muni | Lemberg, Russia |
| Mike Nichols | Berlin, Germany |
| Ramon Novarro | Durango, Mexico |
| Maureen O'Hara | Dublin, Ireland |
| Maureen O' Sullivan | Boyle, Ireland |
| Jennifer O'Neill | Rio de Janeiro, Brazil |
| Merle Oberon | Tasmania |
| Mary Pickford | Toronto, Canada |
| Walter Pidgeon | E. St. John, N.B., Canada |
| Andre Previn | Berlin, Germany |
| Victoria Principal | Fukuoka, Japan |

| | |
|---|---|
| Anthony Quinn | Chihuahua, Mexico |
| Luise Rainer | Vienna, Austria |
| Basil Rathbone | Johannesburg, South Africa |
| Edward G. Robinson | Bucharest, Rumania |
| Gilbert Roland | Juarez, Mexico |
| George Romney | Chihuahua, Mexico |
| Morley Safer | Toronto, Canada |
| Mort Sahl | Montreal, Canada |
| Buffy Sainte-Marie | Craven, Saskatchewan |
| George Sanders | St. Petersburg, Russia |
| Michael Sarrazin | Quebec, Canada |
| Franklin J. Schaffner | Tokyo, Japan |
| Mack Sennett | Quebec, Canada |
| William Shatner | Montreal, Canada |
| Norma Shearer | Montreal, Canada |
| Alexis Smith | Penticton, B.C., Canada |
| Hank Snow | Nova Scotia, Canada |
| Sam Spiegel | Jaroslaw, Poland |
| David Steinberg | Winnipeg, Canada |
| Liv Ullmann | Tokyo, Japan |
| Billy Wilder | Vienna, Austria |
| Fay Wray | Alberta, Canada |
| Alan Young | North Shield, England |
| Henny Youngman | London, England |

## PEOPLE BORN IN THE UNITED STATES BUT YOU DIDN'T THINK SO

| | **Place of Birth** |
|---|---|
| Jules Dassin | Middletown, CT |
| Emil Jannings | Brooklyn, NY |
| Richard Lester | Philadelphia, PA |
| Patrick McGoohan | Astoria, NY |
| Lawrence Welk | Strasburg, ND |
| Anna May Wong | Los Angeles, CA |

# CELEBRITIES FROM BROOKLYN

Brooklyn was founded in 1636 by Dutch settlers. It was named Breukelen ("broken land") after a small town near Utrecht in the Netherlands.

As the New York area grew, Brooklyn mushroomed. It is the largest borough in the City of New York and boasts a population that would make it the fourth largest city in the United States. It is larger than Philadelphia but smaller than Los Angeles.

Brooklyn is not just a part of New York—it is a state of mind. Brooklynites grow up in the fiercely competitive environment of an urban melting pot. Each ethnic group tries to outhustle the other. Being "street-wise" is the equivalent of at least a college education.

The following celebrities were born in Brooklyn and managed to hustle their way to celebritydom:

## BORN IN BROOKLYN, NEW YORK

Clara Bow
Scott Brady
Louis Calhern
Jeff Chandler
Chuck Connors
Vic Damone
Marion Davies
Albert Dekker
Dom DeLuise
Neil Diamond
Tom Drake
Richard Dreyfuss
Vince Edwards
Clifton Fadiman
James Farentino
David Frye
William Gargan
George Gershwin
Jackie Gleason
Lou Gossett
Elliot Gould
Buddy Hackett
Susan Hayward

Walter Hampden
Joseph Heller
Edward Everett Horton
Lena Horne
Emil Jannings
Gabe Kaplan
Danny Kaye
Patsy Kelly
Michael Kidd
Alan King
Carole King
Martin Landau
Abbe Lane
Julius LaRosa
Steve Lawrence
Vincent Lopez
Robert Merrill
Mary Tyler Moore
Zero Mostel
Joseph Papp
S. J. Perelman
Buddy Rich
Joan Rivers

18

Mickey Rooney
John Saxon
Murray Schisgal
Erich Segal
Phil Silvers
Mickey Spillane
Lawrence Spivak

Barbara Stanwyck
Connie Stevens
Barbra Streisand
Gene Tierney
Brenda Vaccaro
Eli Wallach
Mae West

# BIRTHDAYS

**January 1** (Capricorn)
William Fox (studio head) 1879
Charles Bickford (actor) 1889
Xavier Cugat (bandleader) 1900
Dana Andrews (actor) 1909

**January 2**
Ann Sothern (actress) 1912

**January 3**
Marion Davies (actress) 1897
ZaSu Pitts (actress) 1900
Ray Milland (actor) 1907
Victor Borge (pianist) 1909
Betty Furness (actress) 1916

**January 4**
Jane Wyman (actress) 1914
Dyan Cannon (actress) 1937

**January 5**
Jean-Pierre Aumont (actor) 1913

**January 6**
Joey Adams (comedian) 1911
Loretta Young (actress) 1913
Danny Thomas
  (comedian, prod.) 1914

**January 7**
Adolph Zukor (studio head) 1873

**January 8**
José Ferrer (actor, dir.) 1912

Yvette Mimieux (actress) 1941
David Bowie (singer, actor) 1947

**January 9**
Gracie Fields (comedienne) 1898
George Balanchine
  (choreographer) 1904
Gypsy Rose Lee (actress) 1914
Fernando Lamas (actor) 1915
Joan Baez (singer) 1941
Susannah York (actress) 1941

**January 10**
Francis X. Bushman
  (actor) 1883
Ray Bolger (actor) 1904
Paul Henreid (actor) 1908
Gisele MacKenzie
  (actress, singer) 1927
Sal Mineo (actor) 1939

**January 11**
Eva Le Gallienne (actress) 1899
Rod Taylor (actor) 1930

**January 12**
Patsy Kelly (actress) 1910
Luise Rainer (actress) 1910

**January 13**
Robert Stack (actor) 1919
Gwen Verdon (actress) 1926

**January 14**
William Bendix (actor) 1906

Tom Tryon (actor, writer) 1926
Faye Dunaway (actress) 1941

**January 15**
Lloyd Bridges (actor) 1913
Maria Schell (actress) 1926
Margaret O'Brien (actress) 1937

**January 16**
Alexander Knox (actor) 1907
Ethel Merman
   (singer, actress) 1909

**January 17**
Mack Sennett (producer) 1884
James Earl Jones (actor) 1931
Sheree North (actress) 1933
Shari Lewis (puppeteer) 1934

**January 18**
Oliver Hardy (comedian) 1892
Cary Grant (actor) 1904
Danny Kaye
   (actor/comedian) 1913
Muhammad Ali (boxer) 1942

**January 19**
Victor Mature (actor) 1916
John Raitt (singer) 1917
Guy Madison (actor) 1922
Jean Stapleton (actress) 1923
Fritz Weaver (actor) 1926
Dolly Parton (singer) 1946
Desi Arnaz, Jr. (actor) 1953

**January 20**
George Burns (comedian) 1896
Leon Ames (actor) 1903
Joy Adamson (author) 1910
Hugh Marlowe (actor) 1911
Federico Fellini (director) 1920
Patricia Neal (actress) 1926
Edwin Aldrin, Jr.
   (astronaut) 1930
Joan Rivers (comedienne) 1937

Shelley Fabares (actress) 1944
Lorenzo Lamas (actor) 1958

**January 21** (Aquarius)
J. Carroll Naish (actor) 1900
Paul Scofield (actor) 1922
Telly Savalas (actor) 1924?
Benny Hill (comedian) 1925
Mac Davis (singer) 1942
Robby Benson (actor) 1955

**January 23**
Dan Duryea (actor) 1907
Jeanne Morgan (actress) 1928
Chita Rivera
   (actress, singer) 1933
Gil Gerard (actor) 1943

**January 24**
Estelle Winwood (actress) 1883
Ernest Borgnine (actor) 1917

**January 25**
Mildred Dunnock (actress) 1906
Dean Jones (actor) 1935

**January 26**
Jimmy Van Heusen
   (song writer) 1913
Paul Newman (actor) 1925
William Redfield (actor) 1927
Eartha Kitt (singer) 1928
Roger Vadim (director) 1928
Jules Feiffer (cartoonist) 1929

**January 27**
William Randolph Hearst, Jr.
   (publisher) 1908
Skitch Henderson
   (bandleader) 1918
Donna Reed (actress) 1921
Troy Donahue (actor) 1938

**January 28**
Alan Alda (actor) 1936

Mikhail Baryshnikov
(dancer) 1948

**January 29**
Clara Bow (actress) 1905
W. C. Fields (comedian) 1880
John Forsythe (actor) 1918
Paddy Chayevsky (writer) 1923
Noel Harrison
(actor, singer) 1936
Tom Selleck (actor) 19??
Germaine Greer (writer) 1939
Katharine Ross (actress) 1943

**January 30**
David Wayne (actor) 1914
John Ireland (actor) 1915
Dick Martin (comedian) 1922
Dorothy Malone (actress) 1925
Harold Prince
(producer, dir.) 1928
Gene Hackman (actor) 1931
Tammy Grimes (actress) 1934
Vanessa Redgrave (actress) 1937
Boris Spassky
(chess player) 1937

**January 31**
Eddie Cantor (comedian) 1892
Tallulah Bankhead
(actress) 1903
Garry Moore
(TV personality) 1915
Mario Lanza (singer) 1921
Carol Channing
(comedienne) 1923
Joanne Dru (actress) 1923
Norman Mailer (author) 1923
Jean Simmons (actress) 1929
James Franciscus (actor) 1934
Suzanne Pleshette (actress) 1937

**February 1**
John Ford (director) 1895

Clark Gable (actor) 1901
S. J. Perelman (writer) 1904
Hildegarde (singer) 1906

**February 2**
Jascha Heifetz (violinist) 1901
Eddie Foy, Jr.
(dancer, actor) 1905
James Dickey (author, poet) 1923
Shelley Berman (comedian) 1926
Stan Getz (jazz musician) 1927
Elaine Stritch (actress) 1928
Tom Smothers (comedian) 1937

**February 3**
Bibi Osterwald (actress) 1920
Joey Bishop (comedian) 1919
Peggy Ann Garner
(actress) 1932

**February 4**
Ida Lupino (actress) 1918
Betty Friedan (feminist) 1921
Alice Cooper (rock singer) 1948

**February 5**
John Carradine (actor) 1906
Red Buttons
(comedian, actor) 1919

**February 6**
Ronald Reagan
(actor, U.S. president) 1911
Zsa Zsa Gabor (actress) 1923
Rip Torn (actor) 1931
François Truffaut
(director) 1932
Mike Farrell (actor) 1942
Fabian Forte (singer) 1943

**February 7**
Eubie Blake
(pianist, composer) 1883
Buster Crabbe
(actor, athlete) 1908

21

Eddie Bracken (actor) 1920
Keefe Brasselle (actor) 1923

**February 8**
Dame Edith Evans
    (actress) 1888
King Vidor (director) 1895
Ray Middleton (actor) 1907
Lana Turner (actress) 1920
Jack Lemmon (actor) 1925

**February 9**
Peggy Wood (actress) 1892
Carmen Miranda
    (actress, singer) 1909
Kathryn Grayson
    (actress, singer) 1923
Carole King
    (singer, composer) 1941
Mia Farrow (actress) 1946

**February 10**
Jimmy Durante (comedian) 1893
Dame Judith Anderson
    (actress) 1898
Lon Chaney, Jr. (actor) 1906
Joyce Grenfell (actress) 1910
Larry Adler (musician) 1914
Roberta Flack (singer) 1940

**February 11**
Joseph Mankiewicz
    (writer, director) 1909
Eva Gabor (actress) 1925
Kim Stanley (actress) 1925
Virginia Johnson
    (sexologist) 1925
Tina Louise (actress) 1934
Burt Reynolds (actor) 1936

**February 12**
Omar Bradley (general) 1893
Lorne Greene (actor) 1915
Forrest Tucker (actor) 1919

Franco Zeffirelli (director) 1923
Joe Garagiola (baseball player;
    TV personality) 1926

**February 13**
Tennessee Ernie Ford
    (singer) 1919
Eileen Farrell (singer) 1920
Kim Novak (actress) 1933
George Segal (actor) 1936
Carol Lynley (actress) 1942

**February 14**
Jack Benny (comedian) 1894
Thelma Ritter (actress) 1905
Mel Allen
    (sports announcer) 1913
Jimmy Hoffa (labor leader) 1913
James Pike
    (religious leader) 1913
Hugh Downs
    (TV personality) 1921
Florence Henderson
    (actress) 1934

**February 15**
John Barrymore (actor) 1882
Harold Arlen (composer) 1905
Cesar Romero (actor) 1914
Kevin McCarthy (actor) 1914
Harvey Korman
    (actor, comedian) 1927
Claire Bloom (actress) 1931

**February 16**
Chester Morris (actor) 1901
Edgar Bergen
    (ventriloquist) 1903
George F. Kennan
    (diplomat) 1904
Brian Bedford (actor) 1935
Sonny Bono (singer) 1935

## February 17
Marian Anderson (singer) 1902
Arthur Kennedy (actor) 1914
Hal Holbrook (actor) 1925
Alan Bates (actor) 1934

## February 18
Adolph Menjou (actor) 1890
Billy De Wolfe (actor) 1907
Dane Clark (actor) 1915
Bill Cullen (TV personality) 1920
Jack Palance (actor) 1920
Helen Gurley Brown
  (editor) 1922
George Kennedy (actor) 1925

## February 19
Sir Cedric Hardwick
  (actor) 1893
Louis Calhern (actor) 1895
Merle Oberon (actress) 1911
Stan Kenton (musician) 1912
George Rose (actor) 1920
Lee Marvin (actor) 1924

## February 20 (Pisces)
John Daly (TV personality) 1914
Sidney Poitier (actor) 1924
Robert Altman (director) 1925
Nancy Wilson (singer) 1937
Jennifer O'Neill (actress) 1949
Buffy Sainte-Marie (1941)

## February 21
Ann Sheridan (actress) 1915
Sam Peckinpah (director) 1925
Hubert Givenchy
  (fashion designer) 1927
Nina Simone (singer) 1933

## February 22
Luis Buñuel (director) 1900
Sheldon Leonard
  (actor, producer) 1907

Robert Young (actor) 1907
John Mills (actor) 1908

## February 23
Peter Fonda (actor) 1939

## February 24
Marjorie Main (actress) 1890
Abe Vigoda (actor) 1921
James Farentino (actor) 1938

## February 25
Zeppo Marx (comedian) 1901
Jim Backus (actor) 1913
Tom Courtenay (actor) 1937
George Harrison (singer) 1943

## February 26
Robert Alda (actor) 1914
Jackie Gleason (comedian) 1916
Betty Hutton (actress) 1921
Margaret Leighton
  (actress) 1922
Tony Randall (actor) 1924
Fats Domino (singer) 1928
Johnny Cash (singer) 1932

## February 27
Franchot Tone (actor) 1905
James T. Farrell (author) 1904
Joan Bennett (actress) 1910
Peter De Vries (author) 1910
Irwin Shaw (novelist) 1913
Guy Mitchell (actor) 1927
Joanne Woodward (actress) 1930
Elizabeth Taylor (actress) 1932

## February 28
Milt Caniff (cartoonist) 1907
Vincente Minnelli
  (director) 1913
Zero Mostel (actor) 1915
Tommy Tune
  (dancer, choreographer) 1939

Bernadette Peters
(actress, singer) 1949

**February 29**
William Wellman
(director) 1896

**March 1**
David Niven (actor) 1910
Dinah Shore (singer) 1917
Harry Belafonte (singer) 1927

**March 2**
Jennifer Jones (actress) 1919
Desi Arnaz
(bandleader, producer) 1917

**March 3**
Jean Harlow (actress) 1911

**March 4**
Charles Goren
(bridge expert) 1901
Miriam Makeba (singer) 1932

**March 5**
Rex Harrison (actor) 1908
Pier Paolo Pasolini
(director) 1922
Jack Cassidy (actor) 1927
Dean Stockwell (actor) 1936
Eddie Hodges (actor) 1947
Eugene Fodor (violinist) 1950

**March 6**
Ed McMahon
(TV personality) 1923
L. Gordon Cooper, Jr.
(astronaut) 1927

**March 7**
Anna Magnani (actress) 1908
Anthony Armstrong-Jones
(photographer) 1930

**March 8**
Sam Jaffe (actor) 1898

Cyd Charisse
(dancer, actress) 1923
Lynn Redgrave (actress) 1943

**March 9**
Will Geer (actor) 1902
Mickey Spillane (writer) 1918
Andre Courreges
(fashion designer) 1923
Fernando Bujones
(ballet dancer) 1955

**March 10**
Barry Fitzgerald (actor) 1888
David Rabe (playwright) 1940

**March 11**
Lawrence Welk
(bandleader) 1903
Ralph Abernathy
(civil rights leader) 1926

**March 12**
Roger L. Stevens
(producer) 1910
Gordon MacRae (singer) 1921
Edward Albee
(playwright) 1928
Barbara Feldon (actress) 1941
Liza Minnelli
(singer, actress) 1946
James Taylor (singer) 1948

**March 13**
Sammy Kaye (bandleader) 1910

**March 14**
Max Shulman (writer) 1919
Frank Borman (astronaut) 1928
Michael Caine (actor) 1933
Eugene Andrew Cernan
(astronaut) 1934
Rita Tushingham (actress) 1942

**March 15**
George Brent (actor) 1904

MacDonald Carey (actor) 1913
Harry James (bandleader) 1916
Alan Bean (astronaut) 1932

**March 16**
Robert Rossen
  (director, prod.) 1908
Jerry Lewis
  (comedian, director) 1926
Walter Cunningham
  (astronaut) 1932

**March 17**
Alfred Newman
  (composer) 1901
Frederick Brisson
  (producer) 1913
Mercedes McCambridge
  (actress) 1918
Rudolf Nureyev
  (ballet dancer) 1938
Monique Van Vooren
  (actress, author) 1938

**March 18**
Edward Everett Horton
  (actor) 1887
Peter Graves (actor) 1926

**March 19**
Kent Smith (actor) 1907
Ursula Andress (actress) 1938

**March 20**
Ozzie Nelson (actor) 1907
Michael Redgrave (actor) 1908
Larry Elgart (bandleader) 1922
Carl Reiner
  (actor, writer, director) 1922
Ray Goulding (comedian) 1922
Hal Linden (actor) 1931
Jerry Reed (singer) 1937

**March 21** (Aries)
Peter Brooks (director) 1925
Cesar Chavez (labor leader) 1927

James Coco (actor) 1929
Kathleen Widdoes (actress) 1939

**March 22**
Chico Marx (comedian) 1891
Karl Malden (actor) 1914
Marcel Marceau (mime) 1923
Stephen Sondheim
  (composer, lyricist) 1930
William Shatner (actor) 1931
May Britt (actress) 1936

**March 23**
Joan Crawford (actress) 1908
Akira Kurosawa (director) 1910

**March 24**
Fatty Arbuckle (actor) 1887
Byron Janis (pianist) 1928
Steve McQueen (actor) 1930

**March 25**
Ed Begley (actor) 1901
David Lean (director) 1908
Nancy Kelly (actress) 1921
Anita Bryant (singer) 1940
Aretha Franklin (singer) 1942
Elton John (singer) 1947

**March 26**
Tennessee Williams
  (playwright) 1911
Pierre Boulez (conductor) 1925
Leonard Nimoy (actor) 1931
Alan Arkin (actor) 1934
James Caan (actor) 1939
Erica Jong (writer) 1942
Diana Ross (singer) 1944

**March 27**
Gloria Swanson (actress) 1899
Budd Schulberg (writer) 1914
David Janssen (actor) 1930
Michael York (actor) 1942

**March 28**
Nelson Algren (author) 1909
Dirk Bogarde (actor) 1921
Freddie Bartholomew
  (actor) 1924
Ken Howard (actor) 1944

**March 29**
Pearl Bailey (singer) 1918
Eileen Heckart
  (actress) 1919

**March 30**
Frankie Laine (singer) 1913
McGeorge Bundy
  (statesman) 1919
Warren Beatty
  (actor, director) 1937

**March 31**
Henry Morgan
  (comedian, critic) 1915
Richard Kiley (actor) 1922
Sydney Chaplin (actor) 1926
Shirley Jones (actress) 1934
Herb Alpert (musician) 1935
Richard Chamberlain
  (actor) 1935
Israel Horowitz
  (playwright) 1939

**April 1**
Wallace Beery (actor) 1886
George Grizzard (actor) 1928
Jane Powell (actress) 1929
Debbie Reynolds (actress) 1932
Ali MacGraw (actress) 1939

**April 2**
Buddy Ebsen (actor) 1908
Sir Alec Guinness (actor) 1914
Jack Webb
  (actor, producer) 1920
Rita Gam (actress) 1928

**April 3**
Leslie Howard (actor) 1893
George Jessel (entertainer) 1898
Marlon Brando (actor) 1924
Doris Day (actress) 1924
Marsha Mason (actress) 1942
Wayne Newton (singer) 1942

**April 4**
Frances Langford (singer) 1913
Elmer Bernstein
  (composer) 1922

**April 5**
Spencer Tracy (actor) 1900
Chester Bowles (diplomat) 1901
Melvyn Douglas (actor) 1901
Bette Davis (actress) 1908
Gregory Peck (actor) 1916
Arthur Hailey (novelist) 1920
Roger Corman (director) 1926
Frank Gorshin
  (impressionist) 1934
Michael Moriarty (actor) 1941

**April 6**
André Previn (conductor) 1929
Merle Haggard
  (singer, songwriter) 1937
Billy Dee Williams (actor) 1938

**April 7**
James Garner (actor) 1928
Donald Barthelme
  (novelist) 1931
Francis Ford Coppola
  (director) 1939
David Frost
  (producer, entertainer) 1939

**April 8**
Sonja Henie (ice skater) 1912
Carmen McRae (singer) 1922
Franco Corelli

(opera singer) 1923
Jacques Brel
   (singer, composer) 1929
John Gavin
   (actor, diplomat) 1935

## April 9
Ward Bond (actor) 1905
Antal Dorati (conductor) 1906
Hugh Hefner (publisher) 1919
Jean-Paul Belmondo (actor) 1933

## April 10
George Arliss (actor) 1868
Tim McCoy (actor) 1891
Chuck Connors (actor) 1921
Omar Sharif (actor) 1932
David Halberstam (writer) 1934

## April 11
Paul Douglas (actor) 1907
Oleg Cassini
   (fashion designer) 1913
Cameron Mitchell (actor) 1918
Joel Grey (actor) 1932

## April 12
Ann Miller
   (dancer, actress) 1919
David Cassidy (singer) 1950

## April 13
Samuel Beckett
   (playwright) 1906
Howard Keel (singer, actor) 1919

## April 14
Sir John Gielgud (actor) 1904
Rod Steiger (actor) 1925
Bradford Dillman (actor) 1930
Loretta Lynn (singer) 1932
Tony Perkins (actor) 1932
Julie Christie (actress) 1941

## April 15
Roy Clark (singer) 1933
Elizabeth Montgomery
   (actress) 1933

## April 16
Charlie Chaplin (comedian) 1889
Peter Ustinov (actor) 1921
Kingsley Amis (writer) 1922
Lindsay Anderson
   (director) 1923
Henry Mancini (composer) 1923
Edie Adams (actress) 1929
Shani Wallis (actress) 1933
Bobby Vinton (singer) 1935

## April 17
William Holden (actor) 1918
Genevieve (entertainer) 1930

## April 18
Huntington Hartford
   (A&P heir) 1911
Clive Revill (actor) 1930
Charley Pride (singer) 1938
Hayley Mills (actress) 1946

## April 19
Don Adams (comedian) 1927
Hugh O'Brian (actor) 1930
Jayne Mansfield (actress) 1933
Dudley Moore
   (actor, composer) 1935

## April 20 (Taurus)
Harold Lloyd (comedian) 1893
Lionel Hampton (musician) 1914
Nina Foch (actress) 1924
Ryan O'Neal (actor) 1941
Jessica Lange (actress) 1949

## April 21
Anthony Quinn (actor) 1916
Silvana Mangano (actress) 1930

## April 22
Eddie Albert (actor) 1908
Charlotte Rae (actress) 1926
Jack Nicholson (actor) 1937
Glen Campbell (singer) 1938

## April 23
Simone Simon (actress) 1914
Janet Blair (actress) 1921
Shirley Temple Black
   (actress, diplomat) 1928
Sandra Dee (actress) 1942

## April 24
Shirley MacLaine (actress) 1934
Barbra Streisand
   (singer, actress) 1942

## April 25
Ella Fitzgerald (singer) 1918
Melissa Hayden (ballerina) 1928
Al Pacino (actor) 1940

## April 26
Anita Loos (writer) 1893
Bambi Linn (dancer) 1926
Carol Burnett (actress) 1936

## April 27
Jack Klugman (actor) 1922
Anouk Aimee (actress) 1934
Sandy Dennis (actress) 1937

## April 28
Lionel Barrymore (actor) 1878
Robert Anderson
   (playwright) 1917
Carolyn Jones (actress) 1933
Ann-Margret (actress) 1941

## April 29
Tom Ewell (actor) 1909
Celeste Holm (actress) 1919
Keith Baxter (actor) 1933

Rod McKuen
   (singer, composer) 1933

## April 30
Eve Arden (actress) 1912
Corinne Calvet (actress) 1926
Cloris Leachman (actress) 1926

## May 1
Kate Smith (singer) 1909
Glenn Ford (actor) 1916
Danielle Darrieux (actress) 1917
Jack Paar (comedian) 1918
Joseph Heller (novelist) 1923
Scott Carpenter (astronaut) 1925
Judy Collins (singer) 1939

## May 2
Brian Aherne (actor) 1902
Bing Crosby (singer) 1904
Theodore Bikel
   (actor, singer) 1924
King Hussein I
   (ruler of Jordan) 1935
Engelbert Humperdinck
   (singer) 1936

## May 3
Walter Slezak (actor) 1902
Mary Astor (actress) 1906
William Inge (playwright) 1913
Betty Comden
   (writer, lyricist) 1919
James Brown (singer) 1934
Samantha Eggar (actress) 1939

## May 4
Howard Da Silva (actor) 1909
Audrey Hepburn (actress) 1929

## May 5
Freeman F. Gosden (actor) 1899
Tyrone Power (actor) 1914
Alice Faye (actress) 1915

Pat Carroll
(comedienne, actress) 1927

**May 6**
Rudolph Valentino (actor) 1895
Max Orphuls (director) 1902
Stewart Granger (actor) 1913
Orson Welles
(actor, director) 1915

**May 7**
Gary Cooper (actor) 1901
Darren McGavin (actor) 1922
Anne Baxter (actress) 1923
Teresa Brewer (singer) 1931

**May 8**
Fernandel
(actor, comedian) 1903
Don Rickles (comedian) 1926
Peter Benchley (author) 1940
Ricky Nelson (singer, actor) 1940
Melissa Gilbert (actress) 1964

**May 9**
Albert Finney (actor) 1936
Glenda Jackson (actress) 1936
Candice Bergen (actress) 1946

**May 10**
Fred Astaire (dancer) 1899
David O. Selznick
(producer) 1902
Nancy Walker (actress) 1922

**May 11**
Irving Berlin (songwriter) 1888
Phil Silvers (comedian) 1912
Mort Sahl (comedian) 1927
Doug McClure (actor) 1938

**May 12**
Wilfred Hyde-White (actor) 1903
Burt Bacharach (composer) 1929

**May 13**
Daphne Du Maurier

(novelist) 1907
Bea Arthur (actress) 1926

**May 14**
Bobby Darin (singer) 1936

**May 15**
Clifton Fadiman
(critic, writer) 1904
Joseph Cotton (actor) 1905
James Mason (actor) 1909
Constance Cummings
(actress) 1910
Eddy Arnold (singer) 1918
Richard Avedon
(photographer) 1923
Peter Shaffer (playwright) 1926
Anthony Shaffer
(playwright) 1926
Anna Maria Alberghetti
(singer) 1936
Stevie Wonder (singer) 1950

**May 16**
Henry Fonda (actor) 1905
Margaret Sullavan
(actress) 1911
Woody Herman (musician) 1913
Liberace (pianist) 1919

**May 17**
Maureen O'Sullivan
(actress) 1911
Dennis Hooper (actor) 1936
Sugar Ray Leonard (boxer) 1955

**May 18**
Frank Capra (director) 1897
Perry Como (singer) 1913
Pierre Balmain
(fashion designer) 1914
Dame Margot Fonteyn
(ballerina) 1919
Robert Morse (actor) 1931

Reggie Jackson
(baseball player) 1945

**May 19**
David Hartman
(TV personality) 1935

**May 20**
James Stewart (actor) 1908
Moshe Dayan
(Israeli statesman) 1915
George Gobel (comedian) 1920
Cher Bono (singer, actress) 1946

**May 21** (Gemini)
Robert Montgomery (actor) 1904
Raymond Burr (actor) 1917
Dennis Day (singer) 1917
Peggy Cass (comedienne) 1926

**May 22**
Sir Laurence Olivier (actor) 1907
Charles Aznavour
(singer, actor) 1924
Peter Nero (pianist) 1934
Richard Benjamin (actor) 1938
Susan Strasberg (actress) 1938
Michael Sarrazin (actor) 1940

**May 23**
Douglas Fairbanks (actor) 1883
Artie Shaw (bandleader) 1910
Rosemary Clooney (singer) 1928

**May 24**
Lilli Palmer
(actress, author) 1914
Siobhan McKenna (actress) 1923
Bob Dylan (singer) 1941

**May 25**
Jeanne Crain (actress) 1925
Miles Davis (musician) 1926
Leslie Uggams (singer) 1943

**May 26**
Al Jolson (singer) 1886

John Wayne (actor) 1907
Robert Morley (actor) 1908
Peter Cushing (actor) 1913
Peggy Lee (singer) 1920
James Arness (actor) 1923
Alec McCowen (actor) 1925

**May 27**
Vincent Price (actor) 1911
John Cheever (writer) 1912
Christopher Lee (actor) 1922
Lou Gosset (actor) 1936

**May 28**
Carroll Baker (actress) 1935
Gladys Knight (singer) 1944

**May 29**
Bob Hope (comedian) 1903

**May 30**
Mel Blanc (voice-over man) 1908
Benny Goodman (musician) 1909
Hugh Griffith (actor) 1912
Clint Walker (actor) 1927
Keir Dullea (actor) 1936
Michael J. Pollard (actor) 1939

**May 31**
Don Ameche (actor) 1908
Clint Eastwood (actor) 1931

**June 1**
Frank Morgan (actor) 1890
Molly Picon (actress) 1898
Nelson Riddle (conductor) 1921
Joan Caulfield (actress) 1922
Andy Griffith (actor) 1926
Marilyn Monroe (actress) 1926
Pat Boone (singer) 1934
Cleavon Little (actor) 1939

**June 2**
Hedda Hopper (columnist) 1890
Johnny Weissmuller
(swimmer, actor) 1904
Pete Conrad (astronaut) 1930

Sally Kellerman (actress) 1938
Stacy Keach (actor) 1941
Marvin Hamlisch
(pianist, composer) 1944

**June 3**
Paulette Goddard (actress) 1911
Susan Hayward (actress) 1919
Alain Resnais (director) 1922
Tony Curtis (actor) 1925
Colleen Dewhurst (actress) 1926
Allen Ginsberg (poet) 1926

**June 4**
Rosalind Russell (actress) 1908
Charles Collingwood
(TV commentator) 1917
Robert Merrill (baritone) 1919
Gene Barry (actor) 1922

**June 5**
Tony Richardson (director) 1928

**June 6**
Walter Abel (actor) 1898

**June 7**
Jessica Tandy (actress) 1909
Gwendolyn Brooks (poet) 1917
Tom Jones (singer) 1940
Nikki Giovanni (poet) 1943

**June 8**
Robert Preston (actor) 1918
Alexis Smith (actress) 1921
Dana Wynter (actress) 1930
James Darren (actor) 1936
Nancy Sinatra (singer) 1940

**June 9**
S. N. Behrman (writer) 1893
Robert Cummings (actor) 1910
Les Paul (musician) 1916
George Axelrod
(playwright) 1922

**June 10**
Sessue Hayakawa (actor) 1890

Frederick Loewe
(composer) 1904
Sir Terence Rattigan
(writer) 1911
Judy Garland
(singer, actress) 1922
June Haver (actress) 1926
F. Lee Bailey (lawyer) 1933

**June 11**
Jacques Cousteau
(marine biologist) 1910

**June 12**
Uta Hagen (actress) 1919
Vic Damone (singer) 1928
Jim Nabors (actor) 1932

**June 13**
Basil Rathbone (actor) 1892
Paul Lynde (actor) 1926
Richard Thomas (actor) 1951

**June 14**
Burl Ives (singer) 1909
Dorothy McGuire (actress) 1919
Dennis Weaver (actor) 1925

**June 15**
Erik Ericson
(psychoanalyst) 1902
Trini Lopez (singer) 1937

**June 16**
Stan Laurel (comedian) 1890
Jack Albertson (actor) 1910
Katherine Graham
(publisher) 1917
Erich Segal (author) 1937

**June 17**
Ralph Bellamy (actor) 1904
Dean Martin (singer) 1917
Kingman Brewster
(college president) 1919
Beryl Reid (actress) 1920

31

**June 18**
Jeanette MacDonald
   (actress) 1901
Sammy Cahn (composer) 1913
Richard Boone (actor) 1917
Paul McCartney
   (singer, composer) 1942

**June 19**
Guy Lombardo
   (bandleader) 1902
George Voskevec (actor) 1905
Mildred Natwick (actress) 1908
Louis Jourdan (actor) 1920
Nancy Marchand (actress) 1928
Marisa Pavan (actress) 1932
Pier Angeli (singer) 1932
Gena Rowlands (actress) 1936
Malcolm McDowell (actor) 1943

**June 20**
Lillian Hellman
   (author, playwright) 1905
Chet Atkins (guitarist) 1924
Audie Murphy
   (actor, war hero) 1924

**June 21**
Jane Russell (actress) 1921
Judy Holliday (actress) 1922
Maureen Stapleton
   (actress) 1925

**June 22** (Cancer)
Billy Wilder (director) 1906
Gower Champion
   (choreographer) 1921
Joseph Papp
   (producer, director) 1921
Bill Blass
   (fashion designer) 1922
Kris Kristofferson (singer) 1936

**June 23**
Jean Anouilh (playwright) 1910

Larry Blyden (actor) 1925
Bob Fosse
   (choreographer, director) 1927

**June 24**
Phil Harris (actor) 1906
Norman Cousins
   (publisher) 1915
Pete Hamill (writer) 1935

**June 25**
George Abbott (producer) 1889
Sidney Lumet (director) 1924
June Lockhart (actress) 1925
Carly Simon (singer) 1945

**June 26**
Peter Lorre (actor) 1904
Eleanor Parker (actress) 1922

**June 28**
Richard Rodgers
   (composer) 1902
Eric Ambler (writer) 1909
Sally Struthers (actress) 1948

**June 29**
Nelson Eddy (actor, singer) 1901
Frank Loesser (composer)
   1910

**June 30**
Glenda Farrell (actress) 1904
Lena Horne (singer) 1917
Buddy Rich (drummer) 1917
Nancy Dussault (actress) 1936

**July 1**
Olivia De Havilland
   (actress) 1916
Farley Granger (actor) 1925
Leslie Caron (actress) 1931
Karen Black (actress) 1942
Genevieve Bujold (actress) 1942
Dan Aykroyd (comedian) 1952

Princess Diana
   (future queen) 1961

**July 2**
Barry Gray
   (radio talk show host) 1916
Dan Rowan (comedian) 1922

**July 3**
George Sanders (actor) 1906
Dorothy Kilgallen
   (columnist) 1913

**July 4**
Louis Armstrong
   (musician) 1900
George Murphy
   (actor, politician) 1902
Eva Marie Saint (actress) 1924
Neil Simon (playwright) 1927
Stephen Boyd (actor) 1928
Gina Lollobrigida (actress) 1928

**July 5**
Andre Gromyko (diplomat) 1909

**July 6**
Merv Griffin
   (talk show host) 1925
Janet Leigh (actress) 1927
Della Reese (singer) 1932
Vladimir Ashkenazy
   (pianist) 1937

**July 7**
George Cukor (director) 1899
Vittorio De Sica (director) 1901
Pierre Cardin
   (fashion designer) 1922
Vince Edwards (actor) 1928
Ringo Starr
   (singer, drummer) 1940

**July 8**
Billy Eckstine (singer) 1914
Faye Emerson (actress) 1917

Steve Lawrence (singer) 1935
Marcia Rodd (actress) 1940
Kim Darby (actress) 1948

**July 9**
Edward Heath
   (British prime minister) 1916

**July 10**
Saul Bellow (author) 1915
David Brinkley
   (TV journalist) 1920
Arlo Guthrie (singer)
   1947

**July 11**
Yul Brynner (actor) 1920
Tab Hunter (actor) 1931

**July 12**
Buckminster Fuller
   (architect) 1895
Milton Berle (comedian) 1908
Joey Faye (comedian) 1910
Van Cliburn (pianist) 1934
Bill Cosby (comedian) 1937
Cheryl Ladd (actress) 1951

**July 13**
Sidney Blackmer (actor) 1895
Dave Garroway (TV host) 1913

**July 14**
Ken Murray (producer) 1903
Terry-Thomas (actor) 1911
Ingmar Bergman
   (director) 1918
Arthur Laurent
   (playwright) 1918
John Chancellor
   (TV journalist) 1927
Polly Bergen (actress) 1930
Robert Stephens
   (actor, director) 1931
Roosevelt Grier (athlete) 1932

## July 15
Dorothy Fields
  (librettist, lyricist) 1905

## July 16
Barbara Stanwyck
  (actress) 1907
Ginger Rogers
  (actress, dancer) 1911

## July 17
James Cagney (actor) 1900
William Gargan (actor) 1905
Art Linkletter
  (TV personality) 1912
Phyllis Diller (comedienne) 1917
Diahann Carroll (singer) 1931

## July 18
Keye Luke (actor) 1904
Clifford Odets (playwright) 1906
E. G. Marshall (actor) 1910
Hume Cronyn (actor) 1911
Red Skelton (comedian) 1913
John Glenn (U.S. senator) 1921

## July 19
Pat Hingle (actor) 1924
Vicki Carr (singer) 1942

## July 20
Sir Edmund Hillary
  (mountaineer) 1919
Lola Albright (actress) 1925
Sally Ann Howe (actress) 1934
Diana Rigg (actress) 1938
Natalie Wood (actress) 1938

## July 21
Al Hirschfeld (cartoonist) 1903
Don Knotts (comedian) 1924
Robin Williams (comedian) 1952

## July 22 (Leo)
Rose Fitzgerald Kennedy
  (matriarch) 1890

Orson Bean
  (actor, comedian) 1928
Vivien Merchant (actress) 1929
Oscar De La Renta
  (fashion designer) 1932

## July 23
Gloria DeHaven (actress) 1925
Bert Convy (actor) 1934

## July 24
Walter Brennan (actor) 1894
Jack Gilford (actor) 1907

## July 26
Blake Edwards
  (director, producer) 1922
Jason Robards, Jr. (actor) 1922
Stanley Kubrick (director) 1928
Mick Jagger (singer) 1944

## July 27
Keenan Wynn (actor) 1916

## July 28
Rudy Vallee (singer) 1901
Jacques D'Amboise
  (dancer) 1934
Peter Duchin (bandleader) 1937

## July 29
Theda Bara (actress) 1890
William Powell (actor) 1892
Clara Bow (actress) 1905
Thelma Todd (actress) 1905
Richard Egan (actor) 1923
David Warner (actor) 1941

## July 30
Ben Piazza (actor) 1934
Paul Anka (singer) 1941
Peter Bogdanovich
  (director) 1939

## July 31
France Nuyen (actress) 1939

## August 1
Arthur Hill (actor) 1922
Lionel Bart (songwriter) 1930
Geoffrey Holder (dancer) 1930

## August 2
Myrna Loy (actress) 1905
Gary Merrill (actor) 1914
James Baldwin (writer) 1924
Carroll O'Connor (actor) 1924
John Dexter (director) 1925
Peter O'Toole (actor) 1933

## August 3
Dolores Del Rio (actress) 1905
Marilyn Maxwell (actress) 1922
Tony Bennett (singer) 1926
Martin Sheen (actor) 1940

## August 5
John Huston (director) 1906
Robert Taylor (actor) 1911
Neil Armstrong (astronaut) 1930
Loni Anderson (actress) 19??

## August 6
Louella Parsons (columnist) 1881
Billie Burke (actress) 1886
Lucille Ball (actress) 1911
Robert Mitchum (actor) 1917

## August 7
Ann Harding (actress) 1902
Robert Moore
    (actor, director) 1927

## August 8
Sylvia Sidney (actress) 1910
Rudy Gernreich
    (fashion designer) 1922
Dino De Laurentiis
    (producer) 1919
Esther Williams (actress) 1923

Dustin Hoffman (actor) 1937
Connie Stevens (singer) 1938

## August 9
Robert Shaw (actor) 1927

## August 10
Norma Shearer (actress) 1900
Noah Beery, Jr. (actor) 1916
Rhonda Fleming (actress) 1923
Jimmy Dean (singer) 1928
Eddie Fisher (singer) 1928

## August 11
Lloyd Nolan (actor) 1902
Jean Parker (actress) 1915
Arlene Dahl (actress) 1924
Mike Douglas (TV host) 1925

## August 12
Cecil B. De Mille (producer) 1881
Cantinflas (comedian) 1911
Michael Kidd
    (choreographer) 1919
George Hamilton (actor) 1939

## August 13
Bert Lahr (actor, comedian) 1895
Alfred Hitchcock (director) 1899
Buddy Rogers (actor) 1904
Gene Raymond (actor) 1908
Fidel Castro (Cuban leader) 1926

## August 14
Nehemiah Persoff (actor) 1920
Buddy Greco (singer) 1926
Alice Ghostley (actress) 1926
Earl Weaver
    (baseball manager) 1930

## August 15
Ethel Barrymore (actress) 1879
Julia Child (chef) 1912
Wendy Hiller (actress) 1912
Mike Connors (actor) 1921
Janice Rule (actress) 1931

35

## August 16
Ann Blyth (actress) 1928
Robert Culp (actor) 1930
Eydie Gorme (singer) 1932
Anita Gillette (actress) 1936

## August 17
Mae West (actress) 1892
Maureen O'Hara (actress) 1921
Robert De Niro (actor) 1943

## August 18
Shelley Winters (actress) 1922
Roman Polanski (director) 1933
Robert Redford
   (actor, director) 1937

## August 19
Malcolm Forbes
   (publisher) 1919
Jill St. John (actress) 1940

## August 20
Jacqueline Susann (author) 1921
Carla Fracci (dancer) 1936
Isaac Hayes (composer) 1942

## August 21
Count Basie (bandleader) 1904
Mark Crowley (playwright) 1936
Patty McCormack (actress) 1945

## August 22 (Virgo)
Denton Cooley
   (heart surgeon) 1920
Ray Bradbury
   (sci-fi writer) 1920
Valerie Harper (actress) 1940
Cindy Williams (actress) 1947

## August 23
Gene Kelly (dancer, dir.) 1912
Vera Miles (actress) 1929

## August 25
Ruby Keeler (actress) 1909
Van Johnson (actor) 1916
Mel Ferrer (actor) 1917
Leonard Bernstein
   (conductor) 1918
Sean Connery (actor) 1930

## August 26
Christopher Isherwood
   (author) 1904
Ronny Graham
   (actor, songwriter) 1919
Ben Bradlee (editor) 1921

## August 27
Martha Raye (actress) 1916
Tommy Sands (singer) 1937
Tuesday Weld (actress) 1943

## August 28
Charles Boyer (actor) 1899
James Wong Howe
   (cinematographer) 1899
Sam Levene (actor) 1905
Donald O'Connor (actor) 1925
Ben Gazzara (actor) 1930

## August 29
Ingrid Bergman (actress) 1916
George Montgomery (actor) 1916
Richard Attenborough
   (actor, director) 1923
Elliott Gould (actor) 1938

## August 30
Raymond Massey (actor) 1896
Fred MacMurray (actor) 1908
Shirley Booth (actress) 1909
Joan Blondell (actress) 1912
Elizabeth Ashley (actress) 1939

## August 31
Fredric March (actor) 1897

Arthur Godfrey
(TV personality) 1903
Dore Schary
(producer, writer) 1905
Alan Jay Lerner (lyricist) 1918
Richard Basehart (actor) 1919
Buddy Hackett (comedian) 1924
James Coburn (actor) 1928
Warren Berlinger (actor) 1937

**September 1**
Yvonne De Carlo (actress) 1922
Vittorio Gassman
(actor, dir.) 1922

**September 2**
Cleveland Amory (author) 1917
Allen Drury (novelist) 1918
Victor Spinetti (actor) 1933
Richard Castellano (actor) 1934

**September 3**
Alan Ladd (actor) 1913
Kitty Carlisle (actress) 1915
Anne Jackson (actress) 1926
Valerie Perrine (actress) 1943

**September 4**
Morris Carnovsky (actor) 1897
Ida Kaminska (actress) 1899
Henry Ford II (auto maker) 1917
Mitzi Gaynor (actress) 1931

**September 5**
Florence Eldridge
(actress) 1901
Darryl F. Zanuck
(producer) 1902
Bob Newhart (comedian) 1929
Carol Lawrence
(dancer, actress) 1932
Raquel Welch (actress) 1940

**September 6**
Billy Rose (song writer) 1899
Jo Anne Worley (actress) 1937

**September 7**
Taylor Caldwell (novelist) 1900
Michael De Bakey
(heart surgeon) 1908
Elia Kazan (director) 1909
Anthony Quayle (actor) 1913
Peter Lawford (actor) 1923
King Baudouin (Belgium) 1930

**September 8**
Howard Dietz
(lyricist and playwright) 1896
Claude Pepper
(Florida Representative) 1900
Sid Caesar (comedian) 1922
Denise Darcel (actress) 1925
Peter Sellers (actor) 1925

**September 9**
Cliff Robertson (actor) 1925
Sylvia Miles (actress) 1932

**September 10**
Edmund O'Brien (actor) 1915
Yma Sumac (singer) 1927
José Feliciano (singer) 1945

**September 11**
Kristy McNichol (actress) 1962

**September 12**
Maurice Chevalier
(actor, singer) 1888

**September 13**
Ruth McDevitt (actress) 1895
Leland Hayward
(producer, agent) 1902
Claudette Colbert (actress) 1905
Scott Brady (actor) 1924

Mel Tormé (singer) 1925
Jacqueline Bisset (actress) 1944

**September 14**
Milton Eisenhower
(educator) 1899
Jack Hawkins (actor) 1910
Kay Medford (actress) 1920
Charles Evers
(civil rights leader) 1923
Zoe Caldwell (actress) 1933
Nicol Williamson (actor) 1938
Joey Heatherton (actress) 1944

**September 15**
Jean Renoir (director) 1894
Margaret Lockwood
(actress) 1916
Jackie Cooper (actor) 1922

**September 16**
Allen Funt
(TV personality) 1914
Janis Paige (actress) 1922
Lauren Bacall (actress) 1924
B. B. King (singer) 1925
Peter Falk (actor) 1927
Anne Francis (actress) 1930

**September 17**
Roddy McDowall (actor) 1928
Anne Bancroft (actress) 1931
Ken Kesey (novelist) 1935
John Ritter (actor) 1948

**September 18**
Harold Clurman
(producer) 1901
Greta Garbo (actress) 1905
Eddie Anderson (actor) 1905
Rossano Brazzi (actor) 1916
Robert Blake (actor) 1933
Frankie Avalon (singer) 1940

**September 19**
Ernest Truex (actor) 1889

Joseph Pasternak
(producer) 1901
Rosemary Harris (actress) 1930
David McCallum (actor) 1933
Twiggy (model, actress) 1949

**September 20**
Elliot Nugent
(actor, director) 1899
Sophia Loren (actress) 1934

**September 21**
Dawn Addams (actress) 1930
Melvin Van Peebles
(playwright) 1932

**September 22**
Paul Muni (actor) 1895
John Houseman
(producer, director) 1902
Shepperd Strudwick
(actor) 1907
Martha Scott (actress) 1914
Debby Boone (singer) 1956

**September 23** (Libra)
Walter Pidgeon (actor) 1897
Mickey Rooney (actor) 1920
Colin Blakely (actor) 1930
Ray Charles (singer) 1932
Romy Schneider (actress) 1938

**September 24**
Cheryl Crawford
(producer) 1902
Larry Gates (actor) 1915
William Bundy (editor) 1917
Lester Rawlins (actor) 1924
Sheila MacRae
(comedienne) 1924
Anthony Newley
(actor, songwriter) 1931

**September 25**
John Ericson (actor) 1927
Barbara Walters

(TV personality) 1931
Glenn Gould (pianist) 1932
Juliet Prowse (actress) 1936
Mark Hamill (actor) 1951

## September 26
Julie London (singer) 1926
Patrick O'Neal (actor) 1927
Olivia Newton-John
    (singer) 1948

## September 27
George Raft (actor) 1896
William Conrad (actor) 1920
Arthur Penn (director) 1922
Jayne Meadows (actress) 1926
Claude Jarman, Jr. (actor) 1934

## September 28
Elmer Rice (playwright) 1892
Al Capp (cartoonist) 1909
Peter Finch (actor) 1916
Marcello Mastroianni
    (actor) 1924

## September 29
Gene Autry (actor) 1907
Greer Garson (actress) 1908
Virginia Bruce (actress) 1910
Michelangelo Antonioni
    (director) 1912
Stanley Kramer
    (producer, director) 1913
Trevor Howard (actor) 1916
Lizabeth Scott (actress) 1931
Anita Ekberg (actress) 1931
Jerry Lee Lewis (singer) 1935
Madeline Kahn (actress) 1942

## September 30
Kenny Baker (singer, actor) 1912
Deborah Kerr (actress) 1921
Truman Capote (author) 1921
Angie Dickinson (actress) 1931
Johnny Mathis (singer) 1935

## October 1
Stanley Holloway (actor) 1890
George Coulouris (actor) 1903
Vladimir Horowitz
    (pianist) 1904
Walter Matthau (actor) 1920
James Whitmore (actor) 1921
Tom Bosley (actor) 1927
Laurence Harvey (actor) 1928
George Peppard (actor) 1928
Richard Harris (actor) 1933
Julie Andrews
    (actress, singer) 1935
Stella Stevens (actress) 1936

## October 2
Bud Abbott (comedian) 1895
Groucho Marx (comedian) 1895
Graham Greene (novelist) 1904
Marge Champion
    (actress, dancer) 1923
Clay Felker
    (editor, publisher) 1925
Moses Gunn (actor) 1929
Rex Reed (critic) 1940
Don McLean (singer) 1945

## October 3
Warner Oland (actor) 1880
Leo McCarey
    (director, producer) 1895
Gertrude Berg (actress) 1899
Gore Vidal (writer) 1925

## October 4
Charlton Heston (actor) 1924

## October 5
Joshua Logan
    (director, producer) 1908
Donald Pleasence (actor) 1919
Glynis Johns (actress) 1923
Richard Francis Gordon, Jr.
    (actor) 1929
Diane Cilento (actress) 1933

Jeff Conaway (actor) 1950

**October 6**
Janet Gaynor (actress) 1906
Carole Lombard (actress) 1909
Thor Heyerdahl (explorer) 1914
Anne Quayle (actress) 1937

**October 7**
Andy Devine (actor) 1905
Vaughn Monroe (singer) 1912
Sarah Churchill (actress) 1914
Alfred Drake
  (singer, author) 1914
June Allyson (actress) 1923
Diana Lynn (actress) 1926
Gabe Dell (actor) 1930

**October 8**
Rev. Jesse Jackson
  (civil rights leader) 1941

**October 9**
Bruce Catton (historian) 1899
Jacques Tati (actor) 1908
John Lennon (singer) 1940

**October 10**
Helen Hayes (actress)
  1900
Harold Pinter (playwright) 1930
Jerry Orbach (actor) 1935
Ben Vereen (actor) 1946
Tanya Tucker (singer) 1958

**October 11**
Joseph Alsop (journalist) 1910
Jerome Robbins
  (choreographer) 1916
Ron Leibman (actor) 1937

**October 12**
George K. Funston
  (business executive) 1910

**October 13**
Herblock

(political cartoonist) 1909
Cornel Wilde (actor) 1918
Jack MacGowran (actor) 1918
Laraine Day (actress) 1920
Yves Montand (actor) 1921
Pamela Tiffin (actress) 1942

**October 14**
Lillian Gish (actress) 1896
Roger Moore (actor) 1927

**October 15**
Ina Claire (actress) 1895
Mervyn LeRoy (director) 1900
John Kenneth Galbraith
  (economist) 1908
Mario Puzo (writer) 1921
Jean Peters (actress) 1926
Linda Lavin (actress) 1937

**October 16**
Linda Darnell (actress) 1921
Angela Lansbury (actress) 1925
Günter Grass (novelist) 1927

**October 17**
Spring Byington (actress) 1893
Jean Arthur (actress) 1908
Arthur Miller (playwright) 1915
Marsha Hunt (actress) 1917
Rita Hayworth (actress) 1928
Montgomery Clift (actor) 1920
Tom Poston (actor) 1927
Jimmy Breslin (journalist) 1930
William A. Anders
  (astronaut) 1933
Margot Kidder (actress) 1948

**October 18**
Lotte Lenya
  (singer, actress) 1900
Miriam Hopkins (actress) 1902
Sidney Kingsley
  (playwright) 1906
Melina Mercouri (actress) 1925

George C. Scott (actor) 1927

**October 19**
Jack Anderson (columnist) 1922

**October 20**
Anna Neagle (actress) 1908
Will Rogers, Jr. (actor) 1911
Art Buchwald (columnist) 1925

**October 21**
Dizzy Gillespie (trumpeter) 1917

**October 22**
Joan Fontaine (actress) 1917
Dory Previn (singer) 1925
Catherine Deneuve
   (actress) 1943

**October 23** (Scorpio)
James Daly (actor) 1918
Johnny Carson
   (TV entertainer) 1925
Diana Dors (actress) 1931
Michael Crichton (writer) 1942

**October 25**
Henry Steele Commager
   (historian) 1902
Anthony Franciosa (actor) 1928
Helen Reddy (singer) 1941

**October 26**
Jackie Coogan (actor) 1914
Eugene Ionesco
   (playwright) 1912
Rich Little (impressionist) 1935

**October 27**
Leif Erickson (actor) 1911
Teresa Wright (actress) 1918
Nanette Fabray (actress) 1922
Ruby Dee (actress) 1924
Melba Moore (singer) 1945

**October 28**
Elsa Lanchester (actress) 1902
Edith Head
   (costume designer) 1907
Joan Plowright (actress) 1929
Suzy Parker
   (model, actress) 1933
Dody Goodman (actress) 19??

**October 29**
Bela Lugosi (actor) 1884
Perc Westmore (Hollywood
   makeup artist) 1904
Richard Dreyfuss (actor) 1947

**October 30**
Ruth Gordon (actress) 1896
Ruth Hussey (actress) 1914
Henry Winkler (actor) 1945

**October 31**
Ethel Waters
   (actress, singer) 1900
Barbara Bel Geddes
   (actress) 1922
Lee Grant (actress) 1930
Michael Collins (astronaut) 1930
Dale Evans (actress) 1931
Michael Landon (actor) 1936

**November 1**
Victoria de los Angeles
   (soprano) 1924

**November 2**
Paul Ford (actor) 1901
Luchino Visconti (director) 1906
Burt Lancaster (actor) 1913
Ann Rutherford (actress) 1917

**November 3**
Charles Bronson (actor) 1922

**November 4**
Walter Cronkite
   (TV newscaster) 1916

Gig Young (actor) 1917
Art Carney (actor) 1918
Martin Balsam (actor) 1919

**November 5**
Joel McCrea (actor) 1906
Roy Rogers (actor) 1912
Vivien Leigh (actress) 1913
John McGiver (actor) 1913
Elke Sommer (actress) 1941
Donald Madden (actor) 1933
Tatum O'Neal (actress) 1963

**November 6**
Francis Lederer (actor) 1906
Mike Nichols (director) 1931
Sally Field (actress) 1946

**November 7**
Dean Jagger (actor) 1903
Billy Graham (evangelist) 1918
Al Hirt (trumpeter) 1922
Joni Mitchell (singer) 1943

**November 8**
Katharine Hepburn
   (actress) 1909
June Havoc (actress) 1916
Jerome Hines (basso) 1921
Patti Page (singer) 1927
Alain Delon (French actor) 1935

**November 9**
Marie Dressler (actress) 1869
Ed Wynn (actor) 1886
Hedy Lamarr (actress)
   1915

**November 10**
Claude Rains (actor) 1890
Mabel Normand (actress) 1897
Richard Burton (actor) 1925
Roy Scheider (actor) 1935
MacKenzie Phillips
   (actress) 1959

**November 11**
Réné Clair (director) 1898
Pat O'Brien (actor) 1899
Sam Spiegel (producer) 1901
Robert Ryan (actor) 1909
Howard Fast (novelist) 1914
Jonathan Winters
   (comedian) 1925
Bibi Andersson (actress) 1935

**November 12**
Jack Oakie (actor) 1903
Kim Hunter (actress) 1922
Grace Kelly (princess) 1929
Stefanie Powers (1942)

**November 13**
Hermione Baddeley
   (British actress) 1906
Alexander Scourby (actor) 1913
Robert Sterling (actor) 1917
Oskar Werner (actor) 1922
Linda Christian (actress) 1924
Jean Seberg (actress) 1938

**November 14**
Mamie Eisenhower
   (former first lady) 1896
Aaron Copland (composer) 1900
Dick Powell (actor) 1904
Barbara Hutton (heiress) 1912
Veronica Lake (actress) 1919
Brian Keith (actor) 1921
Johnny Desmond (singer,
   actor) 1921

**November 15**
Lewis Stone (actor) 1879
W. Averill Harriman (ex-gov-
   ernor of New York) 1891
Edward Asner (actor) 1929
Petula Clark (singer) 1934
Sam Waterston (actor) 1940

**November 16**
Lawrence Tibbett (actor) 1896
Burgess Meredith (actor) 1908

**November 17**
Lee Strasberg (director) 1901
Mischa Auer (actor) 1905
Rock Hudson (actor) 1925

**November 18**
George Gallup (poll taker) 1901
Johnny Mercer (composer) 1909
Dorothy Collins (singer) 1926
Brenda Vaccaro (actress) 1939

**November 19**
Clifton Webb (actor) 1893
Indira Gandhi
   (political leader) 1917
Alan Young (actor) 1919
Dick Cavett
   (TV personality) 1936

**November 20**
Chester Gould (cartoonist) 1900
Alistair Cooke
   (TV commentator) 1908
Judy Canova (actress) 1916
Gene Tierney (actress) 1920
Kaye Ballard (actress) 1926
Estelle Parsons (actress) 1927
Dick Smothers (comedian) 1939

**November 21**
Eleanor Powell (actress) 1912
Ralph Meeker (actor) 1920
Vivian Blaine
   (actress, singer) 1924
Marlo Thomas (actress) 1943
Goldie Hawn (actress) 1945

**November 22** (Sagittarius)
Hoagy Carmichael
   (songwriter) 1899
Geraldine Page (actress) 1924

Robert Vaughn (actor) 1932

**November 23**
Boris Karloff (actor) 1887
Harpo Marx (comedian) 1893
Victor Jory (actor) 1903

**November 24**
Cathleen Nesbitt (actress) 1889
Garson Kanin
   (playwright, writer) 1912
Geraldine Fitzgerald
   (actress) 1914
William F. Buckley
   (journalist) 1925

**November 25**
Helen Gahagan Douglas
   (ex-U.S. representative) 1900
Ricardo Montalban (actor) 1920

**November 26**
Charles Brackett
   (producer, writer) 1892
Emlyn Williams (actor) 1905
Charles Schulz (cartoonist) 1922
Robert Goulet (singer) 1933
Marian Mercer
   (actress, singer) 1935

**November 27**
David Merrick (producer) 1912
Alexander Dubček (ex-president
   of Czechoslovakia) 1921
Marshall Thompson (actor) 1925

**November 28**
Brooks Atkinson
   (drama critic) 1894
José Iturbi (pianist) 1895
Gloria Grahame (actress) 1925
Hope Lange (actress) 1933
Alexander Godunov
   (dancer) 1949

**November 29**
Busby Berkeley (director) 1895
John Gary (singer) 1932

**November 30**
Gordon Parks (director) 1912
Efrem Zimbalist, Jr. (actor) 1923
Allan Sherman (comedian) 1924
Richard Crenna (actor) 1927
Dick Clark
    (TV personality) 1929

**December 1**
Cyril Ritchard (actor) 1897
Mary Martin
    (singer, actress) 1914
Keith Mitchell (actor) 1928
Woody Allen (actor) 1935
Charlene Tilton (actress) 19??

**December 2**
Adolph Green (lyricist) 1915
Ezra Stone
    (actor, producer) 1917
Alexander Haig
    (U.S. general) 1924
Julie Harris (actress) 1925

**December 3**
Larry Parks (actor) 1914
Phyllis Curtin (soprano) 1927
Jean-Luc Godard (director) 1930
Andy Williams (singer) 1930

**December 4**
Deanna Durbin (actress) 1922
Horst Buchholz (actor) 1933

**December 5**
Fritz Lang (director) 1890
Walt Disney (producer) 1901
Otto Preminger
    (director, producer) 1906
Larry Kert (actor) 1930

**December 6**
William S. Hart (actor) 1870
Lynn Fontanne (actress) 1887
Ira Gershwin (lyricist) 1896
Agnes Moorehead (actress) 1906
Dave Brubeck (pianist) 1920
Wally Cox (actor) 1924
Bobby Van (dancer, actor) 1932

**December 7**
Fay Bainter (actress) 1892
Rod Cameron (actor) 1912
Eli Wallach (actor) 1915
Ellen Burstyn (actress) 1932

**December 8**
George Stevens (director) 1904
David Carradine (actor) 1906
Sammy Davis, Jr.
    (singer, actor) 1925
Flip Wilson (comedian) 1933

**December 9**
Eddie Dowling (actor) 1894
Hermione Gingold (actress) 1897
Emmett Kelly (clown) 1898
Dalton Trumbo
    (screenwriter) 1905
Kirk Douglas (actor) 1916
Douglas Fairbanks, Jr.
    (actor) 1909
Broderick Crawford (actor) 1911
Lee J. Cobb (actor) 1911
Redd Foxx (actor) 1922
Dina Merrill (actress) 1925
Dick Van Patten (actor) 1928
John Cassavetes
    (director, actor) 1929
Beau Bridges (actor) 1941

**December 10**
Una Merkel (actress) 1903
Morton Gould (composer) 1913

44

Dorothy Lamour (actress) 1914
Dennis Morgan (actor) 1920

**December 11**
Victor McLaglen (actor) 1886
Gilbert Roland (actor) 1905
Rita Moreno (actress) 1931

**December 12**
Edward G. Robinson
    (actor) 1893
Frank Sinatra
    (singer, actor) 1915
Connie Francis (singer) 1938

**December 13**
Marc Connelly
    (playwright) 1890
Lillian Roth
    (singer, actress) 1910
Van Heflin (actor) 1910
Dick Van Dyke (actor) 1925
Christopher Plummer
    (actor) 1929
John Davidson (actor) 1941

**December 14**
James H. Doolittle
    (ex-Air Force gen.) 1896
Morey Amsterdam
    (comedian) 1914
Dan Dailey (actor) 1917
Abbe Lane (singer) 1935
Lee Remick (actress) 1935
Patty Duke Astin (actress) 1946

**December 15**
J. Paul Getty
    (billionaire) 1892

**December 16**
Noel Coward
    (composer, author) 1899

Liv Ullmann (actress) 1939

**December 17**
Arthur Fiedler (conductor) 1894
Erskine Caldwell (novelist) 1903
Tommy Steele (singer) 1936

**December 18**
Gladys Cooper (actress) 1888
Christopher Fry
    (playwright) 1907
Abe Burrows
    (playwright, director) 1910
Jules Dassin (director) 1911
Willy Brandt
    (German political leader) 1913
Betty Grable (actress) 1916
Ossie Davis (actor, writer) 1917

**December 19**
Sir Ralph Richardson
    (actor) 1902
Leonid Brezhnev
    (political leader) 1906
Jean Genêt (playwright) 1910
David Susskind
    (TV producer) 1920
Gordon Jackson
    (Scottish actor) 1923
Cicely Tyson (actress) 1939

**December 20**
Sidney Hook (philosopher) 1902
Irene Dunne (actress) 1904
Hortense Calisher (novelist) 1911
Audrey Totter (actress) 1918
Ann Richards (actress) 1919
George Roy Hill (director) 1922

**December 21**
Jane Fonda (actress) 1937
Michael Tilson Thomas
    (conductor) 1944

**December 22** (Capricorn)
Andre Kostelanetz
(orchestra conductor) 1901
Gene Rayburn
(TV personality) 1917
Frank Corsaro
(opera director) 1924

**December 23**
José Greco (dancer) 1918
Harry Guardino (actor) 1925
Elizabeth Hartman
(actress) 1941

**December 24**
Howard Hughes
(billionaire) 1905
Ava Gardner (actress) 1922
Robert Joffrey
(choreographer) 1930
Jill Bennett
(British actress) 1931

**December 25**
Sir Isaac Newton (scientist) 1642
Clara Barton (nurse) 1821
Conrad Hilton
(hotel executive) 1887
Robert Ripley (cartoonist) 1893
Humphrey Bogart (actor) 1899
Clark Clifford
(ex-secretary of defense) 1906
Cab Calloway (bandleader) 1907
Tony Martin (singer) 1914
Rod Serling
(writer, producer) 1924
Sissy Spacek (actress) 1949

**December 26**
Albert A. Gore (ex-senator) 1907
Richard Widmark (actor) 1914

Steve Allen (comedian) 1921
Alan King (entertainer) 1927

**December 27**
Sydney Greenstreet (actor) 1879
Marlene Dietrich (actress) 1901

**December 28**
Earl "Fatha" Hines
(pianist) 1905
Cliff Arquette (actor) 1905
Lew Ayres (actor) 1908
Sam Levenson (humorist) 1911
Lou Jacobi (actor) 1913
Lee Bowman (actor) 1914
Hildegarde Neff (actress) 1925

**December 29**
Thomas Bradley
(mayor, L.A.) 1917
Mary Tyler Moore (actress) 1937
Jon Voight (actor) 1938
Marianne Faithful
(British actress) 1946

**December 30**
Sir Carol Reed (director) 1906
Bert Parks
(TV personality) 1914
Jack Lord (actor) 1930

**December 31**
Jule Styne
(composer, producer) 1905
Dick Kollmar
(actor, producer) 1910
Odetta (folk singer, actress) 1930
Anthony Hopkins
(British actor) 1937
John Denver (singer) 1943
Sarah Miles (actress) 1943

## CELEBRITIES WHO ARE ONLY CHILDREN

An only child usually runs everything around the house except errands, which implies that only children enjoy and command the spotlight and therefore have an edge in life.

If this is true, you might expect a large number of celebrities to be only children; however, for whatever reason, few are. Here are the names of some only children in the celebrity world:

| | | |
|---|---|---|
| Ann-Margret | Keir Dullea | George Peppard |
| Lauren Bacall | Elliot Gould | Cliff Robertson |
| Frank Borman | Fred MacMurray | William Styron |
| Dick Cavett | Ann Miller | François Truffaut |
| Alain Delon | Anthony Newley | Oskar Werner |
| Robert De Niro | Jerry Orbach | |

## CELEBRITIES FROM LARGE FAMILIES

| | Number* of Brothers and Sisters |
|---|---|
| Glen Campbell | 10 |
| Benny Goodman | 10 |
| Roosevelt Grier | 10 |
| Charley Pride | 10 |
| William F. Buckley, Jr. | 9 |
| Walter Annenberg | 8 |

*Does not include the listed celebrity.

| Maurice Chevalier | 8 |
| Florence Henderson | 8 |
| Edward M. Kennedy | 8 |
| José Feliciano | 7 |
| Peggy Lee | 7 |
| Nina Simone | 7 |
| Luis Buñuel | 6 |
| Johnny Cash | 6 |
| Vince Edwards | 6 |
| Mia Farrow | 6 |
| Fritz Mondale | 6 |
| Johnny Mathis | 5 |
| Dick Gregory | 5 |
| Reggie Jackson | 5 |

# CELEBRITY SIBLINGS

The show business bug, like influenza, is often caught by brothers and sisters in the same family.

The following siblings entered show biz, to varying degrees of success:

Marisa Pavan/Pier Angeli
George Sanders/Tom Conway
Olivia De Havilland/
   Joan Fontaine
Ricardo Cortez/Stanley Cortez
Audrey Meadows/
   Jayne Meadows
Gypsy Rose Lee/June Havoc
Peter Fonda/Jane Fonda
Darryl Hickman/
   Dwayne Hickman
Shirley MacLaine/
   Warren Beatty
Catherine Deneuve/
   Françoise Dorléac

Betty Hutton/Marion Hutton
James Arness/Peter Graves
Garson Kanin/Michael Kanin
Lilli Palmer/Maria Palmer
Frank Morgan/Ralph Morgan
Mary Pickford/Jack Pickford
James Cagney/Jeanne Cagney
Lawrence Tierney/Scott Brady
Jean Renoir/Pierre Renoir
John/Lionel/Ethel Barrymore
Marlon Brando/Jocelyn Brando
Joanne Dru/Peter Marshall
Gigi Perreau/Peter Miles
Maximilian Schell/Maria Schell
Abigail van Buren/Ann Landers

# SECOND-GENERATION ACTORS AND ACTRESSES

Actors and actresses who appear frequently on television talk shows often complain that their hours are long and that it's a tough business. Yet a high percentage of their children choose to enter the profession themselves. The hours, in fact, are not great but if one is successful the pay certainly is, and the positive reinforcement of applause and national publicity helps make up for the bad hours. The leverage of a famous family name also seems to have helped more than one aspiring actor. Probably half of all actors use a stage name yet the offspring of already successful theater people rarely change *their* last name. In fact, if the offspring's name isn't sufficiently identifiable with the parent's the child may decide to make it more so to take professional advantage. (Lon Chaney, Jr. and Robert Walker, Jr. are examples.) Here is a partial list of actors and actresses whose sons and daughters decided to pursue the profession of their parents:

| Parents | Children |
| --- | --- |
| Robert Alda | Alan Alda |
| Desi Arnaz, Lucille Ball | Luci Arnaz, Desi Arnaz, Jr. |
| John Barrymore | John Barrymore, Jr. |
| Noah Beery | Noah Beery, Jr. |
| Edgar Bergen | Candice Bergen |
| Helen Broderick | Broderick Crawford |
| Lloyd Bridges | Jeff Bridges, Beau Bridges |
| John Carradine | David and Keith Carradine |
| Charlie Chaplin | Geraldine Chaplin |
| Lon Chaney | Lon Chaney, Jr. |
| Kirk Douglas | Michael Douglas |
| Douglas Fairbanks | Douglas Fairbanks, Jr. |
| John Farrow, Maureen O'Sullivan | Mia Farrow |
| Henry Fonda | Jane Fonda, Peter Fonda |
| Jack Haley | Jack Haley, Jr. |
| Helen Hayes | James MacArthur |
| Alan Ladd | Alan Ladd, Jr., David Ladd |
| Viveca Lindfors | Kris Tabori |
| Gene Lockhart | June Lockhart |
| Mary Martin | Larry Hagman |
| John Mills | Hayley Mills, Juliet Mills |
| Vincente Minnelli, Judy Garland | Liza Minnelli |

| | |
|---|---|
| Robert Mitchum | James Mitchum |
| Zero Mostel | Josh Mostel |
| Ryan O'Neal | Tatum O'Neal |
| Ozzie and Harriet Nelson | Ricky Nelson, David Nelson |
| Christopher Plummer, | |
|    Tammy Grimes | Amanda Plummer |
| John Raitt | Bonnie Raitt |
| Sir Michael Redgrave | Vanessa Redgrave, |
| |    Lynn Redgrave |
| Debbie Reynolds, Eddie Fisher | Carrie Fisher |
| Frank Sinatra | Nancy Sinatra, |
| |    Frank Sinatra, Jr. |
| Lee Strasberg | Susan Strasberg |
| Danny Thomas | Marlo Thomas |
| Ed Wynn | Keenan Wynn |

# THE OCCUPATIONS OF CELEBRITIES' FATHERS

    Celebrities often come from unglamorous backgrounds, and their fathers (and mothers*) have typical jobs. Following this list are lists of offspring of military men and clergymen, but here is a random sample of the other occupations of celebrities' fathers:

| Celebrity | Father's Occupation |
|---|---|
| Lew Alcindor | transit policeman |
| Muhammad Ali | sign painter |
| Woody Allen | jewelry engraver |
| Herb Alpert | clothing designer |
| Don Ameche | bar owner |
| Alan Arkin | industrial draftsman |
| Louis Armstrong | turpentine worker |
| Eddie Arnold | farmer |
| Arthur Ashe | playground caretaker |
| Fred Astaire | salesman |
| Joan Baez | physicist |
| F. Lee Bailey | newspaper ad salesman |

*Times have changed but, mothers of these famous people either did not work or gave up working (as waitresses or secretaries for the most part) to raise their children. In many cases the mother's new occupation became the nurturing of a career for her child or children. The *Celebrity Book of Lists II* will contain the occupations of mothers (teaser: Jacqueline Bisset's mother was a lawyer).

| | |
|---|---|
| Pearl Bailey | minister |
| Kaye Ballard | construction worker |
| Orson Bean | campus policeman |
| Alan Bates | insurance broker |
| Warren Beatty | realtor;<br>    superintendent of schools |
| Joey Bishop | machinist; bicycle shop owner |
| Bill Blass | wholesale hardware dealer |
| Jean-Paul Belmondo | sculptor |
| Shirley Temple Black | banker |
| Dirk Bogarde | art editor |
| Richard Boone | corporate lawyer |
| William F. Buckley, Jr. | oil magnate |
| Michael Caine | fish market porter |
| Johnny Carson | utility company lineman and<br>    operations manager |
| Johnny Cash | farmer |
| John Cassavetes | businessman |
| Dick Cavett | English teacher |
| Maurice Chevalier | house painter |
| Julia Child | farm consultant |
| Richard Chamberlain | manufacturing plant owner |
| Julie Christie | tea plantation manager |
| Petula Clark | hospital orderly |
| Sean Connery | long-haul truck driver |
| Bill Cosby | Navy mess steward |
| Miles Davis | dentist |
| Ruby Dee | railroad porter and waiter |
| Olivia De Havilland | patent attorney |
| Sandy Dennis | mail clerk |
| James Dickey | lawyer |
| James Garner | upholsterer; carpenter |
| Ben Gazzara | carpenter |
| Jean-Luc Godard | doctor |
| Cary Grant | clothing firm presser |
| Lorne Greene | shoemaker |
| Merv Griffin | stockbroker |
| Tammy Grimes | hotel and club owner |
| Buddy Hackett | upholsterer |
| George Harrison | school bus driver |
| Katharine Hepburn | doctor |
| Benny Hill | pharmacist |

| | |
|---|---|
| Dustin Hoffman | furniture designer |
| Trevor Howard | insurance underwriter |
| Glenda Jackson | bricklayer, construction jobber |
| James Earl Jones | actor |
| Louis Jourdan | hotel owner |
| Stacy Keach | dialogue coach |
| Alan King | handbag cutter |
| Jessica Lange | traveling salesman |
| Angela Lansbury | lumber merchant |
| Peggy Lee | railroad station agent |
| John Lennon | merchant marine |
| Jerry Lewis | nightclub singer |
| John V. Lindsay | investment banker |
| Fred MacMurray | violinist |
| Paul McCartney | cotton salesman |
| Norman Mailer | accountant |
| Lee Marvin | advertising executive |
| Marcello Mastroianni | carpenter |
| Johnny Mathis | chauffeur; painter; handyman |
| Robert Mitchum | railroad worker |
| Jeanne Moreau | restaurant owner |
| Robert Morse | theater chain owner; record shop manager |
| George Murphy | track coach |
| Jim Nabors | policeman |
| Joe Namath | steel millworker |
| Patricia Neal | transportation manager |
| Bob Newhart | heating engineer |
| Anthony Newley | shipping clerk |
| Jack Nicklaus | drugstore owner |
| Patti Page | railroad foreman |
| George Peppard | building contractor |
| Harry Reasoner | superintendent of schools |
| Ronald Reagan | shoe salesman |
| Robert Redford | accountant |
| Della Reese | factory worker |
| Lee Remick | department store owner |
| Joan Rivers | doctor |
| Cliff Robertson | rancher |
| Ginger Rogers | electrical engineer |
| Jessica Savitch | clothing merchant |
| Maximilian Schell | poet; playwright |

| | |
|---|---|
| Romy Schneider | actor |
| George C. Scott | mine surveyor; executive |
| Jean Seberg | pharmacist |
| Omar Sharif | timber merchant |
| Robert Shaw | doctor |
| Dinah Shore | department store owner |
| Maggie Smith | public health doctor |
| Ringo Starr | house painter |
| Barbra Streisand | teacher |
| Senator John Tower | Methodist minister |
| Twiggy | TV set carpenter |
| John Updike | teacher |
| Rudy Vallee | drugstore owner |
| Dick Van Dyke | trucking agent |
| Robert Vaughn | radio actor |
| Barbara Walters | nightclub owner |
| Fritz Weaver | economist |
| Raquel Welch | engineer |
| Richard Widmark | salesman |
| Paul Williams | architectural engineer |
| Tom Wolfe | college professor |
| Natalie Wood | set designer |

# CELEBRITY "MILITARY BRATS"
## Sons and Daughters of Military Men

| | **Father** |
|---|---|
| John Denver | Air Force lieutenant colonel |
| Kris Kristofferson | Air Force general (pilot) |
| Swoosie Kurtz | Air Force, B-17 pilot |
| Christopher Lee | British colonel |
| Steve McQueen | Navy pilot |
| Jim Morrison | Navy rear admiral |
| Priscilla Presley | Navy pilot (father) |
| | Air Force major (stepfather) |
| Victoria Principal | Air Force master sergeant |
| James Woods | Army |
| Faye Dunaway | Army sergeant |

# FAMOUS CHILDREN OF CLERGYMEN

|  | **Father** |
|---|---|
| Pearl Bailey (singer) | denomination of ministry not known |
| Ingmar Bergman (Swedish movie director) | Lutheran minister |
| Erskine Caldwell (novelist) | Presbyterian minister |
| Alistair Cooke (TV commentator) | Methodist minister |
| Rita Coolidge (singer) | Baptist minister |
| William O. Douglas (Supreme Court justice) | Presbyterian minister |
| Aretha Franklin (singer) | Baptist minister |
| David Frost (producer) | Methodist minister |
| Leon Jaworski (lawyer) | Evangelical minister |
| Melvin Laird (former U.S. secretary of defense) | Presbyterian minister |
| Henry Luce (publisher) | Presbyterian minister |
| Laurence Olivier (actor) | Anglican minister |
| Walter Matthau (actor) | Eastern Rite Catholic priest |
| George McGovern (former U.S. senator) | Methodist minister |
| Walter Mondale (former U.S. vice-president) | Methodist minister |
| Agnes Moorehead (actress) | Presbyterian minister |
| Huey P. Newton (black activist) | Baptist minister |
| Dean Rusk (former U.S. secretary of state) | Presbyterian minister |
| William Saroyan (writer) | Presbyterian minister |
| Albert Schweitzer (humanitarian) | Lutheran minister |
| Erich Segal (author, professor) | Jewish rabbi |
| Nina Simone (singer) | Methodist minister |
| Fran Tarkenton (former athlete) | Methodist minister |
| John Tower (U.S. senator) | Methodist minister |
| Virginia Wade (tennis player) | Anglican minister |
| DeWitt Wallace (publisher) | Presbyterian minister |

# CELEBRITIES WHO HAVE FOUR OR MORE CHILDREN

| | | | |
|---|---|---|---|
| Frankie Avalon | 8 | Burt Lancaster | 5 |
| Michael Landon | 8 | Cloris Leachman | 5 |
| Norman Mailer | 8 | Jack Nicklaus | 5 |
| Werner Erhard | 7 | Gregory Peck | 5 |
| Dean Martin | 7 | Jason Robards | 5 |
| Muhammad Ali | 6 | Charles Schulz | 5 |
| Charles Bronson | 6 | Leonard Bernstein | 4 |
| Jerry Lewis | 6 | Pat Boone | 4 |
| Loretta Lynn | 6 | Marlon Brando | 4 |
| Paul Newman | 6 | Anita Bryant | 4 |
| Sidney Poitier | 6 | Glen Campbell | 4 |
| Roy Rogers | 6 | Neil Diamond | 4 |
| George C. Scott | 6 | Kirk Douglas | 4 |
| Johnny Cash | 5 | Bob Hope | 4 |
| Bill Cosby | 5 | Hal Linden | 4 |
| Phil Donahue | 5 | Ed McMahon | 4 |
| Bob Dylan | 5 | Ricky Nelson | 4 |
| Jim Henson | 5 | Dick Van Dyke | 4 |
| Jesse Jackson | 5 | Richard Pryor | 4 |

# DOUBLE TAKES: CELEBRITY TWINS

**Famous Twins**

Montgomery Clift
Laraine Day
William Randolph Hearst*
Lewis Lehrman
Liberace*

John Lindsay
Elvis Presley*
Ed Sullivan*
Jim Thorpe

*Twin died at birth or in infancy.

**Twins Who Are Both Famous**
Pier Angeli and Marisa Pavan
John and Roy Boulting
Tim and Tom Gullikson
Ann Landers and Abigail Van Buren
Anthony and Peter Shaffer

**Famous Parents of Twins**
Ed Asner
Alan Bates
Jim Brown
Mia Farrow
Andy Gibb
Henry Mancini
Rick Nelson
Eric Severeid
James Stewart
Margaret Thatcher

# UNUSUAL NAMES OF SHOW BUSINESS CHILDREN

Show business people can be a creative lot when it comes to the naming of their children. One does suspect that some of these names were inspired by certain stimulants and mystical visions. However, the names *are* distinctive and the odds are that few of the children's friends and classmates will have those *same* names. Here is a sampling of the unusual names of some show business children:

| Parent(s) | Children's Names |
|---|---|
| Cher and Greg Allman | Elijah Blue |
| Sonny and Cher Bono | Chastity |
| David Bowie | Zowie |
| David Carradine, Barbara Hershey | Free |
| Aretha Franklin | Kecalf (acronym of Ken E. Cunningham, the father, and Aretha L. Franklin) |
| Elliot Gould | Sam Bazooka |
| Mick and Bianca Jagger | Jade |

| Tony Perkins | Elvis, Osgood |
| Mia Farrow, Andre Previn | Lark Song, Summer Song |
| Sylvester Stallone | Sage Moonblood |
| Frank Zappa | Moon Unit, Dweezil, Diva, and |
| | Ahmet Emuukha Rodan |

# FAMOUS ILLEGITIMATE CHILDREN

Being an illegitimate child is often a stigma, but sometimes it is an inspiration. The Reverend Jesse Jackson, an admitted illegitimate child, once commented that he became successful as a result of trying to prove himself legitimate. The following well-known people were born illegitimate but didn't let that stand in the way of success.

Guillaume Apollinaire (French poet)
Sarah Bernhardt (actress)
Willy Brandt (German statesman)
Paul Cezanne (French artist)
Alexander Hamilton (U.S. secretary of treasury)
Jesse Jackson (civil rights leader)
Jenny Lind (Swedish soprano)
Jack London (novelist)
Malcolm X (black leader)
Marilyn Monroe (actress)
Maria Montessori (educator)
Juan Peron (Argentine dictator)
August Strindberg (Swedish playwright)
Richard Wagner (German composer)
Booker T. Washington (educator)

# MARRIED THE MOST

"Marriage is the most licentious of human institutions—
that is the secret of its popularity."

——George Bernard Shaw

| | Number of Times Married |
|---|---|
| Stan Laurel | 8 |
| Alan Jay Lerner | 8 |
| Marie McDonald | 8 |
| Mickey Rooney | 8 |
| Artie Shaw | 8 |
| Elizabeth Taylor | 7 |
| Lana Turner | 7 |
| Louis Armstrong | 6 |
| Rex Harrison | 6 |
| Dick Haymes | 6 |
| DeWolf Hopper | 6 |
| Hedy Lamarr | 6 |
| Norman Mailer | 6 |
| Claude Rains | 6 |
| Lili St. Cyr | 6 |
| Gloria Swanson | 6 |
| Constance Bennett | 5 |
| George Brent | 5 |
| Arlene Dahl | 5 |
| Henry Fonda | 5 |
| Clark Gable | 5 |
| Rita Hayworth | 5 |
| Ginger Rogers | 5 |
| Johnny Weissmuller | 5 |
| Tammy Wynette | 5 |

# HOLLYWOOD MARRIAGES
## YOU MAY NOT REMEMBER

Lola Albright—Jack Carson
Constance Bennett—Gilbert Roland
Joan Blondell—Dick Powell
Ava Gardner—Mickey Rooney
Ruby Keeler—Al Jolson

Carole Lombard—William Powell
Suzanne Pleshette—Troy Donahue
Eleanor Powell-Glenn Ford
Luise Rainer—Clifford Odets
Martha Raye—Ed Begley; Billy Rose
Jean Simmons—Stewart Granger
Barbara Stanwyck—Robert Taylor
Gloria Swanson—Wallace Beery
Shirley Temple—John Agar
Lupe Velez—Johnny Weissmuller
Shelley Winters—Farley Granger; Anthony Franciosa

## CELEBRITIES WHO NEVER MARRIED

Groucho Marx was fond of saying that marriage was the chief cause of divorce. The following people avoided or are avoiding divorce the easy way—by never taking the vow:

Kaye Ballard
Warren Beatty
Truman Capote
Richard Chamberlain
Montgomery Clift
Roy Cohn
Greta Garbo
Sir John Gielgud
Halston
Marvin Hamlisch
Edward Everett Horton

Tab Hunter
Paul Lynde
Sal Mineo
Jim Nabors
Joe Namath
Ramon Novarro
Mack Sennett
Lily Tomlin
Gore Vidal
Clifton Webb

## HOLLYWOOD MARRIAGES: TWENTY YEARS PLUS

Studio contracts are honored more seriously than marriage contracts in Hollywood, or so it seems. Here are some luminaries who deserve special Oscars for having stayed together for at least twenty years:

Bob and Dolores Hope (49 years)
Lloyd and Dorothy Bridges (44 years)

Robert and Dorothy Mitchum (42 years)
Dennis and Geraldine Weaver (42 years)
Mike and Genevieve Douglas (40 years)
Garson Kanin and Ruth Gordon (40 years)
Perry and Roselle Como (39 years)
James and Gloria Stewart (33 years)
Ronald and Nancy Reagan (30 years)
Gregory and Veronique Peck (27 years)
Alan and Arlene Alda (25 years)
Robert and Lola Redford (24 years)
Paul Newman and Joanne Woodward (24 years)
Walter and Carol Matthau (23 years)
Carroll and Nancy O'Connor (21 years)
Jack and Felicia Lemmon (20 years)

Honorable mention: Jerry and Patti Lewis (36 years)—divorced in 1980.

# Who's Really Who | 3.

## THE REAL NAMES OF FAMOUS PEOPLE

Celebrities often become famous bearing names other than the ones appearing on their birth certificates. Changing one's name is as American as apple pie and the Fourth of July. Names are shortened or Americanized for "marquee value"; numerologists suggest spelling changes; a woman adopts the maiden name of her mother or, like most married women, she adopts her husband's last name; immigration officials arbitrarily change names—the reasons are varied.

Names like Itzkowitz, Kubelsky, Sarkesian, and Beedle are the real names of some very famous people. Jewish, Russian, Polish, and German names abound—names like Kominski, Konopka, and Heimberger.

Here are the real names of almost one thousand celebrities:

Abdul-Jabbar, Kareem
   Ferdinand Lewis
   Alcindor, Jr.

Abzug, Bella
   Bella Savitsky

Adams, Edie
   Elizabeth Edith Enke

Adams, Joey
   Joseph Abramowitz

Adams, Nick
   Nicholas Adamshock

Aimée, Anouk
   Françoise Sorya

Albert, Eddie
   Edward Albert Heimberger

Alda, Robert
   Alphonso D'Abruzza

Ali, Muhammad
   Cassius Marcellus Clay, Jr.

Allen, Fred
   John F. Sullivan

Allen, Mel
    Melvin Allen Israel

Allen, Woody
    Allen Stewart Konigsberg

Allyson, June
    Ella Geisman

Alton, Robert
    Robert Alton Hart

Ameche, Don
    Dominic Felix Amici

Andrews, Julie
    Julia Elizabeth Wells

Angeli, Pier
    Anna Maria Pierangeli

Angeles, Victoria de los
    Victoria Gamez Cima

Annabella
    Suzanne Georgette
    Carpentier

Ann-Margret
    Ann-Margret Olson

Anthony, John J.
    Lester Kroll

Arden, Elizabeth
    Florence Nightingale
    Graham

Arden, Eve
    Eunice Quedens

Arlen, Harold
    Hyman Arluck

Arlen, Richard
    Richard Van Mattemore

Arliss, George
    George Augustus Andrews

Armstrong, Henry
    Henry Jackson

Armstrong, Robert
    Donald Robert Smith

Arness, James
    James Aurness

Arno, Peter
    Curtis Arnoux Peters

Arno, Sig
    Siegfried Aron

Arnold, Edward
    Guenther Schneider

Arthur, Bea
    Bernice Frankel

Arthur, Jean
    Gladys Greene

Ashley, Elizabeth
    Elizabeth Ashley Cole

Astaire, Adele
    Adele Austerlitz

Astaire, Fred
    Frederick Austerlitz

Astor, Mary
    Lucile Vasconcells
    Langhanke

Atlas, Charles
    Angelo Siciliano

Auer, Mischa
    Mischa Ounskowski

Aumont, Jean-Pierre
    Jean Pierre Salomons

Avalon, Frankie
    Francis Avalonne

Axis Sally (Berlin)
Mildred Gillars Sisk

Axis Sally (Rome)
Rita Louise Zucca

Aznavour, Charles
Varenaugh Aznavourian

Bacall, Lauren
Betty Joan Perske

Baker, Wee Bonnie
Evelyn Nelson

Balanchine, George
Georgi Melitonovitch
Balanchivadze

Ballard, Kaye
Catherine Gloria Balotta

Bancroft, Anne
Anne Marie Italiano

Bara, Theda
Theodosia Goodman

Bari, Lynn
Marjorie Schuyler Fisher

Barr, Candy
Juanita Slusher

Barr, Richard
Richard Baer

Barrie, Mona
Mona Smith

Barrie, Wendy
Margaret Wendy Jenkins

Barry, Don
Donald Barry D'Acosta

Barry, Gene
Eugene Klass

Barrymore, Ethel
Ethel Blythe

Barrymore, Lionel
Lionel Blythe

Barrymore, John
John Blythe

Bart, Lionel
Lionel Begleiter

Bartok, Eva
Eva Sjöke

Bates, Florence
Florence Rabe

Baxter, Keith
Keith Baxter-Wright

Bayes, Nora
Dora Goldberg

Beame, Abraham
Abraham David Birnbaum

Bean, Orson
Dallas Frederick Burroughs

Beatty, Warren
Warren Beaty

Bel Geddes, Barbara
Barbara Geddes Lewis

Bellamy, Madge
Margaret Philpot

Ben-Gurion, David
David Green

Bennett, Bruce
Herman Brix

Benny, Jack
Benjamin Kubelsky

Benton, Barbi
Barbara Klein

Berg, Gertrude
  Gertrude Edelstein

Bergen, Polly
  Nellis Paulina Burgin

Berkeley, Busby
  William Berkely Enos

Berle, Milton
  Milton Berlinger

Berlin, Irving
  Israel Baline

Bernhardt, Sarah
  Rosine Bernard

Big Bopper
  Jiles Perry Richardson

Bishop, Joey
  Joseph Abraham Gottlieb

Black, Karen
  Karen Blanche Ziegler

Blaine, Vivian
  Vivienne Stapleton

Blair, Betsy
  Betsy Boger

Blair, Janet
  Martha Lafferty

Blake, Amanda
  Beverly Louise Neill

Blake, Robert
  Michael Gubitosi

Blane, Sally
  Elizabeth Jane Young

Bloom, Claire
  Claire Blume

Blue, Ben
  Ben Bernstein

Bly, Nellie
  Elizabeth Cochrane

Blyden, Larry
  Ivan Lawrence Blieden

Blythe, Betty
  Elizabeth Blythe Slaughter

Bogarde, Dirk
  Derek Van Den Bogaerde

Bono, Cher
  Cherilyn Sarkesian (later
  LaPiere)

Booth, Shirley
  Thelma Booth Ford

Borge, Victor
  Borge Rosenbaum

Borgnine, Ernest
  Ermes Effron Borgnino

Boyd, Stephen
  William Millar

Brady, Scott
  Gerald Tierney

Brand, Max
  Frederick Faust

Brandon, Henry
  Henry Kleinbach

Brandt, Willy
  Herbert Ernst Karl Frahm

Brent, George
  George Brent Nolan

Brice, Fanny
  Fannie Borach

Bridges, Beau
  Lloyd Vernet Bridges III

Britt, May
  Maybritt Wilkens

Brodie, Steve
  John Stevens

Bronson, Charles
  Charles Bunchinsky
  (later Buchinsky or
  Buchinski)

Brooke, Hillary
  Beatrice Sofie Mathilda
  Peterson

Brooks, Geraldine
  Geraldine Stroock

Brooks, Leslie
  Leslie Gettman

Brooks, Mel
  Melvin Kaminsky

Brown, Vanessa
  Smylla Brind

Bruce, David
  Marden McBroom

Bruce, Lenny
  Leonard Alfred Schneider

Bruce, Virginia
  Helen Virginia Briggs

Bryan, Jane
  Jane O'Brien

Brynner, Yul
  Taidje Khan

Bubbles, John
  John William Sublett

Buck, Pearl
  Pearl Comfort Sydenstricker

Burgess, Anthony
  John Anthony Burgess
  Wilson

Burke, Billie
  Mary William Ethelbert
  Appleton Burke

Burns, George
  Nathan Birnhaum

Burr, Raymond
  William Stacey Burr

Burstyn, Ellen
  Edna Rae Gillooly

Burton, Richard
  Richard Jenkins

Buttons, Red
  Aaron Chwatt

Byrnes, Edd "Kookie"
  Edward Breitenberger

Cabot, Bruce
  Jacques de Bujac

Cahn, Sammy
  Sam Cohen (later Cohn or
  Kahn)

Caine, Michael
  Maurice J. Micklewhite

Calhern, Louis
  Carl Henry Vogt

Calhoun, Rory
  Francis Timothy Durgin

Callan, Michael
  Martin Caliniff

Callas, Maria
  Maria Calogeropoulos

Calvet, Corinne
  Corinne Dibos

Cameron, Rod
  Rod Cox

Cannon, Dyan
  Samile Diane Friesen

Cantinflas
  Mario Moreno August

Cantor, Eddie
  Isidore Itzkowitz

Capote, Truman
  Truman Streckfus Persons

Capp, Al
  Alfred Gerald Caplin

Capucine
  Germaine Lefebvre

Carlisle, Kitty
  Catherine Conn

Carol, Sue
  Evelyn Lederer

Carradine, John
  Richmond Reed Carradine

Carroll, Diahann
  Carol Diahann Johnson

Carroll, John
  Julian La Faye

Carroll, Lewis
  Charles Lutwidge Dodgson

Carroll, Nancy
  Ann La Hiff

Carson, Jeannie
  Jean Shufflebottom

Cassidy, Hopalong
  William Lawrence Boyd

Cassini, Oleg
  Oleg Loiewski-Cassini

Castle, Irene
  Irene Foote

Castle, William
  William Schloss

Chambers, Whittaker
  J. Vivian Chambers

Champion, Marge
  Marjorie Celeste Belcher

Chandler, Jeff
  Ira Grossel

Chaney, Lon, Jr.
  Creighton Chaney

Chaplin, Lita Grey
  Lillita Louise McMurray

Charo
  Maria Rosario Pilar Martinez
  Melina Baeza

Charisse, Cyd
  Tula Ellice Finklea

Charles, Ray
  Ray Charles Robinson

Checker, Chubby
  Ernest Evans

Cheshire, Maxine
  Maxine Hall

Chisholm, Shirley
  Shirley Anita St. Hill

Christian, Linda
  Blanca Rosa Welter

Christie, Dame Agatha
  Agatha Mary Clarissa Miller

Christo
  Christo Javacheff

Claire, Ina
   Ina Fagan

Clark, Dane
   Bernard Zanville

Clarke, Mae
   Mary Klotz

Clive, Colin
   Clive Greig

Cobb, Lee J.
   Lee Jacoby (or Jacob)

Colbert, Claudette
   Lily Chauchoin

Colby, Anita
   Anita Katherine Counihan

Cole, Nat King
   Nathaniel Adams Coles

Coleman, Cy
   Seymour Kaufman

Collins, Dorothy
   Marjorie Chandler

Comden, Betty
   Betty Cohen

Como, Perry
   Pierino Roland Como

Connors, Chuck
   Kevin Joseph Connor

Connors, Mike
   Krekor "Kirk" Ohanian

Conrad, Robert
   Conrad Robert Falk

Conway, Tom
   Thomas Sanders

Cooper, Alice
   Vincent Damon Furnier

Cooper, Gary
   Frank James Cooper

Cord, Alex
   Alexander Viespi

Corrigan, Ray "Crash"
   Ray Benard

Cortez, Ricardo
   Jacob Krantz (or Kranz)

Cortez, Stanley
   Stanislaus Krantz

Cosell, Howard
   Howard William Cohen

Costello, Lou
   Louis Cristillo

Court, Margaret
   Margaret Smith

Crabbe, Buster
   Clarence Linden Crabbe

Crawford, Cheryl
   Cheryl Kingsley

Crawford, Joan
   Lucille LeSueur

Crist, Judith
   Judith Klein

Cristal, Linda
   Victoria Maya

Crosby, Bing
   Harry Lillis Crosby

Cummings, Constance
   Constance Halverstadt

Curtis, Tony
   Bernard Schwartz

Curtiz, Michael
   Mihaly Kertesz

D'Amboise, Jacques
   Jacques Joseph D'Amboise
   Ahearn

Damita, Lily
   Lillian Carre

Damone, Vic
   Vito Farinola

Darcel, Denise
   Denise Billecard

Darin, Bobby
   Walden Robert Cassotto

Darnell, Linda
   Monetta Eloyse Darnell

Darren, James
   James Ercolani

Darro, Frankie
   Frank Johnson

Da Silva, Howard
   Howard Silverblatt

Davies, Marion
   Marion Douras

Davis, Gail
   Betty Jeanne Grayson

Dawn, Hazel
   Hazel Letout

Day, Doris
   Doris Kappelhof

Day, Laraine
   Laraine Johnson

Dean, Dizzy
   Jay Hanna Dean

Deane, Martha
   Marian Young Taylor

De Carlo, Yvonne
   Peggy Yvonne Middleton

Dee, Ruby
   Ruby Ann Wallace

Dee, Sandra
   Alexandra Zuck

Del Rio, Dolores
   Lolita Dolores . . . Asúnsolo
   Martinez

Deneuve, Catherine
   Catherine Dorléac

Dennis, Patrick
   Edward Everett Tanner III

Denver, John
   Henry John Deutschendorf, Jr.

Derek, John
   Derek Harris

De Wolfe, Billy
   William Andrew Jones

Diamond, Legs
   John T. Nolan

Dickinson, Angie
   Angeline Brown

Diddley, Bo
   Elias McDaniel

Dietrich, Marlene
   Maria Magdalene Dietrich
   (later Von Losch)

Diller, Phyllis
   Phyllis Driver

Dix, Richard
   Ernest Carlton Brimmer

Dixon, Jean
   Jeane Pinckert

Dominguin, Luis Miguel
Luis Miguel Gonzalez Lucas

Donahue, Troy
Merle Johnson

Dorn, Philip
Hein Van Der Niet
(later Fritz Van Dongen)

Dors, Diana
Diana "Daisy" Fluck

D'Orsay, Fifi
Yvonne Lussien

Douglas, Kirk
Issur Danielovitch Demsky

Douglas, Melvyn
Melvin Hesselberg

Douglas, Mike
Michael Delaney Dowd, Jr.

Dove, Billy
Lillian Bohny

Dowling, Eddie
Joseph Nelson Goucher

Drake, Alfred
Alfred Capurro

Drake, Tom
Alfred Alderdeiss

Dressler, Marie
Leila Kerber

Dru, Joanne
Joanne la Cock

Drummond, Bulldog
Hector McNeil

Dvorak, Ann
Ann McKim

Dylan, Bob
Robert Zimmerman

Ebsen, Buddy
Christian Rudolph Ebsen, Jr.

Edwards, Blake
William Blake McEdwards

Edwards, Vince
Vincent Edward Zoino

Elaine
Elaine Kaufman

Eldridge, Florence
Florence McKechnie

Elliot, Cass
Ellen Naomi Cohen

Elliott, William
Gordon Nance

Eliot, George
Mary Ann Evans

Ellington, Duke
Edward Kennedy Ellington

Erhard, Werner
John Paul "Jack" Rosenberg

Evans, Dale
Frances Octavia Smith

Evelyn
Evelyn Kaye Klein

Everett, Chad
Ray Cramton

Ewell, Tom
S. Yewell Tompkins

Fabian
Fabian Anthony Forte

Fabray, Nanette
Ruby Bernadette Nanette
Fabares

Fairbanks, Douglas
Douglas Elton Thomas
Ulman

Faith, Adam
Terence Nelhams

Falkenburg, Jinx
Eugenia Lincoln Falkenburg

Farrow, Mia
Maria de Lourdes Villiers
Farrow

Faye, Alice
Alice Leppert

Faye, Joey
Joseph Antony Palladino

Fernandel
Fernand Joseph Desire
Contandin

Ferrer, José
José Vicente Ferrer Otero y
Cintron

Fetchit, Stepin
Lincoln Theodore Perry

Fields, Gracie
Grace Stansfield

Fields, Jackie
Jacob Finkelstein

Fields, W.C.
William Claude Dukenfield

Fitzgerald, Barry
William Joseph Shields

Flanagan, Bud
Robert Winthrop

Fleming, Rhonda
Marilyn Louis

Foch, Nina
Nina Fock

Fontaine, Joan
Joan De Havilland

Fontanne, Lynn
Lily Louise

Fonteyn, Dame Margot
Margaret Hookham

Ford, Gerald R., Jr.
Leslie Lynch King, Jr.

Ford, Glenn
Gwyllyn Ford

Ford, John
Sean O'Feeney

Ford, Mary
Colleen Summers

Ford, Paul
Paul Ford Weaver

Ford, Wallace
Sam Grundy

Forest, Mark
Lou Degni

Forrest, Sally
Katherine Scully Feeney

Forrest, Steve
William Forrest Andrews

Forsythe, John
John Lincoln Freund

Foster, Phil
Philip Feldman

Foster, Susanna
Suzanne Larson

Fox, William
William Fried (or Fuchs)

Foxx, Redd
John Elroy Sanford

Franciosa, Anthony
    Anthony Papaleo

Francis, Connie
    Concetta Franconero

Francis, Kay
    Katherine Gibbs

Friedan, Betty
    Betty Naomi Goldstein

Friendly, Fred
    Ferdinand Wachenheimer

Frye, David
    David Shapiro

Gabin, Jean
    Alexis Moncourge

Garbo, Greta
    Greta Lovisa Gustaffson

Garfield, John
    Julius Garfinkel

Garland, Judy
    Frances Gumm

Garner, James
    James Bumgarner

Gary, John
    John Gary Strader

Gary, Romain
    Romain Kacew

Gaynor, Janet
    Laura Gainor

Gaynor, Mitzi
    Francesca Mitzi Marlene
    de Czanyi Von Gerber

Gavin, John
    John Anthony Golenor

Genet
    Janet Flanner

Genevieve
    Ginette Marguerite Auger

George, Gladys
    Gladys Clare

Gibbs, Georgia
    Fredda Lipson

Gibson, Hoot
    Edmund Richard Gibson

Gilbert, John
    John Pringle

Gilbert, Lou
    Lou Gitlitz

Gilford, Jack
    Jacob Gellman

Gillespie, Dizzy
    John Birks Gillespie

Gloria Jean
    Gloria Jean Schoonover

Goddard, Paulette
    Pauline Levee (or Levy)

Golden, Harry
    Harry Goldenhurst

Goldwyn, Samuel
    Samuel Goldfisch

Gordon, Bert
    Barney Gorodetsky

Gordon, Max
    Michael Salpeter

Gordon, Ruth
    Ruth Gordon Jones

Gould, Elliott
    Elliot Gouldstein

Graham, Sheilah
    Lily Sheil

Graham, Virginia
  Virginia Komiss

Grahame, Gloria
  Gloria Hallward

Granger, Stewart
  James Stewart

Grant, Cary
  Archibald Alexander Leach

Grant, Kathryn
  Olive Kathryn Grandstaff

Grant, Lee
  Lyova Haskell Rosenthal

Graves, Peter
  Peter Aurness

Gray, Barry
  Bernard Yaroslaw

Gray, Colleen
  Doris Jensen

Gray, Sally
  Constance Stevens

Grayson, Kathryn
  Zelma Hedrick

Graziano, Rocky
  Rocco Barbella

Green, Mitzi
  Elizabeth Keno

Greene, Lorne
  Lorne Green

Gregory, Paul
  Jason Lenhart

Grey, Joel
  Joel Katz

Grey, Nan
  Eschal Miller

Grey, Zane
  Pearl Zane Gray

Grofe, Ferde
  Ferdinand Rudolphe von Grofe

Guest, C. Z.
  Lucy Douglas Cochrane

Gwynne, Anne
  Marguerite Gwynne Trice

Hackett, Buddy
  Leonard Hacker

Hadley, Reed
  Reed Herring

Hagen, Jean
  Jean Shirley Verhagen

Hale, Alan
  Rufus Alan McKahan

Hall, Gus
  Arvo Kusta Halberg

Hall, Huntz
  Henry Hall

Hall, James
  James Brown

Hall, Jon
  Charles Hall Locher

Hall, Monty
  Monte Halparin

Halston
  Roy Halston Frowick

Harding, Ann
  Dorothy Gatley

Harlow, Jean
  Harlean Carpentier

Harrison, Rex
  Reginald Carey Harrison

Hart, Dolores
Dolores Hicks

Harvey, Laurence
Larushka Mischa Skikne

Haver, June
June Stovenour

Havoc, June
June Hovick

Hayden, Melissa
Mildred Herman

Hayden, Russell
Hayden Michael Lucid

Hayden, Sterling
John Hamilton

Hayes, Helen
Helen Hayes Brown

Hayes, Peter Lind
Joseph Conrad Lind, Jr.

Hayward, Louis
Seafield Grant

Hayward, Susan
Edythe Marrener

Hayworth, Rita
Margarita Casino

Heflin, Van
Emmet Evan Haflin, Jr.

Henderson, Skitch
Lyle Russell Cedric
Henderson

Henreid, Paul
Paul Von Hernreid

Henry, O.
William Sidney Porter

Hepburn, Audrey
Audrey Hepburn-Ruston

Herblock
Herbert L. Block

Hildegarde
Hildegarde Loretta Sell

Hill, Steven
Solomon Berg

Hobson, Laura Z.
Laura Zametkin

Hoey, Dennis
Samuel David Hyams

Holden, Fay
Fay Hamilton

Holden, William
William Franklin Beedle

Holiday, Billie
Eleanora Fagan

Holliday, Judy
Judith Tuvim

Holman, Libby
Elizabeth Holzman

Holt, Tim
John Charles Holt, Jr.

Hope, Bob
Leslie Townes Hope

Hopper, Hedda
Elda Furry

Horton, Robert
Mead Howard Horton

Houdini, Harry
Ehrich Weiss

Houseman, John
Jacques Haussmann

Howard, John
John Cox

Howard, Leslie
Leslie Howard Stainer

Howard, Moe and Shemp
Moe and Shemp Horowitz

Howe, James Wong
Wong Tung Jim

Hoyt, John
John Hoysradt

Hudson, Rock
Roy Scherer, Jr.
(later Roy Fitzgerald)

Humperdinck, Engelbert
Arnold Dorsey

Hunter, Jeffrey
Henry McKinnies, Jr.

Hunter, Kim
Janet Cole

Hunter, Ross
Martin Fuss

Hunter, Tab
Arthur Andrew Gelien

Hussey, Ruth
Ruth Carol O'Rourke
Huston, Walter
Walter Houghston

Hutton, Betty
Betty June Thornberg

Hutton, Marion
Marion Thornberg

Hutton, Robert
Robert Bruce Winne

Ian, Janis
Janis Fink

Indiana, Robert
Robert Clarke

Ingram, Rex
Reginald Hitchcock

Innes, Michael
John Innes MacKintosh
Stewart

Irving, George
George Irving Shelasky

Irving, Jules
Jules Israel

Jack, Beau
Sidney Walker

Jagger, Dean
Dean Jeffries

James, Joni
Joan Carmella Babbo

Jannings, Emil
Theodor Emil Janez

Janssen, David
David Harold Meyer

Jeffreys, Ann
Ann Carmichael

Jenkins, Allen
Allen McGonegal

Jimmy the Greek
Demetrios George Synodinos
(later James G. Snyder)

Joffrey, Robert
Abdullah Jaffa Bey Khan

John, Elton
  Reginald Kenneth Dwight

Johnny (Philip Morris)
  Johnny Roventini

Jolson, Al
  Asa Hesselson
  (later Asa Yoelson)

Jones, Candy
  Jessica Wilcox

Jones, Jennifer
  Phyllis Isley
  (later Walker)

Jones, Spike
  Lindley Armstrong Jones

Jones, Tom
  Thomas Jones Woodward

Jorgensen, Christine
  George Jorgensen, Jr.

Jourdan, Louis
  Louis Gendre

Kabibble, Ish
  Merwyn A. Bogue

Karloff, Boris
  William Henry Platt

Kaye, Danny
  David Daniel Kominski

Kaye, Nora
  Nora Koreff

Kazan, Elia
  Elia Kazanjoglous

Kazan, Lainie
  Lainie Levine

Keaton, Buster
  Joseph Frank Keaton

Keel, Howard
  Harold Keel

Keith, Brian
  Robert Keith, Jr.

Keith, Ian
  Keith Ross

Keith, Ricky
  Ricky Thibodeaux

Kendall, Kay
  Justine McCarthy
  (or Kay Kendall McCarthy)

Kendall, Suzy
  Frieda Harrison

Kerr, Deborah
  Deborah Kerr-Trimmer

Kerr, Jean
  Bridget Jean Collins

Kidd, Michael
  Milton Greenwald

King, Alan
  Irvin Alan Kniberg

King, Alexander
  Alexander Koenig

King, B. B.
  Riley B. King

King, Billie Jean
  Billy Jean Moffitt

Kingman, Dong
  Dong Moy Shu

Kingsley, Sidney
  Sidney Kirschner

Kirk, Phyllis
  Phyllis Kirkegaard

Knickerbocker, Cholly
  Igor Loiewski-Cassini

Knight, Ted
Tadewurz Wladziu Konopka

Kyser, Kay
James Kern Kyser

Lahr, Bert
Irving Lahrheim

Laine, Frankie
Frank Paul Lo Vecchio

Lake, Arthur
Arthur Silverlake

Lake, Veronica
Constance Ockleman

Lamarr, Hedy
Hedwig Kiesler

La Marr, Barbara
Reatha Watson

Lanchester, Elsa
Elsa Sullivan

Landers, Ann
Esther Pauline Friedman

Landers, Lew
Lewis Friedlander

Landis, Carole
Frances Ridste

Landon, Michael
Michael Orowitz

Lane, Abbe
Francine Lassman

Lane, Allan "Rocky"
Harry Albershart

Lane, Burton
Burton Levy

Lane, Lola
Dorothy Mullican

Lang, June
June Vlasek

Lang, Pearl
Pearl Lack

Langtry, Lily
Emily Le Breton

Lansky, Meyer
Maier Suchowljansky

Lanson, Snooky
Roy Landman

Lanza, Mario
Alfred Arnold Cocozza

La Rue, Jack
Gaspare Biondolillo

Lassie
Pal

Latimore, Frank
Frank Kline

Laurel, Stan
Arthur Stanley Jefferson

Laurie, Piper
Rosetta Jacobs

Lawrence, Carol
Carol Maria Laraia

Lawrence, Gertrude
Gertrud Lawrence-Klasen

Lawrence of Arabia
Thomas Edward Lawrence

Lawrence, Mary Wells
Mary Georgene Berg

Lawrence, Steve
Sidney Liebowitz

Layton, Joe
Joseph Lichtman

Le Carre, John
    David John Moore Cornwell

Lee, Canada
    Lionel Canegata

Lee, Gypsy Rose
    Rose Louise Hovick

Lee, Lila
    Augusta Appel

Lee, Michele
    Michele Dusiak

Lee, Peggy
    Norma Engstrom

Lee, Pinky
    Pinkus Leff

Leek, Sybil
    Sybil Falk

Leigh, Janet
    Jeanette Morrison

Leigh, Vivien
    Vivian Mary Hartley

Lemmon, Jack
    John Uhler Lemmon III

Lenin, Nikolai
    Vladimir Ilyich Ulyanov

Lenya, Lotte
    Karoline Balmauer

Leonard, Benny
    Benjamin Leiner

Leonard, Sheldon
    Sheldon Bershad

Lepke, Louis
    Louis Buchalter

Le Roy, Baby
    Le Roy Winnebrenner

Le Roy, Hal
    John Le Roy Schotte

Leslie, Joan
    Joan Brodell

Levene, Sam
    Samuel Levine

Lewis, Jerry
    Joseph Levitch

Lewis, Joe E.
    Joe Klewan

Lewis, Shari
    Shari Hurwitz

Lewis, Ted
    Theodore Leopold Friedman

Liberace
    Wladziu Valentino Liberace

Lillie, Beatrice
    Constance Sylvia Munston

Lincoln, Elmo
    Otto Elmo Linkenhelter

Linden, Hal
    Harold Lipshitz

Lindsay, Margaret
    Margaret Kies

Lisi, Virni
    Virna Peralisi

Livingstone, Mary
    Sadie Marks

Lockwood, Gary
    John Gary Yusolfsky

Lockwood, Margaret
    Margaret Day

Logan, Ella
    Ella Allan

Lom, Herbert
  Herbert Charles Angelo
  Kuchacevich ze
  Schluderpacheru

Lombard, Carol
  Carol Jane Peters

London, Julie
  Julie Peck

Lord, Jack
  John Joseph Ryan

Loren, Sophia
  Sofia Scicolone

Lorre, Peter
  Lazlo Loewenstein

Louis, Joe
  Joe Louis Barrow

Louise, Anita
  Anita Louise Fremault

Louise, Tina
  Tina Blacker

Love, Bessie
  Juanita Horton

Lowery, Robert
  Robert L. Hanke

Loy, Myrna
  Myrna Williams

Lugosi, Bela
  Bela Blasko

Lukas, Paul
  Paul Lukacs

Lupescu, Magda
  Elena Wolff

Lynn, Diana
  Dolly Loehr

Lynn, Jeffrey
  Ragnar Godfrey Lind

Lynn, Loretta
  Loretta Webb

Lyons, Leonard
  Leonard Sucher

Mabley, Jackie "Moms"
  Loretta Mary Aiken

Mack, Ted
  William Edward Maguiness

Madison, Noel
  Noel Moscovitch

Mahoney, Jock
  Jacques O'Mahoney

Main, Marjorie
  Mary Tomlinson

Malden, Karl
  Mladen Sekulovich

Malo, Gina
  Janet Flynn

Manners, David
  Rauff de Ryther Acklom

Mansfield, Jayne
  Jayne Palmer

Mansfield, Katherine
  Katherine Mansfield
  Beauchamp Murry

March, Fredric
  Frederick McIntyre Bickel

Marciano, Rocky
  Rocco Marchegiano

Marisol
  Marisol Escobar

Marlowe, Hugh
  Hugh Hipple

Marlowe, Julia
  Sarah Frances Ford

Marlowe, Marion
  Marion Townsend

Marshall, Brenda
  Ardis Akerson

Marshall, Peter
  Pierre la Cock

Marshall, Tully
  T. M. Phillips

Martin, Dean
  Dino Crocetti

Martin, Ross
  Martin Rosenblatt

Martin, Tony
  Alvin Morris

Marx Brothers
  Groucho—Julius
  Chico—Leonard
  Harpo—Adolph
  Zeppo—Herbert
  Gummo—Milton

Mason, Jackie
  Jacob Masler

Mason, Shirley
  Leona Flugrath

Massey, Ilona
  Ilona Hajmassey

Maurois, André
  Emile Herzog

Maxwell, Lois
  Lois Hooker

Maxwell, Marilyn
  Marvel Maxwell

May, Elaine
  Elaine Berlin

May, Joe
  Joseph Mandel

Mazurki, Mike
  Mikhail Mazurwski

Meadows, Audrey
  Audrey Cotter

Meadows, Jayne
  Jayne Cotter

Meeker, Ralph
  Ralph Rathgeber

Meir, Golda
  Gold Mabovitz
  (later Meyerson)

Melba, Dame Nellie
  Helen Porter Mitchell

Merchant, Vivien
  Ada Thompson

Merman, Ethel
  Ethel Zimmerman

Merrick, David
  David Margulies
  (or Margulois)

Merrill, Dina
  Nedenia Hutton

Merrill, Robert
  Moishe Miller

Mesta, Perle
  Perle Skirvin

Middleton, Robert
  Samuel G. Messer

Miles, Peter
  Gerlad Perreau

Miles, Vera
Vera Ralston

Milland, Ray
Reginald Truscott-Jones

Miller, Ann
Lucy Ann Collier

Miller, Marvin
Marvin Mueller

Milligan, Spike
Terence Alan Milligan

Minter, Mary Miles
Juliet Shelby

Miranda, Carmen
Maria da Carmo Miranda da Cunha

Mitchell, Guy
Al Cernick

Mitchell, Joni
Roberta Joan Anderson

Monroe, Marilyn
Norma Jeane Mortensen (or Baker)

Montana, Bull
Luigi Montagna

Montand, Yves
Ivo Montand Livi

Montez, Lola
Eliza Gilbert

Montez, Maria
Maria de Santo Silas

Montgomery, George
George Montgomery Letz

Moody, Ron
Ronald Moodnick

Moore, Archie
Archibald Lee Wright

Moore, Colleen
Kathleen Morrison

Moore, Garry
Thomas Garrison Morfit

Moore, Melba
Beatrice Moore

Moore, Terry
Helen Koford

Moravia, Alberto
Alberto Pincherle

Moreno, Rita
Rosita Dolores Alverio

Morgan, Dennis
Stanley Morner

Morgan, Frank
Francis Wupperman

Morgan, Harry
Harry Bratsburg

Morgan, Henry
Henry Lerner Von Ost, Jr.

Morgan, Michele
Simone Roussel

Morgan, Ralph
Ralph Wupperman

Morris, Wayne
Bert De Wayne Morris

Mostel, Zero
Samuel Joel Mostel

Muhammad, Elijah
Elijah Poole

Muni, Paul
Muni Weisenfreund

Munsel, Patrice
Patrice Munsil

Murnau, F. W.
  F. W. Plumpe

Murray, Arthur
  Arthur Murray Teichman

Murray, Jan
  Murray Janofsky

Murray, Kathryn
  Kathryn Kohnfelder

Murray, Ken
  Don Court

Murray, Mae
  Marie Adrienne Koenig

Murrow, Edward R.
  Egbert Roscoe Murrow

McBain, Ed
  Evan Hunter (né Lombino)

McDowell, Malcolm
  Malcolm Taylor

McFarland, Spanky
  George Emmett McFarland

McKay, Jim
  James Kenneth McManus

MacKenzie, Gisele
  Marie Marguerite Louise
  Gisele La Fleche

MacLaine, Shirley
  Shirley MacLean Beaty

McQueen, Butterfly
  Thelma McQueen

Naldi, Nita
  Anita Donna Dooley

Nebel, Long John
  John Zimmerman
  (later John "Jack" Knebel)

Negri, Pola
  Apolonia Mathias-Chalupec

Nelson, Barry
  Gene Berg

Nelson, Harriet
  Peggy Lou Snyder

Nerina, Nadia
  Nadine Judd

Nero, Peter
  Bernie Nierow

Neruda, Pablo
  Neftali Ricardo Reyes y
  Basoalto

Newmar, Julie
  Julia Newmeyer

Niblo, Fred
  Federico Nobile

Nichols, Mike
  Michael Igor Peschkowsky

Nidetch, Jean
  Jean Slutsky

Noonan, Tommy
  Thomas Noon

Normand, Mabel
  Mabel Fortescue

North, Sheree
  Dawn Bethel

Novak, Kim
  Marilyn Novak

Novarro, Ramon
  Ramon Samaniegoes

Nye, Carrie
  Carrie Nye McGeoy

Nye, Louis
  Luis Nyestadt

Oakie, Jack
Lewis Delaney Offield

Oakley, Annie
Phoebe Annie Oakley Mozee

Oberon, Merle
Merle O'Brien Thompson

Obolensky, Serge
Serge Platonovitch Obolensky
Neledinsky Meletsky

O'Brian, Hugh
Hugh J. Krampe

O'Brien, Margaret
Angela Maxine O'Brien

O'Brien, Dave
David Barclay

O'Brien, Pat
William Joseph O'Brien, Jr.

Odetta
Odetta Holmes

O'Hara, Maureen
Maureen FitzSimmons

O'Keefe, Dennis
Edward "Bud" Flanagan

Orwell, George
Eric Arthur Blair

Owens, Jesse
James Cleveland Owens

Page, Anita
Anita Pomares

Page, Gale
Sally Rutter

Page, Patti
Sally Anne Fowler

Paget, Deborah
Debralee Griffin

Paige, Janis
Donna Mae Jaden

Paige, Robert
John Arthur Page

Palance, Jack
Walter Palanuik

Palmer, Lilli
Lilli Peiser

Papp, Joseph
Joseph Papirofksy

Parker, Dorothy
Dorothy Rothschild

Parker, Suzy
Cecilia Parker

Parks, Bert
Bert Jacobson

Parks, Larry
Samuel Klausman

Parsons, Louella
Louella Oettinger

Paul VI, Pope
Giovanni Battista Montini

Pavan, Marisa
Marisa Pierangeli

Pearl, Minnie
Sarah Ophelia Colley Cannon

Peerce, Jan
Jacob Pinkus Perelmuth

Perreau, Gigi
Ghislaine Perreau-Saussine

Peters, Bernadette
Bernadette Lazzara

Peters, Roberta
Roberta Peterman

Peters, Susan
  Suzanne Carnahan

Phillips, Michelle
  Holly Michelle Gilliam

Piaf, Edith
  Edith Giovanna Gassion

Pickens, Slim
  Louis Bert Lindley

Pickford, Mary
  Gladys Mary Smith

Pinza, Ezio
  Fortunato Pinza

Plummer, Christopher
  Arthur Christopher Ormf

Pollard, Michael J.
  Michael J. Pollack

Pollard, Snub
  Harold Fraser

Porter, Sylvia
  Sylvia Field Feldman

Post, Emily
  Emily Price

Powell, Jane
  Suzanne Burce

Powers, Stefanie
  Stefanie Federkiewicz

Prentiss, Paula
  Paula Ragusa

Preston, Robert
  Robert Preston Meservey

Previn, Dory
  Dory Langan

Pucci, Emilio
  Marchese di Barsento

Qualen, John
  John Oleson

Rae, Charlotte
  Charlotte Lubotsky

Raft, George
  George Ranft

Rand, Sally
  Helen Gould Beck

Ray, Aldo
  Aldo de Re

Ray, Nicholas
  Raymond N. Kienzle

Raye, Martha
  Margie Yvonne Reed
  (or O'Reed)

Raymond, Gene
  Raymond Guion

Reed, Donna
  Donna Bella Mullenger

Reems, Harry
  Herbert Streicher

Reese, Della
  Deloreese Patricia Early

Reinhardt, Max
  Max Goldman

Remarque, Erich Maria
  Erich Paul Remark

Renaldo, Duncan
  Renaldo Duncan

Renay, Liz
  Pearl Elizabeth Dobbins

Rey, Fernando
  Fernando Arambillet

Reynolds, Marjorie
  Marjorie Moore

83

Rice, Elmer
    Elmer Reizenstein

Rich, Irene
    Irene Luther

Richard, Little
    Richard Wayne Penniman

Richards, Renée
    Richard Raskind

Ritter, Tex
    Woodward Maurice Ritter

Ritz, Al
    Al Joachim

Rivers, Joan
    Joan Molinsky

Rivers, Larry
    Yitzroch Loiza Grossberg

Robbins, Harold
    Francis Kane

Robbins, Jerome
    Jerome Rabinowitz

Robinson, Edward G.
    Emanuel Goldenberg

Robinson, Sugar Ray
    Walker Smith, Jr.

Rogers, Ginger
    Virginia McMath

Rogers, Roy
    Leonard Slye

Roland, Gilbert
    Luis Antonio Damaso de
    Alonso

Romanoff, Mike
    Harry F. Gerguson

Rooney, Mickey
    Joe Yule, Jr.

Rose, Billy
    William Samuel Rosenberg

Ross, Barney
    Barnet Rasofsky

Roth, Lillian
    Lillian Rutstein

Rothko, Mark
    Marcus Rothkovich

Russell, Lillian
    Helen Louise Leonard

Russell, Pee Wee
    Charles Ellsworth Russell III

Rydell, Bobby
    Robert Riderelli

Sabu
    Sabu Dastagir

Sagan, Françoise
    Francoise Quoirez

St. Cyr, Lili
    Marie Van Schaak

Saint James, Susan
    Susan Miller

St-Laurent, Yves
    Henri Donat Mathieu

Sakall, S. Z.
    Eugene Gero Szakall

Saki
    Hector Hugh Munro

Sales, Soupy
    Milton Hines

Sand, George
    Amandine Lucille Aurore
    Dudevant (née Dupin)

Sanda, Dominique
    Dominique Varaigne

Sawyer, Joseph
  Joseph Sauer

Saxon, John
  Carmen Orrico

Scaasi, Arnold
  Arnold Isaacs

Scala, Gia
  Giovanna Scoglio

Schneider, Romy
  Rosemarie Albach-Retty

Schultz, Dutch
  Arthur Flegenheimer

Scott, Gordon
  Gordon M. Werschkul

Scott, Elizabeth
  Emma Matzo

Scott, Randolph
  Randolph Crane

Sennett, Mack
  Michael Sinnott

Seuss, Dr.
  Theodor Seuss Geisel

Shapp, Milton
  Milton Jerrold Shapiro

Sharif, Omar
  Michael Shalhoub

Sharkey, Jack
  Joseph Paul Zukauskas

Shaw, Artie
  Arthur Isaac Arshawsky

Shawn, Dick
  Richard Schulefand

Shean, Al
  Alfred Schoenberg

Shearer, Moira
  Moira Shearer King

Sheen, Bishop Fulton
  Peter John Sheen

Sheen, Martin
  Ramon Estevez

Sheridan, Ann
  Clara Lou Sheridan

Shirley, Anne
  Dawn Evelyneen Paris

Shor, Toots
  Bernard Shor

Shore, Dinah
  Frances "Fanny" Rose Shore

Sidney, Sylvia
  Sophie Kosow

Signoret, Simone
  Simone Kaminker

Sills, Beverly
  Belle "Bubbles" Miriam Silverman

Silvers, Phil
  Philip Silversmith

Simone, Nina
  Eunice Kathleen Waymon

Simpson, Adele
  Adele Smithline

Simpson, O. J.
  Orenthal James Simpson

Singleton, Penny
  Mariana Dorothy McNulty

Skelton, Red
  Richard Bernard Skelton

Slick, Grace
  Grace Wing

Smith, Adam
George J. Goodman

Smith, Red
Walter Wellesley Smith

Smith and Dale
Joseph Seltzer and
Clarles Marks

Sommer, Elke
Elke Schletz

Sothern, Ann
Harriet Lake

Sothern, Georgia
Hazel Anderson

Sparks, Ned
Edward Sparkman

Spillane, Mickey
Frank Morrison

Stalin, Joseph
Josif V. Dzhugashvili

Stanislavski
Konstantin Sergeyevitch
Alekseyev

Stanley, Kim
Patricia Kimberly Reid

Stanwyck, Barbara
Ruby Stevens

Stapleton, Jean
Jeanne Murray

Starr, Ringo
Richard Starkey

Steele, Bob
Robert North Bradbury, Jr.

Steele, Tommy
Tommy Hicks

Sten, Anna
Anjuchka Stenska

Stendhal
Marie Henri Beyle

Sterling, Jan
Jane Sterling Adriance

Sterling, Robert
William Sterling Hart

Stevens, Connie
Concetta Ingolia

Stevens, Craig
Gail Shekles

Stevens, Inger
Inger Stensland

Stevens, K. T.
Gloria Wood

Stevens, Risë
Risë Steenberg

Stewart, Elaine
Elsy Steinberg

St. John, Jill
Jill Oppenheim

Stone, George E.
George Stein

Stone, Irving
Irving Tennenbaum

Stoppard, Tom
Thomas Straussler

Storm, Gail
Josephine Owaissa Cottle

Stuart, Lyle
Lionel Simon

Sturges, Preston
Edmund P. Biden

Styne, Jule
  Jules Stein

Sullivan, Barry
  Patrick Barry

Sumac, Yma
  Emperatriz Chavarri Yma
  Sumac

Suzy
  Aileen Elder (later Mehle)

Talbot, Lyle
  Lisle Henderson

Talmadge, Richard
  Ricardo Metzetti

Tate, Allen
  John Orley

Tati, Jacques
  Jacques Tatischeff

Taylor, Estelle
  Estelle Boylan

Taylor, Kent
  Louis Weiss

Taylor, Laurette
  Laurette Cooney

Taylor, Robert
  Spangler Arlington Brugh

Terry, Alice
  Alice Taafi

Terry, Don
  Donald Locher

Thomas, Danny
  Amos Jacobs

Thomas, Terry-
  Thomas Terry Hoar-Stevens

Thumb, Tom
  Charles Sherwood Stratton

Tim, Tiny
  Herbert Khaury

Titian
  Tiziano Vecelli

Tito
  Josip Broz (ovich?)

Tittle, Y. A.
  Yelberton Abraham Tittle

Todd, Ann
  Ann T. Mayfield

Todd, Mike
  Avrom Goldenborgen

Tokyo Rose
  Iva Ikuko Toguri D'Aquino

Topol
  Chaim Topol

Torn, Rip
  Elmore Torn

Torres, Raquel
  Paula Marie Osterman

Tracy, Arthur
  Harry Rosenberg

Trapp, Maria
  Maria Augusta Kutschera

Traver, Robert
  John Donaldson Voelker

Treacher, Arthur
  Arthur T. Veary

Trotsky, Leon
  Lev Davidovich Bronstein

Troyat, Henri
  Lev Tarassov

Tucker, Richard
  Reuben Ticker

Tucker, Sophie
  Sophie Kalish (later Abuza)

Tufts, Sonny
  Bowen Charleston Tufts III

Tunney, Gene
  James Joseph Tunney

Turner, Lana
  Julia Jean Turner

Turner, Tina
  Annie Mae Bullock

Twain, Mark
  Samuel Langhorne Clemens

Twiggy
  Leslie Hornby

Twitty, Conway
  Harold Jenkins

Tyler, Tom
  Vincent Markowsky

Tynan, Kenneth
  Kenneth Peacock

Ukulele Ike
  Cliff Edwards

Vadim, Roger
  Roger Vadim Plemiannikow

Valens, Richie
  Richard Venezuela

Valentino
  Valentino Garavani

Valentino, Rudolph
  Rodolpho Gugielmi di
  Valentino d'Antonguolla

Vallee, Rudy
  Hubert Prior Vallee

Valli, Alida
  Alida Maria Altenburger

Valli, Virginia
  Virginia McSweeney

Van Buren, Abigail
  Pauline Esther Friedman

Van Doren, Mamie
  Joan Lucille Olander

Van Heusen, Jimmy
  Edward Chester Babcock

Van Peebles, Melvin
  Melvin Peebles

Velez, Lupe
  Guadeloupe Velez de
  Villalobos

Venuta, Benay
  Venuta Rose Crooke

Vera-Ellen
  Vera Ellen Westmeyr Rohe

Vickers, Martha
  Martha MacVicar

Villa, Pancho
  Doroteo Arango

Vincent, Gene
  Gene Vincent Craddock

Vinson, Helen
  Helen Rules

Visconti, Luchino
  Count Don Luchino Visconti
  di Modrone

Vitti, Monica
  Monica Luisa Ceciarelli

Von Sternberg, Josef
  Josef Stern

Von Stroheim, Erich
  Hans Erich Maria Stroheim
  von Nordenwall

Walcott, Jersey Joe
  Arnold Raymond Cream

Walker, Nancy
  Nancy Swoyer

Wallace, Irving
  Irving Wallechinsky

Wallace, Jean
  Jean Wallasek

Wallace, Mike
  Myron Wallace

Walter, Bruno
  Bruno Walter Schlesinger

Wanger, Walter
  Walter Feuchtwanger

Ward, Burt
  Bert John Gervais, Jr.

Warhol, Andy
  Andy Warhola

Warner, H. B.
  Henry Bryan Warner
  Lickford

Warner, Jack
  Jack Waters

Warwick, Dionne
  Marie Dionne Warrick

Wayne, David
  David M. Meakan

Wayne, John
  Marion Robert Morrison
  (later Marion Michael
  Morrison)

Waxman, Franz
  Franz Wachsmann

Weaver, Charlie
  Cliff Arquette

Webb, Clifton
  Webb Parmelee Hollenbeck

Welch, Raquel
  Raquel Tejada

Weld, Tuesday
  Susan Ker Weld

West, Adam
  William Anderson

West, Dame Rebecca
  Cecily Isabel Fairfield

West, Nathanael
  Nathan Weinstein

Whalen, Michael
  Joseph Shovlin

White, Jesse
  Jesse Wiedenfeld

Wilder, Billy
  Samuel Wilder

Williams, Tennessee
  Thomas Lanier Williams

Williams, William B.
  William Breitbard

Wilson, Flip
  Clerow Wilson

Wilson, Johnny
  John Panica

Wilson, Marie
  Katherine Elizabeth White

Winchell, Walter
  Walter Winechel

Windsor, Marie
  Emily Marie Bertelson

Winslow, George "Foghorn"
  George Wenzlaff

Windsor, Claire
　　Clara Viola Cronk

Winters, Shelley
　　Shirley Schrift

Winwood, Estelle
　　Estelle Goodwin

Wonder, Stevie
　　Steveland Judkins
　　(later Steveland Morris)

Wong, Anna May
　　Liu Tsong Wong

Wood, Natalie
　　Natasha Gurdin

Woodlawn, Holly
　　Harold Danhaki

Woolley, Monty
　　Edgard Montillion Woolley

Wray, John
　　John Malloy

Wyman, Jane
　　Sarah Jane Fulks

Wynn, Ed
　　Isaiah Edwin Leopold

Wynter, Dana
　　Dagmar Spencer-Marcus

Young, Chic
　　Murat Bernard Young

Young, Gig
　　Byron Ellsworth Barr

Young, Loretta
　　Gretchen Young

Zorina, Vera
　　Eva Brigitta Hartwig

# FANCY FULL NAMES

Fancy names seem to work well on Wall Street but not in show business. Long names don't fit on marquees and also scare off the masses. That's why Hollywood gave us all the Chads, Tabs, and Rocks. Here are a few actors who used shorter versions of their real WASPy-sounding full names:

| Full Names | Better Known As |
| --- | --- |
| Lewis Frederick Ayres III | Lew Ayres |
| Alexander Crichlow Barker, Jr. | Lex Barker |
| John Charles Holt, Jr. | Tim Holt |
| John Uhler Lemmon III | Jack Lemmon |
| Charles Robert Redford, Jr. | Robert Redford |
| Clifford Parker Robertson III | Cliff Robertson |
| Bowen Charleston Tufts III | Sonny Tufts |

# *WHO'S WHO* TRIVIA

Of the 75,000 people listed in *Who's Who in America*, most are not show business or media celebrities but rather are people of accomplishment in many different professions. Within the 3,810 pages of the two volumes, several entries stand out because of their uniqueness. The following persons have noteworthy entries:

**The First Entry**
Herbert Aach—A New York City artist
**The Youngest Person***
Tatum O'Neal—Born November 5, 1963; actress and daughter of actor Ryan O'Neal.
**The Longest Entry**
Isaac Asimov—Author and biochemist; most of his 221 books are listed.
**The Last Entry**
George J. Zytaruk—Of North Bay Canada; president of Nipissing University College.

---

*Other young people listed are actress Kristy McNichol (born September 11, 1962); actress Jodie Foster (born November 19, 1962); tennis player Tracy Austin (born December 12, 1962); and jockey Steve Cauthen (born May 1, 1960).

# CELEBRITY HIGH SCHOOLS
## CELEBRITY PREPPIES

Edward Albee (Rye Country Day, Lawrenceville, Valley Forge Military Academy, Choate)
Jane Alexander (Beaver Country Day)
Greg Allman (Castle Heights Military Academy)
Walter Annenberg (Peddie)
F. Lee Bailey (Kimball Union Academy)
Peter Benchley (Exeter)
Stephen Birmingham (Hotchkiss)
Shirley Temple Black (Westlake)
Humphrey Bogart (Trinity, Andover)
Peter Bogdanovich (Collegiate)
Marlon Brando (Shattuck Military Academy)
William F. Buckley, Jr. (Millbrook)
McGeorge Bundy (Groton)
George Bush (Andover)
James Caan (Rhodes School)
Truman Capote (Trinity)
John Carradine (Episcopal Academy)
John Chancellor (De Paul Academy)
Chevy Chase (Dalton)
Julia Child (Katherine Branson School)
Jill Clayburgh (Brearley)
Natalie Cole (Northfield-Mt. Hermon)
Bruce Dern (Choate)
Keir Dullea (George School)

Mia Farrow (Marymount, Cygnet House)
Millicent Fenwick (Foxcroft)
Mark Fidrych (Worcester Academy)
Jane Fonda (Emma Willard)
Jodie Foster (Lyçee Francais)
John Frankenheimer (LaSalle Military Academy)
John Gavin (St. John's Military Academy, Villanova Prep)
Tammy Grimes (Beaver Country Day)
David Hartman (Mt. Hermon)
Abbie Hoffman (Worcester Academy)
Jack Lemmon (Andover)
G. Gordon Liddy (St. Benedict's Prep)
John V. Lindsay (Buckley, St. Paul's)
Lee Marvin (St. Leo's Prep)
George Murphy (Pawling)
Jackie Onassis (Miss Porter's)
George Plimpton (Exeter)
Cole Porter (Worcester Academy)
Lee Remick (Miss Hewitt's)
Joan Rivers (Ethical Culture, Adelphi Academy)
Cesar Romero (Collegiate)
Robert Ryan (Loyola Academy)
J. D. Salinger (Valley Forge Military Academy)
Randolph Scott (Woodberry Forest)
Carly Simon (Riverdale Girls' School)
George Steinbrenner (Culver Military Academy)
James Stewart (Mercersburg)
Garry Trudeau (St. Paul's)
Ted Turner (Georgia Military Academy)
Cyrus Vance (Kent)
Gore Vidal (Exeter)
Barbara Walters (Fieldston, Birch Wathen)
Sigourney Weaver (Ethel Walker)
Tom Wolfe (St. Christopher's)

## CELEBRITIES WHO ATTENDED
## DEWITT CLINTON HIGH SCHOOL, BRONX, NEW YORK

George Cukor   '17?
Richard Rodgers   '18?
Lionel Trilling   '21?
Burt Lancaster   '31
Daniel Schorr   '33
Don Adams   '35?
William Kunstler   '36
Martin Balsam   '37?
Paddy Chayevsky   '39

Richard Avedon   '41
James Baldwin   '42
Neil Simon   '44
Bruce Jay Friedman   '47
Judd Hirsch   '52
Robert Klein   '58
Nate Archibald   '66
Jimmy Walker   ?
Fats Waller   ?

## CELEBRITIES WHO ATTENDED
## ERASMUS HIGH SCHOOL, BROOKLYN, NEW YORK

Barbra Streisand   '59
Lainie Kazan   '56
Gabe Kaplan   '63
Donny Most   '70
Neil Diamond   '57
Jeff Chandler   '35

Barbara Stanwyck   ?
Sid Luckman   '35
Gilbert Price   '60
Mickey Spillane   ?
Bernard Malamud   '32
Diana Trilling   '21

## CELEBRITIES WHO ATTENDED
## NEW TRIER HIGH SCHOOL, WINNETKA, ILLINOIS

Ralph Bellamy   '22
Charlton Heston   '41
Rock Hudson   '44
Hugh O'Brian   '48

Bruce Dern   '54
Ann-Margret   '59
Penny Milford   '66

## GRADUATES OF HOLLYWOOD, CALIFORNIA,
## HIGH SCHOOL

Fay Wray   '24
Lana Turner   ?
Jason Robards   '39
Alan Hale, Jr.   '38
James Garner   ?
Nanette Fabray   '40

Carol Burnett   '51
Sally Kellerman   '55
Linda Evans   '60
Stefanie Powers   '60
John Ritter   '66
Charlene Tilton   '76

# FAMOUS HIGH SCHOOL DROPOUTS

Richard Avedon
Harry Belafonte
Robert Blake
Sonny Bono
David Bowie
Michael Caine
Glen Campbell
George Carlin
John Chancellor
Cher
Roger Daltrey
Bo Derek
Lola Falana
Carrie Fisher
Redd Foxx

James Garner
Andy Gibb
Marjoe Gortner
Cary Grant
Gene Hackman
Merle Haggard
Lena Horne
Tom Jones
Eartha Kitt
Evel Knievel
Jerry Lewis
Loretta Lynn
Rod McKuen*
Steve McQueen

Dean Martin
Lee Marvin
Elaine May
Robert Mitchum
Roger Moore
Al Pacino
Sidney Poitier
Richard Pryor
Anthony Quinn
Vidal Sassoon
Frank Sinatra
John Travolta
Peter Ustinov
Robert Wagner

*Grammar school dropout.

# HIGH SCHOOL CHEERLEADERS WHO MADE GOOD

Ann-Margret
Ellen Burstyn
Dyan Cannon
Eydie Gorme
Patty Hearst
Vicky Lawrence

Cybill Shepherd
Dinah Shore
Carly Simon
Meryl Streep
Lily Tomlin
Raquel Welch

# COLLEGES AND UNIVERSITIES ATTENDED BY CELEBRITIES

Abdul-Jabbar, Kareem
Albee, Edward
Albert, Eddie
Alda, Alan
Alexander, Jane
Alpert, Herb
Altman, Robert
Ameche, Don

UCLA
Trinity College
U. of Minnesota
Fordham U.
Sarah Lawrence
USC
U. of Missouri
Loras College, Marquette U.,
    Georgetown U.

| | |
|---|---|
| Amory, Cleveland | Harvard College |
| Andrews, Dana | Sam Houston State |
| Ann-Margret | Northwestern U. |
| Arkin, Alan | Bennington College, |
| | L.A. City College |
| Ashe, Arthur | UCLA |
| Ashley, Elizabeth | Louisiana State U. |
| Asner, Ed | U. of Chicago |
| Bacharach, Burt | McGill U. |
| Bailey, F. Lee | Harvard College, |
| | Boston U. Law School |
| Balsam, Martin | New School for Social Research |
| Barthelmess, Richard | Trinity College |
| Bean, Orson | Harvard College |
| Beatty, Warren | Northwestern U. |
| Bellow, Saul | Northwestern U. |
| Belushi, John | U. of Michigan, others |
| Benchley, Peter | Harvard College |
| Benjamin, Richard | Northwestern U. |
| Bergen, Candice | U. of Pennsylvania |
| Bernstein, Leonard | Harvard College |
| Bickford, Charles | MIT |
| Black, Karen | Northwestern U. |
| Blackmer, Sidney | U. of North Carolina |
| Blyden, Larry | U. of Houston |
| Bombeck, Erma | U. of Dayton |
| Boone, Pat | Columbia U. |
| Bosley, Tom | De Paul U. |
| Boyer, Charles | Sorbonne |
| Brackett, Charles | Williams College, |
| | Harvard Law School |
| Brokaw, Tom | U. of South Dakota |
| Brooks, Mel | Brooklyn College |
| Browne, Roscoe Lee | Lincoln U., Middlebury, |
| | Columbia, U. |
| Bryant, Anita | Northwestern U. |
| Buckley, William F. | Yale College |
| Burnett, Carol | UCLA |
| Burr, Raymond | Stanford U. Columbia U., |
| | U. of Calif. |
| Burton, Richard | Oxford U. |

| | |
|---|---|
| Caan, James | Hofstra U. |
| Capra, Frank | Calif. Institute of Technology |
| Carradine, David | San Francisco State College |
| Carradine, Keith | Colorado State College |
| Carson, Johnny | U. of Nebraska |
| Carter, Jimmy | U.S. Naval Academy |
| Cassavetes, John | Mohawk College, Colgate |
| Cavett, Dick | Yale U. |
| Chamberlain, Richard | Pomona College |
| Channing, Carol | Bennington College |
| Chapin, Harry | USAF Academy, Cornell U. |
| Chase, Chevy | Haverford College, Bard College |
| Child, Julia | Smith College |
| Christie, Julie | Brighton Technical College |
| Clayburgh, Ji˙ | Sarah Lawrence College |
| Coburn, James | Los Angeles City College |
| Connors, Jimmy | UCLA |
| Convy, Bert | UCLA |
| Coolidge, Rita | Florida State U. |
| Cooper, Gary | Wesleyan College (Montana); Grinnell |
| Cooper, Merian C. | U.S. Naval Academy |
| Coppola, Francis Ford | Hofstra U. |
| Corman, Roger | Stanford U., Oxford U. |
| Cosby, Bill | Temple U., U. of Massachusetts |
| Cosell, Howard | NYU |
| Crisp, Donald | Oxford U. |
| Cronkite, Walter | U. of Texas |
| Cronyn, Hume | Ridley College, McGill U. |
| Crosby, Bing | Gonzaga U. |
| Daly, James | Cornell U. |
| Da Silva, Howard | Carnegie Tech. |
| Davidson, John | Denison U. |
| Davis, Mac | Emory U. |
| Dean, James | UCLA |
| Dee, Ruby | Hunter College |
| Denver, John | Texas Tech. |
| Dern, Bruce | U. of Pennsylvania |
| Diamond, Neil | New York U. |
| Dickinson, Angie | Glendale College |
| Diller, Phyllis | Bluffton College |

| | |
|---|---|
| Donahue, Phil | U. of Notre Dame |
| Douglas, Michael | U. of California (Santa Barbara) |
| Downs, Hugh | Bluffton College |
| Drake, Alfred | Brooklyn College |
| Duchin, Peter | Yale U. |
| Dunaway, Faye | U. of Florida |
| Dunnock, Mildred | Goucher College, Columbia U. |
| Dussault, Nancy | Northwestern U. |
| Dylan, Bob | U. of Minnesota |
| Eastwood, Clint | L.A. City College |
| Erving, Julius | U. of Massachusetts |
| Ewell, Tom | U. of Wisconsin |
| Fabray, Nanette | L.A. City College |
| Falk, Peter | Hamilton College, the New School, Syracuse U. |
| Fawcett, Peter | U. of Texas |
| Flack, Roberta | Howard U. |
| Fonda, Henry | U. of Minnesota |
| Fonda, Jane | Vassar College |
| Fonda, Peter | U. of Omaha |
| Ford, Paul | Dartmouth College |
| Ford, Ruth | U. of Mississippi |
| Forsythe, John | U. of North Carolina |
| Foster, Jodie | Yale U. |
| Frost, David | Cambridge U. |
| Garfunkel, Art | Columbia U. |
| Gavin, John | Stanford U. |
| Gazzara, Ben | City College of N.Y. |
| Geer, Will | U. of Chicago, Columbia U. |
| George, Phyllis | North Texas State College |
| Gere, Richard | U. of Massachusetts |
| Ghostley, Alice | U. of Oklahoma |
| Greene, Lorne | Queen's University (Ontario) |
| Gregory, Dick | Southern Illinois U. |
| Griffin, Merv | San Mateo Jr. College, Stanford U., U. of San Francisco |
| Grimes, Tammy | Stephens College |
| Grizzard, George | U. of North Carolina |
| Gunn, Moses | U. of Kansas |
| Hagen, Uta | U. of Wisconsin |
| Halston | U. of Indiana |

| | |
|---|---|
| Hamill, Mark | L.A. City College |
| Harris, Emmylou | U. of North Carolina |
| Harris, Julie | Yale School of Drama |
| Harrison, Rex | Liverpool College |
| Hartman, David | Duke U. |
| Hawn, Goldie | American U. |
| Hayward, Leland | Princeton U. |
| Hefner, Hugh | U. of Illinois |
| Hepburn, Katharine | Bryn Mawr College |
| Heston, Charlton | Northwestern U. |
| Hill, Arthur | U. of British Columbia |
| Hill, George Roy | Yale, Trinity College (Dublin) |
| Hingle, Pat | U. of Texas |
| Hoffman, Dustin | Santa Monica College |
| Holbrook, Hal | Denison U. |
| Holden, William | Pasadena College |
| Houseman, John | Clifton College (England) |
| Howard, Ken | Amherst College, Yale School of Drama |
| Ives, Burl | Eastern Ill. State Teachers College |
| Jackson, Kate | U. of Mississippi, Birmingham U. |
| Jaffe, Sam | CCNY, Columbia U. |
| Jagger, Mick | London School of Economics |
| Jenner, Bruce | San Jose State College |
| Jones, James Earl | U. of Michigan |
| Kahn, Madeline | Hofstra U. |
| Kazan, Elia | Williams College, Yale School of Drama |
| Keach, Stacy | U. of Calif. (Berkeley), Yale School of Drama |
| Kennedy, Arthur | Carnegie Tech. |
| Kert, Larry | L.A. City College |
| Kiley, Richard | Loyola U. |
| King, Billy Jean | UCLA |
| Kissinger, Henry | Harvard U. |
| Klugman, Jack | Carnegie Tech. |
| Kristofferson, Kris | Pomona College, Oxford U. |
| Lancaster, Burt | NYU |
| Lasser, Louise | Brandeis U. |
| Lavin, Linda | William and Mary |

| | |
|---|---|
| MacGraw, Ali | Wellesley College |
| McMahon, Ed | Catholic U. |
| MacMurray, Fred | Carroll College |
| Mailer, Norman | Harvard College |
| Majors, Lee | Eastern Kentucky State College |
| Marshall, Penny | U. of New Mexico |
| Martin, Steve | UCLA |
| Mathis, Johnny | San Francisco State College |
| Meredith, Burgess | Amherst College |
| Midler, Bette | U. of Hawaii |
| Milnes, Sherrill | Drake U. |
| Murphy, George | Yale U. |
| Nabors, Jim | U. of Alabama |
| Nader, Ralph | Princeton U., |
| | Harvard Law School |
| Namath, Joe | U. of Alabama |
| Neal, Patricia | Northwestern U. |
| Newhart, Bob | Loyola U. |
| Newman, Paul | Kenyon College, |
| | Yale School of Drama |
| Nichols, Mike | U. of Chicago |
| Nicklaus, Jack | Ohio State U. |
| Niven, David | Sandhurst Military Academy |
| | (England) |
| Nixon, Richard M. | Whittier College, |
| | Duke U. School of Law |
| Nolte, Nick | Pasadena City College |
| O'Brien, Pat | Marquette U. |
| O'Connor, Carroll | National U. (Dublin) |
| Onassis, Jacqueline | Vassar College |
| Orbach, Jerry | U. of Illinois, Northwestern U. |
| Pauley, Jane | U. of Indiana |
| Peck, Gregory | U. of California (Berkeley) |
| Peppard, George | Purdue U., Carnegie Tech. |
| Perkins, Anthony | Rollins College, Columbia U. |
| Piazza, Ben | Princeton U. |
| Plimpton, George | Harvard College |
| Price, Vincent | Yale, U. of London |
| Radner, Gilda | U. of Michigan |
| Rae, Charlotte | Northwestern U. |
| Raitt, Bonnie | Radcliffe College |
| Randall, Tony | Northwestern U. |

| | |
|---|---|
| Rather, Dan | Sam Houston State Teachers College |
| Reagan, Nancy | Smith College |
| Reagan, Ronald | Eureka College |
| Reasoner, Harry | Stanford U., U. of Minnesota |
| Redford, Robert | U. of Colorado, Pratt Institute |
| Reilly, Charles Nelson | U. of Connecticut |
| Reynolds, Burt | Florida State College |
| Rich, Charlie | U. of Arkansas |
| Ritter, John | USC |
| Rivers, Joan | Barnard College |
| Robertson, Cliff | Antioch College |
| Rogers, Mr. (Fred) | Dartmouth College, Rollins College |
| Rogers, Kenny | U. of Houston |
| Ronstadt, Linda | U. of Arizona |
| Rowlands, Gena | U. of Wisconsin |
| Sales, Soupy | Marshall College |
| Savalas, Telly | Columbia U. |
| Savitch, Jessica | Ithaca College |
| Scheider, Roy | Franklin and Marshall |
| Schell, Maximilian | U. of Zurich, U. of Munich |
| Scott, George C. | U. of Missouri |
| Seaver, Tom | USC |
| Seberg, Jean | Iowa State U. |
| Segal, George | Haverford College, Columbia U. |
| Shalit, Gene | U. of Illinois |
| Sharif, Omar | Victoria College |
| Shaw, Irwin | Brooklyn College |
| Shields, Brooke | Princeton U. |
| Shore, Dinah | Vanderbilt U. |
| Simon, Carly | Sarah Lawrence College |
| Simon, Neil | NYU |
| Simon, Paul | Queens College |
| Simpson, O. J. | USC |
| Slick, Grace | Finch College |
| Smith, Jaclyn | Trinity College (Texas) |
| Smothers, Tom and Dick | San Jose State College |
| Snyder, Tom | Marquette U. |
| Somers, Suzanne | Lone Mountain College |
| Sondheim, Stephen | Williams College |

| | |
|---|---|
| Spielberg, Stephen | Calif. State College (Long Beach) |
| Stallone, Sylvester | U. of Miami |
| Steinem, Gloria | Smith College |
| Stewart, Jimmy | Princeton U. |
| Streisand, Barbra | Yeshiva U. |
| Susskind, David | Harvard College |
| Sutherland, Donald | U. of Toronto |
| Thomas, Marlo | USC |
| Tiegs, Cheryl | Calif. State (LA) |
| Tomlin, Lily | Wayne State U. |
| Torn, Rip | Texas A & M, U. of Texas |
| Tune, Tommy | Lon Morris College, U. of Texas, U. of Houston |
| Updike, John | Harvard College |
| Vallee, Rudy | U. of Maine, Yale U. |
| Vaughn, Robert | U. of Minnesota, L.A. State College, USC |
| Voight, Jon | Catholic U. |
| Wallace, Mike | U. of Michigan |
| Wallach, Eli | U. of Texas, CCNY |
| Walters, Barbara | Sarah Lawrence |
| Warhol, Andy | Carnegie Tech. |
| Waterston, Sam | Yale U. |
| Weaver, Fritz | U. of Chicago |
| Widmark, Richard | Lake Forest College |
| Williams, Cindy | Los Angeles City College |
| Williams, Robin | College of Marin |
| Winkler, Henry | Emerson College, Yale School of Drama |
| Winters, Jonathan | Kenyon College |
| Wolfe, Tom | Washington and Lee, Yale U. |
| Woodward, Joanne | Louisiana State U. |
| York, Michael | Oxford U. |
| Zeffirelli, Franco | U. of Florence |

## ACADEMIC HONORS

| | |
|---|---|
| Pat Boone | Magna cum laude, Columbia University |
| Helen Gurley Brown | Honor roll, high school |
| Connie Francis | Honor roll, high school |

| | |
|---|---|
| Betty Friedan | Honor roll, high school |
| Marvin Hamlisch | Cum laude, Queens College |
| Henry Kissinger | Summa cum laude, Harvard College |
| Kris Kristofferson | Phi Beta Kappa, Pomona College |
| Ann Landers | Honor roll, high school |
| Art Linkletter | Honor roll, high school |
| Shirley MacLaine | Honor roll, high school |
| Rex Reed | Honor roll, high school |
| Joan Rivers | Phi Beta Kappa, Barnard College |
| Mr. Rogers | Magna cum laude, Rollins College |
| Philip Roth | Magna cum laude, Bucknell |
| Barbra Streisand | Honor roll, high school |
| Sally Struthers | Honor roll, high school |
| Tom Tryon | Cum laude, Yale |
| John Updike | Summa cum laude, Harvard College |
| Abigail Van Buren | Honor roll, high school |
| Tom Wolfe | Cum laude, Washington and Lee U. |

# RHODES SCHOLAR CELEBRITIES

Cecil J. Rhodes, British imperialist and diamond/gold millionaire, established in his 1899 will scholarships for British Commonwealth and American students to study at Oxford University. Unlike most scholarships, which are based on either scholarship or need, Rhodes scholarships are for scholar-athletes, for men (and women, since 1975) who are not "merely bookworms" but who have a "fondness of manly outdoor sports" and the "moral force of character and instincts to lead." Of the 4,000 people who have won Rhodes scholarships since 1903, the first year of the awards, slightly less than half have been Americans. Rhodes scholars' "track records" are excellent, as the following list will attest:

Carl Albert (former U.S. representative, speaker of the house)
Daniel J. Boorstin (librarian of Congress)
David Boren (U.S. senator, Oklahoma)

John Brademas (president of New York University)
Bill Bradley (U.S. senator, New Jersey)
Richard Celeste (governor, Ohio)
Bill Clinton (governor, Arkansas)
Charles Collingwood (TV commentator)
Peter Dawkins (brig. general, U.S. Army)
Hedley Donovan (former editor-in-chief, Time Inc.)
J. William Fulbright (U.S. senator, Arkansas)
Pat Haden (lawyer, ex-pro football player)
Kris Kristofferson (singer, composer)
Elliott H. Levitas (U.S. representative, Georgia)
Richard Lugar (U.S. senator, Indiana)
Willie Morris (writer)
Larry Pressler (U.S. senator, South Dakota)
Bernard W. Rogers (general, Supreme Allied Commander)
Dean Rusk (former U.S. secretary of state)
Paul Sarbanes (U.S. senator, Maryland)
Adam Smith (writer—né George J. Goodman)
Howard K. Smith (TV commentator)
Stansfield Turner (U.S. admiral; head of CIA)
Robert Penn Warren (author)
Byron "Whizzer" White (Supreme Court justice)

## PREVIOUS OCCUPATIONS OF CELEBRITIES

All celebrities, according to the media, are "overnight successes." Before they became successes, however, they usually did something else in order to pay the rent.

If you're curious about what celebrities were doing the day before they became overnight successes, here are some examples:

| | **Previous Occupation** |
|---|---|
| Edward Albee | Western Union messenger; advertising copywriter |
| Eddie Arnold | ambulance and hearse driver |
| Lauren Bacall | theater usher |
| Warren Beatty | bar piano player; bricklayer's helper; "sandhog" on Lincoln Tunnel construction |
| Tony Bennett | singing waiter |
| Richard Boone | truck driver; roustabout |
| William F. Buckley, Jr. | Spanish instructor at Yale |
| Carol Burnett | hatcheck girl |
| Glenn Campbell | cotton picker |
| John Chancellor | hospital orderly; carpenter's assistant; trailer truck parker |
| Sean Connery | bricklayer; coffin polisher; theater usher; milk delivery man; model; Royal Navy sailor |
| Bill Cosby | shoe salesman |

| | |
|---|---|
| Joan Crawford | department store sales clerk; chorus girl |
| Ruby Dee | translator |
| Keir Dullea | carpenter's apprentice |
| Allen Funt | ad agency art director |
| James Garner | chauffeur; gas station attendant; waiter; hod carrier; poolroom manager |
| Robert Goulet | disc jockey; stationery salesman at Gimbels |
| Dick Gregory | postal clerk; jet engine inspector |
| Dustin Hoffman | toy demonstrator; typist; psychiatric attendant |
| Alan King | drummer; bandleader |
| Fred MacMurray | saxophone player; bandleader |
| Dean Martin | bootleg runner; boxer; gas station attendant |
| Lee Marvin | plumber's apprentice |
| Walter Matthau | floor scrubber; cement-bag hauler; boxing instructor |
| Sherrill Milnes | high school music teacher |
| Robert Mitchum | coal miner; ditchdigger; boxer; ghostwriter; shoe salesman |
| George Murphy | coal loader; Wall St. messenger |
| Jim Nabors | typist |
| Bob Newhart | advertising copywriter; accountant |
| Anthony Newley | office boy |
| George Peppard | disc jockey |
| Ronald Reagan | sports announcer |
| Robert Redford | artist; oil-field worker |
| Joan Rivers | fashion coordinator |
| Cliff Robertson | reporter |
| Barbra Streisand | switchboard operator; theater usher |
| Senator John Tower | radio announcer |
| Dick Van Dyke | advertising executive |
| Barbara Walters | ad agency secretary |
| Raquel Welch | cocktail lounge waitress |

| | |
|---|---|
| Paul Williams | oil-field worker; insurance clerk |
| Nicol Williamson | metalworker |
| Jonathan Winters | apricot picker; factory worker |

## Stage and Screen Debuts: Humble Beginnings

The secret of getting ahead in show business, it has been said, is getting *started*. Aspiring actors and actresses often take roles of questionable merit just to get their careers launched, and, regardless of the size or quality of the roles, debut performances often leave much to be desired. Lines are fluffed, cues are missed, props are jostled, and the like. For example:

**Sir Laurence Olivier,** one of the greatest actors of all time, in his first professional stage appearance (in a Brighton, England variety show) tripped over the scenery and fell into the footlights, prompting the audience to howl with laughter. Olivier learned the hard way one of the basic rules of acting: don't bump into the props or scenery.

**Jason Robards, Jr.,** another great actor, had a noteworthy stage debut, but for a different reason. Robards played the *rear end* of the cow in a Children's World Theatre production of *Jack and the Bean-stalk*, not exactly a pithy Eugene O'Neill role. Robards, incidentally, was twenty-five years old at the time!

And even the articulate **Rex Harrison** had some problems in his first professional stage performance. Rex was supposed to say, "Fetch a doctor . . . baby," but he nervously blurted out, "Fetch . . . a baby doctor"!

If great performers like Olivier, Robards, and Harrison had shaky starts in their acting careers, you can imagine what kinds of debuts other actors have had. The following are examples of some of those noteworthy stage and screen debuts:

**John Barrymore** made his appearance as a last minute substitute in the Philadelphia production of *Captain Jinks of the Horse Marines* in which his sister Ethel starred. When Barrymore walked onstage, he forgot his lines and ad libbed, "I've blown up, old chap. Where do we go from here?"

**Julie Andrews** made her singing debut at age six as Nod in *Winkin', Blinkin', and Nod.* In the play she wore a one-piece pajama outfit that buttoned at the seat. During her performance, the seat unbuttoned to reveal her pink panties as she pirouetted.

After reciting a Falstaff speech at his first stage audition, **Sir Ralph Richardson** was told by the troupe manager, "That is quite awful. It is shapeless, senseless, badly spoken. . . . You could never, never be any good as Falstaff." (Richardson's portrayal of Falstaff in 1945 was generally considered to be a remarkable performance and the best of his distinguished career!)

**Helen Hayes** made her first professional stage appearance in a male role: as Prince Charles in a 1905 Washington, DC, production of *The Royal Family*. She was five years old at the time.

**Spencer Tracy** played the part of a robot in one of his first stage performances: the Theatre Guild's production of Karel Capek's *R.U.R.* in the early 1920s.

**Anthony Hopkins** was fired after his first professional stage appearance at the Library Theatre in Manchester, England, because he had difficulty remembering even a few lines of dialogue.

**James Cagney**'s first professional stage job was as a chorus *girl* in a female impersonation act at Keith's Eighty-First Street Theatre in New York City.

**James Dean**'s first professional acting job was in a Coca-Cola commercial in the early 1950s. The action took place at a merry-go-round where Dean handed out Cokes to people on the wooden horses.

Sprightly **Sandy Duncan** played an Oriental in her first stage appearance. She was one of the Siamese children in a Dallas State Fair Music Hall production of *The King and I*.

**Lonnie Price,** who played the lead role in *Master Harold and the Boys*, made his stage debut as a *cockroach* in a summer theater production sponsored by Lincoln Center. He was eight years old at the time.

In her first professional appearances, ten-year-old **Ann Miller** performed a tap dance act at the local Lions Club for $5 a night.

**Margaret Hamilton,** the wicked witch in the movie classic *The Wizard of Oz*, is a preppie. She made her stage debut in her senior year at the Hathaway Brown School in Cleveland. Miss Hamilton played the part of Sir Peter Antrobus, an old Englishman, in a production of *Pomander Walk*.

One of **Elizabeth Ashley**'s first professional acting jobs was as the "Chiffon-light Jello Pudding and Pie Filling Girl" on the television game show "The Price Is Right."

The legendary **Sarah Bernhardt** tried to commit suicide after her first three stage appearances.

**Gilda Radner**'s first movie appearance was in *The Last Detail*. She played a chanting Buddhist and had only one line.

**Geraldine Chaplin** made her screen debut at the age of seven in her father's film *Limelight*, in which she uttered the line "Mrs. Alsop is out."

**Penny Marshall** of television's "Laverne and Shirley" made her television debut on "Ted Mack's Amateur Hour" in the mid-1950s. She was a member of a precision dancing troupe known as the Marshalettes.

Born in 1925, **Sammy Davis, Jr.,** made his movie debut in 1933 in the title role of *Rufus Jones for President*. In the movie he played a boy who dreams that he is elected president of the United States.

At age seventeen, **Mary Tyler Moore** appeared as a three-inch tall pixie ("Happy Hotpoint") in a Hotpoint appliance commercial.

Regarding his first movie performance (in *The Silver Chalice*), **Paul Newman** said that he delivered his lines "with the emotional fervor of a New York Central conductor announcing local stops." And the critics agreed with him.

In his first American movie, **Errol Flynn** played a corpse laid out on a marble slab. (*The Case of the Curious Bride*, 1934).

Olympic swimmer, **Johnny Weissmuller** made his motion picture debut, in *Glorifying the American Girl*, as an Adonis-figure wearing a fig leaf.

**John Travolta** made his film debut in the budget horror movie *The Devil's Rain*. (1975). He wore a mask and uttered the line, "Blasphemer! Get him, he is a blasphemer!"

**Johnny Carson**'s first stage appearance was as a bumblebee in a grammar school health pageant. His first professional appearance was as a magician ("The Great Carsoni"). Carson, thirteen years old at the time, was paid $3 to perform at the Norfolk, Nebraska, Rotary Club.

"Good Morning America" host **David Hartman** made his Broadway debut in the original Broadway production of *Hello Dolly*. He played the role of Rudolph, the German headwaiter.

In **Raul Julia**'s first-grade stage debut, he played the part of the Devil in a play written by American nuns who ran the school.

**Charles Bronson** won his first movie role (*You're in the Navy Now*) because of his unusual ability to belch on cue!

When **Ellen Burstyn** (née Edna Rae Gillooly) made her Broadway debut in *Fair Game* (1957), her stage name was Ellen McRae.

**Bette Midler** made her movie debut in the film *Hawaii* (1965), in which she appeared as a missionary's wife who was always seasick.

# CELEBRITY ROOTS: THE ETHNIC ORIGINS OF FAMOUS PEOPLE

The astonishing success of Alex Haley's Pulitzer Prize-winning book *Roots* ignited national interest among most Americans, not only blacks, to trace their ancestry and find their "roots."

Not necessarily the "Great Melting Pot" it is often called, America definitely is a nation of many immigrant groups living together and, in some cases, intermarrying. No other nation has such diversity in its population.

Reflecting the general population, celebrities also have diverse backgrounds. The following section is a random sampling of the ethnic origins of famous people, including a few prominent foreigners well-known to Americans:

| | |
|---|---|
| Albertson, Jack | German-Jewish, Russian-Jewish |
| Alexander, Jane | Irish |
| Ali, Muhammad | Negro, Irish |
| Allen, Woody | Orthodox Jewish |
| Alpert, Herb | Russian-Jewish, Hungarian-Jewish |
| Ameche, Don | Italian, German, Irish, Scottish |
| Anderson, John | Swedish |
| Ann-Margret | Swedish |
| Asner, Edward | Orthodox Jewish |
| Bacall, Lauren | German-Jewish, Rumanian-Jewish |
| Baez, Joan | Mexican, English, Irish, Scottish |

| | |
|---|---|
| Ball, Lucille | Irish, Scottish, English, French |
| Bancroft, Anne | Italian |
| Belushi, John | Albanian |
| Bisset, Jacqueline | Scottish, English, French |
| Blume, Judy | Orthodox Jewish |
| Bossy, Mike | English, Austrian, Ukrainian |
| Bowie, David | Anglo-Catholic, Jewish |
| Bradlee, Benjamin | English, German, Polish |
| Brando, Marlon | French, English, Irish, Dutch |
| Bronson, Charles | Lithuanian, Russian |
| Brooks, Mel | Russian-Jewish, Polish-Jewish |
| Bryant, Anita | French, Dutch, English, Scottish, Irish, Cherokee Indian |
| Brynner, Yul | Swiss-French, Gypsy |
| Burstyn, Ellen | Irish |
| Caan, James | Dutch-Jewish, German-Jewish |
| Cahn, Sammy | Polish-Jewish |
| Campanella, Roy | Italian, Negro |
| Caron, Leslie | French, American |
| Cher | Armenian, Turkish, French, Cherokee Indian |
| Clavell, James | Irish, English, Scottish |
| Cronkite, Walter | Dutch |
| Danner, Blythe | German |
| De Bakey, Dr. Michael | Lebanese |
| De Niro, Robert | Italian, Jewish |
| Dewhurst, Colleen | Irish, Scottish, English |
| Diamond, Neil | Polish-Jewish, Russian-Jewish |
| Didion, Joan | English, Alsatian |
| Donahue, Phil | Irish |
| Duncan, Sandy | Irish, Cherokee Indian |
| Erhard, Werner | Russian-Jewish, English, Swedish |
| Fawcett, Farrah | French, English, Choctaw Indian |
| Feinstein, Diane | Jewish, Russian-Catholic |
| Fidrych, Mark | Polish, Danish |
| Fonda, Jane | Italian, Dutch, English |
| Frankenheimer, John | Jewish, Irish |
| Francis, Arlene | Armenian, English |
| Gerulaitis, Vitas | Lithuanian |

114

| | |
|---|---|
| Gielgud, Sir John | Lithuanian, Polish, English |
| Goldwater, Barry | Polish-Jewish, English |
| Grade, Sir Lew | Russian-Jewish |
| Haley, Alex | Negro, Irish |
| Harper, Valerie | Spanish, English, Scottish, Irish, Welsh, French |
| Harris, Franco | Negro, Italian |
| Hartman, David | Dutch, Swiss, English German |
| Hawn, Goldie | Jewish, English |
| Hill, George Roy | Irish |
| Irving, John | Scottish |
| Jackson, Anne | Irish, Croatian |
| Jackson, Henry | Norwegian |
| Joel, Billy | Alsatian-Jewish, Russian-Jewish, English |
| Kazan, Elia | Greek |
| Korman, Harvey | Russian-Jewish |
| Levine, Joseph E. | Russian-Jewish |
| Liberace | Italian, Polish |
| Liddy, G. Gordon | German, Italian, Scottish |
| Little, Rich | English, Irish |
| Mabley, Moms | Negro, Irish, Cherokee Indian |
| Marshall, Penny | Italian |
| Martin, Billy | Portuguese, Italian |
| Mason, Marsha | Irish, English, Russian, German |
| Miller, Ann | Irish, French, Cherokee Indian |
| Minnelli, Vincente | Italian, French |
| Mitchum, Robert | Irish, Norwegian, American Indian |
| Newton-John, Olivia | Welsh, German-Jewish |
| Nimoy, Leonard | Russian-Jewish |
| Olivier, Sir Laurence | English, French |
| Orbach, Jerry | Irish, Jewish |
| Parton, Dolly | Dutch, Irish, Cherokee Indian |
| Pinter, Harold | Sephardic Jewish |
| Porter, Sylvia | Russian-Jewish |
| Prinze, Freddie | Hungarian-Jewish, Puerto Rican |
| Quinn, Anthony | Mexican (Aztec), Irish |
| Regine | Polish-Jewish |
| Rivera, Geraldo | Puerto Rican, Jewish |

| | |
|---|---|
| Ronstadt, Linda | German, Mexican |
| Safer, Morley | Austrian-Jewish |
| Sedaka, Neil | Sephardic Jewish |
| Sheen, Martin | Spanish, Irish |
| Simon, Carly | German, Spanish, Jewish |
| Sliwa, Curtis | Polish, Italian |
| Spacek, Sissy | Czecholovakian |
| Spock, Dr. Benjamin | Dutch, English |
| Springsteen, Bruce | Dutch, Italian |
| Stallone, Sylvester | Italian, French |
| Stargell, Willie | Negro, Seminole Indian |
| Steinbrenner, George | German, Irish |
| Streep, Meryl | Dutch |
| Struthers, Sally | Norwegian, Scottish |
| Te Kanawa, Kiri | Maori, Irish, English |
| Theroux, Paul | French-Canadian, Italian |
| Tormé, Mel | Russian-Jewish |
| Travolta, John | Italian, Irish |
| Troyanos, Tatiana | Greek, German |
| Tune, Tommy | English, Shawnee Indian |
| Uris, Leon | Russian-Jewish, Polish-Jewish |
| Vinton, Bobby | Polish, Lithuanian |
| Voight, Jon | Czechoslovakian |
| Wallace, Mike | Russian-Jewish |
| Wambaugh, Joseph | Irish, German |
| Weaver, Dennis | Irish, Scottish, English Cherokee and Osage Indian |
| Welch, Raquel | Bolivian, Spanish |
| Welk, Lawrence | Alsatian-German |
| Winkler, Henry | German-Jewish |
| Zanuck, Darryl | Swiss |

# FAMOUS ACTORS OF ORIENTAL DESCENT

Oriental actors and actresses rarely get sufficient credit for the many movies they have been in. Almost without exception, Orientals became character actors and stereotypes and were, therefore, limited in their role potential. Perhaps the biggest insult was when Orientals were not given any key leads in the movie *The Good Earth*, and, of course, the three major Charlie Chans (Sidney Toler, Warner Oland, Roland Winters) were not of Oriental heritage. For the record, here are major Oriental actors and actresses, their specific heritages, and major credits:

116

| | **Heritage** | **Major Credits** |
|---|---|---|
| Philip Ahn | Korean | *The General Died at Dawn* (1936)<br>*I Was an American Spy* (1951)<br>Thoroughly Modern Millie (1967) |
| Sessue Hayakawa | Japanese | *The Typhoon* (1914)<br>*Tokyo Joe* (1949)<br>*The Bridge on the River Kwai* (1957) |
| Nancy Kwan | Chinese-English | *The World of Suzie Wong* (1960)<br>*Flower Drum Song* (1961)<br>*Arrivederci Baby* (1966) |
| Burt Kwouk | Chinese | *Goldfinger* (1964)<br>*You Only Live Twice* (1968)<br>*The Return of the Pink Panther* (1975) and other Inspector Clouseau movies. |
| Bruce Lee | Chinese | *Fist of Fury* (1972)<br>*Enter the Dragon* (1973)<br>*The Way of the Dragon* (1973) |
| Keye Luke | Chinese | *Charlie Chan in Paris* (1934) and others<br>*First Yank in Tokyo* (1945)<br>*Kung Fu* (1942–1974) TV series |
| Toshiro Mifune | Japanese | *Rashomon* (1950)<br>*Seven Samurai* (1954)<br>*Yojimbo* (1961)<br>*Hell in the Pacific* (1968) |
| France Nuyen | Franco-Chinese | *South Pacific* (1958)<br>*A Girl Named Tamiko* (1963)<br>*One More Train to Rob* (1971) |

| | | |
|---|---|---|
| Miyoshi Umeki | Japanese | *Sayonara* (1957)<br>*Flower Drum Song* (1961)<br>*A Girl Named Tamiko* (1963) |
| Anna May Wong | Chinese | *Red Lantern* (1919)<br>*The Thief of Baghdad* (1924)<br>*Bombs Over Burma* (1942)<br>*Portrait in Black* (1960) |

## ROMAN CATHOLIC CELEBRITIES

Alan Alda
Anne Bancroft
Brigitte Bardot
Jacqueline Bisset
Robert Blake
Charles Bronson
William Buckley
Ellen Burstyn
Catherine Deneuve
Robert De Niro
Angie Dickinson
Phil Donahue
Mike Douglas
Chris Evert Lloyd
Mia Farrow
Farrah Fawcett
Albert Finney
Graham Greene
Merv Griffin
Sir Alec Guinness
Valerie Harper

Richard Harris
Audrey Hepburn
Gene Kelly
Grace Kelly
Ted Knight
Burt Lancaster
Liberace
Kenny Loggins
Claudine Longet
Sophia Loren
George Lucas
Ali MacGraw
Rod McKuen
Ed McMahon
Kristy McNichol
Chuck Mangione
Marcello Mastroianni
Johnny Mathis
Liza Minnelli
Mary Tyler Moore

Bob Newhart
Nick Nolte
Carroll O'Connor
Ryan O'Neal
Tony Orlando
Peter O'Toole
Al Pacino
Bernadette Peters
Sidney Poitier
Richard Pryor
Anthony Quinn
Lee Remick
Debbie Reynolds
Linda Ronstadt
Yves St. Laurent
Brooke Shields
Frank Sinatra
Tom Snyder
Suzanne Somers
Bruce Springsteen

## CELEBRITY EPISCOPALIANS

Fred Astaire
Carol Burnett
Walter Cronkite
Werner Erhard

Jane Fonda
Stacy Keach
Tom Seaver

# FAMOUS PEOPLE WHO CONVERTED FROM JUDAISM TO CHRISTIANITY

| | **Denomination Converted To** |
|---|---|
| Michael Blumenthal (presidential aide) | Presbyterian |
| Bob Dylan (singer, composer) | Vineyard Christian Fellowship |
| Bobby Fischer (chess champion) | Worldwide Church of God |
| Robert Neumann (U.S. ambassador) | Catholic |
| Eugene Ormandy (conductor) | Unspecified |
| Boris Pasternak (author) | Unspecified |
| James Schlesinger (presidential aide) | Lutheran |

# FAMOUS CONVERTS TO JUDAISM

Carroll Baker (actress)
Rod Carew (baseball player)
Jim Croce (songwriter)
Sammy Davis, Jr. (singer)
Carolyn Jones (actress)
Marilyn Monroe (actress)
John Newman (baseball player)
Eleanor Parker (actress)
Elizabeth Taylor (actress)

<table>
<tr><td>

*Sex*

</td><td>

**7.**

</td></tr>
</table>

# FIRST SEX EXPERIENCES OF CELEBRITIES

Some celebrities have revealed surprising details about their pasts, especially about their first sex experiences.

Like most first sex experiences, they tend to be either anticlimactic or traumatic. The following are representative first sex experiences of celebrities:

**Liberace** (pianist), 13 years old: "Like, I lost my virginity, if you can call it that, when I was about thirteen. I think I was raped. I was playing piano . . . she was a big, chesty broad who sang blues songs. She was a very good-looking woman, and kind of wild, but she was old enough to be my mother—in her thirties. . . . It was a warm summer night and she was driving some kind of covered hardtop car. After a while she pulled over and stopped on the side of this dirt road and all of a sudden this hand started coming up my leg and she said, 'Oh, you're a big boy, aren't you?' Then she took it out and started gobbling it. I didn't quite know what was happening, but I liked it. I liked it. I was all ready in a few minutes for a repeat. Then she crawled over on my lap and screwed me. It was very fast, like, would you believe about five strokes?"

**Victoria Principal** (actress), 17 years old: "It was a month before my eighteenth birthday that I finally lost my virginity. . . . We were in the front seat. To have gotten in the back would have seemed too premeditated and I was still holding on to some vestige of propriety. It was very short and there was no particular pain or pleasure, no particular physical sensation. In fact, afterward I thought, 'Jesus, there's got to be more than this. If not, I'm going back to the other stuff because petting was a lot of fun.'"

**Art Buchwald** (columnist), 15 years old: In a Long Island hotel where Buchwald was working for the summer. "There was a chambermaid up there who must have been around thirty. She wasn't that bad looking. And about the first week I was working there, it just happened: I lost my virginity. We were in her room and she had on a bathrobe over her pajamas, and I had on pajamas, too. I think she just seduced me."

**Dyan Cannon** (actress), 17 years old: "It was a nice Jewish boy who made love to me first. If I was going to do it, it had to be with a nice Jewish boy. He was gorgeous and all the girls wanted him. He looked like Jean-Paul Belmondo, only more perfect. . . . There wasn't any foreplay. None. We just walked in, sat down on this afghan on the sofa, and awkwardly went to it. There was nothing poetic about it at all. . . . After he left I looked down and there was blood all over the afghan. I went hysterical. My mother had knitted that afghan and put it on our yellow velvet couch so it wouldn't get dirty. I rinsed the blood out of it under the cold water faucet."

**Lou Rawls** (singer), 13 years old: "This lady couldn't have been a day under forty, and she was fat, super fat. . . . She pulled my pajamas down so that my little butt was sticking out. Then she pulled her nightgown up and pulled the covers up on top of us. It was hot and sweaty and she had me. She just kept hunching and going 'Uh, Uh, Uh' until finally she let out this one big yell and her arms flew out. That was the first time she let me go since she pulled me up there, so I rolled off, and pretty soon she starts snoring. I think I balled a wrinkle. There wasn't any sensation for me, no orgasm or anything. I was embarrassed and just felt like I was paying her for the food."

**Nora Ephron** (writer), 19 years old: While a junior at Wellesley College, with a Harvard student. "We finally did it in his dormitory room at Harvard, on his bed. It was over very quickly, and I don't remember much physical sensation one way or the other. It didn't hurt and it wasn't terribly pleasant. Just a kind of nothing feeling. I remember thinking, 'My God, is this it? Is this what I've been going through all this torment about?' It was very disappointing."

**Bob Guccione** (publisher of *Penthouse* magazine), 15 years old: "My first real bounce was when I was fifteen, with a girl named Violet. She was dark-haired, very delicate and feminine looking, very sexy, very white skin. . . . Then we got over into the back seat of the car, fumbling and feeling and scrambling for each other, and I couldn't get it up. . . . Anyway, this girl had patience, or a terrible need, and finally at the end of a couple of hours I got there, lost my virginity in a blaze of glory, like a meteorite flashing across the sky—hot, ferocious and fast."

**Joan Rivers** (comedienne), 20 years old: "The first time I slept with someone was a devastating experience. It was like 'This is it!' It was like the biggest thing in my life, and it was with a guy I'd known since I was fourteen. . . . And I was giving him the supreme gift that Joan Wallinsky could bestow on anybody. I was very dramatic about the whole thing, a lot of looks and no talk and all that junk. Physically, it was like nothing. You read in the books, 'She took to it like an animal.' I just said, 'Huh, is it over?' The whole thing lasted about a minute and a half, including buying the dress."

**Rudy Vallee** (singer), 6 years of age: "Don't ask me how, but I screwed for the first time when I was about six years old. I don't remember much about it. We were all so young. There were four or five of us, and we all went up to the icehouse near the beaver pond behind Valentine School and screwed this girl. I don't remember much about her except that she wasn't very attractive. How the hell four or five of us happened to gang up on her that afternoon, I don't know. Hell, she invited us. There was no raping or anything. It was all very sweet and gentle and relaxed. I was so young that I didn't even know why we were doing it."

**Grace Slick** (singer), 18 years old: "Fucking, until you got in college, wasn't particularly well looked upon. I didn't lose my cherry until the night I graduated from high school, Castilleja, old Castle A, which is a girls' school. . . . I was out with a guy who lived in Carmel. . . . We had a lot to drink and we were all kind of drunk. It took a long time, maybe four hours, because you weren't supposed to be doing it, essentially . . . I didn't bleed, and it wasn't painful at all. I was horny and I enjoyed it a lot. Balling is always good, and sometimes it just knocks your brain out. The first time you ball somebody is always excellent. . . ."

**Jack Lemmon** (actor), 18 years old: "The first time I had an affair I was in a parked car in a parking lot in Harvard Square. I had just gotten to Harvard and had ended up that evening with a girl I had met several times. She was old—twenty-two or twenty-three—not a student, working in the bookstore. . . . It was an old Model A or something. . . . We're in the seat and I can't get over this shift and I'm trapped, and I'm going fucking crazy and I'm sweating and it's just the most uncomfortable god-damned thing you can imagine. Finally, I'm upside down. . . . She had just had her panties off and I had my Navy bell-bottoms—I was in the Reserve—pulled down. . . . Jesus

Christ, it was not at all touching. I didn't feel guilty, just disappointed. You had visions, you know, of the deep thrust. But instead—up, down, up, down."

**Sally Kellerman** (actress), 21 years old: "I don't know what the guy did. I met him somewhere. I was working as a waitress. . . . He had a place in the Valley and we went to his place. I was frightened. Emotionally. Physically too, probably because I didn't know what was coming. . . . I was panicked. I was horrified, horrified. Afterwards he felt like being close, and I said, 'Oh, please, don't talk about it.'"

**Erica Jong** (writer), 18 years old: "My first fuck was with somebody I was in love with and it was tender and romantic. He was a sophomore at Columbia when I was a freshman at Barnard, and he was short and dark and intense and brilliant and garrulous and manic, and we were in love. . . . It was in his apartment off campus, and there was candlelight and wine and nice music and considerable fumbling. . . . I don't remember it being painful or bad, but nor do I remember the earth moving either, not like Dottie Renfrew in *The Group*, who experiences orgasm her first time."

**Maya Angelou** (writer, poet), 7 years old: Raped by her mother's boyfriend. "Then he was holding me too tight to move and his pants were open and his 'thing' was standing out and he grabbed down my bloomers. And then there was the pain and I passed out."

# CELEBRITY SEX QUOTES

Sex, according to etiquette, should be the opposite of the weather. Nobody should *talk* about it but everyone should try to *do* something about it. Occasionally, however, celebrities have some comments about sex and here are representatives of celebrity quotations about sex and related topics:

**Woody Allen**

"I'm a practicing heterosexual . . . but bisexuality immediately doubles your chances for a date on Saturday night."

**Brigitte Bardot**

"I wish I had invented sex. Sex is No. 1!"

**John Barrymore**

"The trouble with life is that there are so many beautiful women and so little time."

**Helen Gurley Brown**

"One of the paramount reasons for staying attractive is so you can have somebody to go to bed with."

**Anita Bryant**

"If God had meant to have homosexuals, he would have created Adam and Bruce."

**Angie Dickinson**

"I dress for women—and I undress for men."

**Britt Ekland**

"Sex is as important as food and drink."

**Farrah Fawcett**

"Sweaty is sexy."

**W. C. Fields**

"Some things are better than sex, and some things are worse, but there's nothing exactly like it."

**Zsa Zsa Gabor**

"The only place men want depth in a woman is in her decolletage."

**George Gilder**

"The fact is there hasn't been a thrilling new erogenous zone discovered since de Sade."

**Katharine Hepburn**

"The male sex, as a sex, does not universally appeal to me. I find the men today less manly; but a woman of my age is not in a position to know exactly how manly they are."

**Xaviera Hollander**

"A prostitute is a girl who knows how to give as well as take."

**Barbara Howar**

"Honey, I've never taken up with a congressman in my life. I'm such a snob. I've never gone below the Senate."

**Bianca Jagger**

"Homosexuals make the best friends because they care about you as a woman and are not jealous. They love you but don't try to screw up your head."

**Erica Jong**

"You see an awful lot of smart guys with dumb women, but you hardly ever see a smart woman with a dumb guy."

**Alfred Kinsey**

"The only unnatural sex act is that which you cannot perform."

**Loretta Lynn**

"Really, that little deelybob is too far away from the hole; it should be built right in. I think the doctors should operate on you and put it right there."

**Groucho Marx**

"Whoever named it necking was a poor judge of anatomy."

**Joe Namath**

"If you aren't going all the way, why go at all?"

**Dolly Parton**

"If I hadn't had them, I would have had some made."

**Leontyne Price**

"A healthy sex life. Best thing in the world for a woman's voice."

**Victoria Principal**

"Older guys like to receive head but they don't like to give it."

**Gilda Radner**

"I can always be distracted by love, but eventually I get horny for my creativity."

**Elizabeth Ray**

"I may never go down in history . . . but I am certainly going down on it."

**Linda Ronstadt**

"I wish I had as much in bed as I get in the newspapers."

**George Bernard Shaw**

"We are not taught to think decently on sex subjects, and consequently we have no language for them except indecent language."

**Brook Shields**

"What does 'Good in Bed' mean to me? When I'm sick and I stay home from school propped up with lots of pillows watching TV and my mom brings me soup—that's good in bed."

**Frank Sinatra**

"If I had as many love affairs as you have given me credit for, I would now be speaking to you from a jar in the Harvard Medical School."

**Elizabeth Taylor**

"I've only slept with the men I've been married to. How many women can make that claim?"

**James Thurber**

"The female sex today is beginning to take a little interest in sex whereas mine is beginning to take little interest in anything else."

**Lily Tomlin**

"There will be sex after death—we just won't be able to feel it."

**Barbara Walters**

"I didn't get ahead by sleeping with people. Girls take heart!"

**Andy Warhol**

"Sex *is* work."

**Raquel Welch**

"I love being a world-famous sex object. But I had to do a live show to show everybody I was more than just a cash register with glands."

## CELEBRITY RHINOPLASTY

Rhinoplasty is plastic surgery on the nose, in common parlance, a nose job. It is as common in Hollywood as a tonsillectomy in Muscatine, Iowa, or a *bris* in Great Neck, Long Island

In fact, the average Los Angeles plastic surgeon probably makes more money than the average movie star! Here is a list of celebrities who have kept Los Angeles plastic surgeons living in the style to which they have grown accustomed:

**Women**

| | | **Men** |
|---|---|---|
| Fanny Brice | Rita Moreno | Milton Berle |
| Barbara Eden | Suzanne Pleshette | Vic Damone |
| Nanette Fabray | Stefanie Powers | Joel Grey |
| Rhonda Fleming | Jill St. John | George Hamilton |
| Annette Funicello | Talia Shire | Al Jolson |
| Eva Gabor | Dinah Shore | Alan King |
| Zsa Zsa Gabor | Sissy Spacek | Dean Martin |
| Mitzi Gaynor | Jan Sterling | Cameron Mitchell |
| Lee Grant | Marlo Thomas | Peter O'Toole |
| Juliette Greco | Vera-Ellen | Bobby Van |
| Joan Hackett | Raquel Welch | |
| Carolyn Jones | Marie Wilson | |
| Carole Landis | Dana Wynter | |
| Marilyn Monroe | | |

By the way, Danny Thomas, Barbra Streisand, and Jamie Farr have not had nose jobs.

# TOUPEE OR NOT TOUPEE: THAT IS THE QUESTION

"Hollywood rug," "scalp doily," and "divot" are all slang terms for a hairpiece or toupee. It is a commonly used device for keeping leading men youthful-looking and employed, lest they become character actors. Although vanity may be one factor, it is the studios who usually instigate the wearing of most "rugs" to preserve their investments and to give the public what they think it wants: the image of perpetual youth. Actually it is a rare actor or performer who doesn't end up wearing one before retirement or death (Yul Brynner and Telly Savalas are notable exceptions!). Here is a *partial* list of leading men and celebrities who wear or have worn toupees on or off the screen:

| | | |
|---|---|---|
| Brian Aherne | Henry Fonda | George Raft |
| Fred Astaire | Rex Harrison | Charles Nelson Reilly |
| Tony Bennett | Van Heflin | Carl Reiner |
| Jack Benny | Charlton Heston | Rob Reiner |
| Humphrey Bogart | Gene Kelly | Burt Reynolds |
| Charles Boyer | Fred MacMurray | Peter Sellers |
| Lee J. Cobb | Fredric March | Frank Sinatra |
| Sean Connery | Ray Milland | Jimmy Stewart |
| Gary Cooper | Robert Montgomery | Franchot Tone |
| Howard Cosell | David Niven | Andy Warhol |
| Bing Crosby | Laurence Olivier | John Wayne |
| Brian Donlevy | | |

# CELEBRITY TATTOOS

Tattoos were formerly only for drunken sailors and marines but are now becoming chic in celebrity circles. Here are a few of the celebrities who have tattoos:

| Celebrity | Description and Location of Tattoo |
|---|---|
| Gregg Allman | A coyote on his forearm |
| Joan Baez | A flower on the small of her back |
| Pearl Bailey | A heart on her thigh |
| Glen Campbell | A dagger on his arm |
| Cher | Flower designs on her derriere |

128

| | |
|---|---|
| Sean Connery | "Mum & Dad" and "Scotland Forever" on his forearm |
| Peter Fonda | Dolphins (whereabouts not known) |
| Barry Goldwater | Navajo tattoos on his left hand |
| Ringo Starr | A half-moon and shooting star on his arm |
| Flip Wilson | A winged number "13" and a cross |

# THE LONG AND THE SHORT: HEIGHTS OF FAMOUS MEN

| | Height | | Height |
|---|---|---|---|
| Lew Alcindor | 7'1½" | Peter O'Toole | 6'3" |
| James Arness | 6'6" | Vincent Price | 6'3" |
| Tommy Tune | 6'6" | Michael Redgrave | 6'3" |
| Sen. Bill Bradley | 6'5" | George Sanders | 6'3" |
| Sterling Hayden | 6'5" | James Stewart | 6'3" |
| Ken Howard | 6'5" | Fritz Weaver | 6'3" |
| Oscar Robertson | 6'4½" | Steve Allen | 6'2½" |
| Chevy Chase | 6'4" | Lee Marvin | 6'2½" |
| Clint Eastwood | 6'4" | Victor Mature | 6'2½" |
| John Gavin | 6'4" | Spiro Agnew | 6'2" |
| Harvey Korman | 6'4" | Richard Boone | 6'2" |
| Ralph Nader | 6'4" | Louis Calhern | 6'2" |
| George Plimpton | 6'4" | Johnny Cash | 6'2" |
| Robert Ryan | 6'4" | Sean Connery | 6'2" |
| Tom Selleck | 6'4" | Bruce Dern | 6'2" |
| John Wayne | 6'4" | Melvyn Douglas | 6'2" |
| Orson Welles | 6'3½" | Vince Edwards | 6'2" |
| Muhammad Ali | 6'3" | Jesse Jackson | 6'2" |
| James Beard | 6'3" | Sen. Edward Kennedy | 6'2" |
| Gary Cooper | 6'3" | Jim Nabors | 6'2" |
| Jimmy Dean | 6'3" | Joe Namath | 6'2" |
| James Dickey | 6'3" | Sidney Poitier | 6'2" |
| John Frankenheimer | 6'3" | Arnold Schwarzenegger | 6'2" |
| James Garner | 6'3" | Ralph Bellamy | 6'1½" |
| Elliot Gould | 6'3" | Lorne Greene | 6'1½" |
| John V. Lindsay | 6'3" | Arthur Ashe, Jr. | 6'1" |
| Victor McLaglen | 6'3" | | |

| | Height | | Height |
|---|---|---|---|
| Warren Beatty | 6'1" | John Travolta | 6' |
| William F. Buckley, Jr. | 6'1" | Gore Vidal | 6' |
| Richard Chamberlain | 6'1" | Tom Wolfe | 6' |
| Henry Fonda | 6'1" | Robert Young | 6' |
| Errol Flynn | 6'1" | Alan Bates | 5'11" |
| Clark Gable | 6'1" | Orson Bean | 5'11" |
| Cary Grant | 6'1" | Mike Douglas | 5'11" |
| James Earl Jones | 6'1" | Johnny Carson | 5'11" |
| Robert Mitchum | 6'1" | David Frost | 5'11" |
| Edwin Newman | 6'1" | Ben Gazzara | 5'11" |
| Basil Rathbone | 6'1" | George Hamilton | 5'11" |
| Ronald Reagan | 6'1" | Paul McCartney | 5'11" |
| George Segal | 6'1" | Johnny Mathis | 5'11" |
| Dick Van Dyke | 6'1" | Ricardo Montalban | 5'11" |
| Herb Alpert | 6' | George Murphy | 5'11" |
| Don Ameche | 6' | Burt Reynolds | 5'11" |
| Alan Arkin | 6' | Cliff Robertson | 5'11" |
| Eddy Arnold | 6' | Robert Shaw | 5'11" |
| Jean-Paul Belmondo | 6' | Lewis Stone | 5'11" |
| Bill Blass | 6' | Richard Widmark | 5'11" |
| Sid Caesar | 6' | Spencer Tracy | 5'10½" |
| Glen Campbell | 6' | Frank Borman | 5'10" |
| John Chancellor | 6' | Marlon Brando | 5'10" |
| Roy Clark | 6' | Maurice Chevalier | 5'10" |
| Bill Cosby | 6' | Merv Griffin | 5'10" |
| Kirk Douglas | 6' | Louis Jourdan | 5'10" |
| Keir Dullea | 6' | Steve McQueen | 5'10" |
| Albert Finney | 6' | Marcello Mastroianni | 5'10" |
| Robert Goulet | 6' | Robert Redford | 5'10" |
| Pat Hingle | 6' | Rod Steiger | 5'10" |
| Danny Kaye | 6' | Robert Vaughn | 5'10" |
| Stacy Keach | 6' | Joey Bishop | 5'9½" |
| Jerry Lewis | 6' | Edward Asner | 5'9" |
| Fred MacMurray | 6' | Fred Astaire | 5'9" |
| Dean Martin | 6' | F. Lee Bailey | 5'9" |
| Jack Nicklaus | 6' | George Burns | 5'9" |
| George Peppard | 6' | John Cassavetes | 5'9" |
| Tyrone Power | 6' | James Dean | 5'9" |
| Ralph Richardson | 6' | Giancarlo Giannini | 5'9" |
| Maximillian Schell | 6' | Steve Lawrence | 5'9" |
| Paul Scofield | 6' | Paul Newman | 5'9" |
| George C. Scott | 6' | Oskar Werner | 5'9" |

| | Height | | Height |
|---|---|---|---|
| Anthony Newley | 5'8½" | Dustin Hoffman | 5'6" |
| Louis Armstrong | 5'8" | George Gobel | 5'5½" |
| Dick Cavett | 5'8" | Senator John Tower | 5'5½" |
| Billy Joel | 5'8" | Peter Lorre | 5'5" |
| Norman Mailer | 5'8" | Alan Ladd | 5'4½" |
| Robert Morse | 5'8" | Roman Polanski | 5'4" |
| Bob Newhart | 5'8" | Charles Aznavour | 5'3" |
| Ringo Starr | 5'8" | Mickey Rooney | 5'3" |
| Robin Williams | 5'8" | Paul Williams | 5'2" |
| Lee Trevino | 5'7½" | Willie Shoemaker | 4'11" |
| Humphrey Bogart | 5'7" | Johnny Roventini | 3'11" |
| Gary Moore | 5'7" | Herve Villechaize | 3'10" |
| Claude Rains | 5'7" | Gary Coleman | 3'7" |
| Edward G. Robinson | 5'7" | Michu | 2'9" |
| Paul Anka | 5'6" | Kenny Baker | 2'8" |
| Sammy Davis, Jr. | 5'6" | | |

# HEIGHT OF FAMOUS WOMEN

| | Height | | Height |
|---|---|---|---|
| Julia Child | 6' | Farrah Fawcett | 5'6" |
| Margaux Hemingway | 6' | Lillian Gish | 5'6" |
| Susan Anton | 5'11½" | Goldie Hawn | 5'6" |
| Vanessa Redgrave | 5'11" | Glenda Jackson | 5'6" |
| Loretta Lynn | 5'10" | Billie Jean King | 5'6" |
| Carol Channing | 5'8½" | Lee Remick | 5'6" |
| Jill Clayburgh | 5'8½" | Dinah Shore | 5'6" |
| Jessica Lange | 5'7½" | Twiggy | 5'6" |
| Carol Burnett | 5'7" | Leslie Uggams | 5'6" |
| Jane Fonda | 5'7" | Raquel Welch | 5'6" |
| Diane Keaton | 5'7" | Marilyn Monroe | 5'5½" |
| Ruby Keeler | 5'7" | Moira Shearer | 5'5½" |
| Peggy Lee | 5'7" | Kay Ballard | 5'5" |
| Melina Mercouri | 5'7" | Joan Caulfield | 5'5" |
| Rosalind Russell | 5'7" | Sandy Dennis | 5'5" |
| Gene Tierney | 5'7" | Marlene Dietrich | 5'5" |
| Diana Lynn | 5'6½" | Tammy Grimes | 5'5" |
| Shirley MacLaine | 5'6½" | Dorothy Lamour | 5'5" |
| Elizabeth Ashley | 5'6" | Marjorie Main | 5'5" |
| Lucille Ball | 5'6" | Ginger Rogers | 5'5" |
| Theda Bara | 5'6" | Jessica Savitch | 5'5" |

| | | | |
|---|---|---|---|
| Lizabeth Scott | 5'5" | Alice Faye | 5'3" |
| Barbra Streisand | 5'5" | Judy Garland | 5'3" |
| Barbara Walters | 5'5" | Miriam Hopkins | 5'3" |
| Jeanne Crain | 5'4½" | Loretta Young | 5'3" |
| Claudette Colbert | 5'4" | Carole Lombard | 5'2½" |
| Linda Darnell | 5'4" | Sally Field | 5'2" |
| Catherine Deneuve | 5'4" | Eva Gabor | 5'2" |
| Phyllis Diller | 5'4" | Sonja Henie | 5'2" |
| Paulette Goddard | 5'4" | Veronica Lake | 5'2" |
| Florence Henderson | 5'4" | Carmen Miranda | 5'2" |
| Betty Hutton | 5'4" | Linda Ronstadt | 5'2" |
| Liza Minnelli | 5'4" | Sissy Spacek | 5'2" |
| Patti Page | 5'4" | Natalie Wood | 5'2" |
| Lilli Palmer | 5'4" | Connie Francis | 5'1½" |
| Romy Schneider | 5'4" | Petula Clark | 5'1" |
| Sylvia Sidney | 5'4" | Ruby Dee | 5'1" |
| Maggie Smith | 5'4" | Debbie Reynolds | 5'1" |
| Mae West | 5'4" | Geraldine Chaplin | 5' |
| Shelley Winters | 5'4" | Patty Duke Astin | 5' |
| Clara Bow | 5'3½" | Janet Gaynor | 5' |
| Peggy Fleming | 5'3½" | Margaret Hamilton | 5' |
| Betty Grable | 5'3½" | Molly Picon | 5' |
| Shirley Temple | 5'3½" | Gloria Swanson | 4'11" |
| Imogene Coca | 5'3" | Nancy Walker | 4'11" |

# CELEBRITY EYE COLORS

## BLUE-EYED

| | |
|---|---|
| Eddie Albert | Tony Bennett |
| Woody Allen | Robby Benson |
| Julie Andrews | Candice Bergen |
| Paul Anka | Jacqueline Bisset |
| Ann-Margret | Karen Black |
| Ed Asner | Bill Blass |
| Tracy Austin | Debbie Boone |
| F. Lee Bailey | Pat Boone |
| Lucille Ball | Bjorn Borg |
| Mikhail Baryshnikov | David Bowie |
| Peter Benchley | Marlon Brando |

Jeff Bridges
Dr. Joyce Brothers
William F. Buckley, Jr.
Richard Burton
James Caan
Michael Caine
Truman Capote
Princess Caroline
Jimmy Carter
Richard Chamberlain
Carol Channing
Prince Charles
Julie Christie
Petula Clark
Jill Clayburgh
Joe Cocker
Walter Cronkite
John Davidson
Bette Davis
Mac Davis
John Denver
Bruce Dern
Phil Donahue
Kirk Douglas
Clint Eastwood
Mia Farrow
Albert Finney
Jane Fonda
Peter Fonda
Bob Fosse
Jodie Foster
David Frost
Greta Garbo
Art Garfunkel
Crystal Gayle
Phyllis George
Marjoe Gortner
Robert Goulet
Billy Graham
Lee Grant
Merv Griffin
Alec Guinness

Gene Hackman
Halston
Mark Hamill
Richard Harris
Deborah Harry
David Hartman
Goldie Hawn
Margaux Hemingway
Katharine Hepburn
Bob Hope
Mick Jagger
Waylon Jennings
Pope John Paul II
Sen. Edward M. Kennedy
Billy Jean King
Carole King
Evel Knievel
Ted Knight
Kris Kristofferson
Cheryl Ladd
Burt Lancaster
Angela Lansbury
Steve Lawrence
Jack Lemmon
Kenny Loggins
Loretta Lynn
Rod McKuen
Shirley MacLaine
Fred MacMurray
Kristy McNichol
Norman Mailer
Lee Majors
Steve Martin
Lee Marvin
Bette Midler
Sarah Miles
Robert Mitchum
George Murphy
Anne Murray
Joe Namath
Ricky Nelson
Bob Newhart

Paul Newman
Olivia Newton-John
Mike Nichols
Jack Nicholson
Jack Nicklaus
David Niven
Nick Nolte
Ted Nugent
Carroll O'Connor
Ryan O'Neal
Tatum O'Neal
Peter O'Toole
Dolly Parton
Jane Pauley
George Peppard
George Plimpton
Ronald Reagan
Robert Redford
Vanessa Redgrave
Lee Remick
Debbie Reynolds
Charlie Rich
John Ritter
Cliff Robertson
Kenny Rogers
Roy Rogers
Charles Schulz

George C. Scott
George Segal
Brooke Shields
Carly Simon
Frank Sinatra
Suzanne Somers
Ringo Starr
James Stewart
Barbra Streisand
Sally Struthers
David Susskind
Donald Sutherland
Toni Tennille
Cheryl Tiegs
Mel Tillis
John Travolta
Gore Vidal
Jon Voight
Robert Wagner
Andy Warhol
Richard Widmark
Andy Williams
Cindy Williams
Paul Williams
Robin Williams
Tom Wolfe
Michael York

## BROWN-EYED

Kareem Abdul-Jabbar
Alan Alda
Muhammad Ali
Cleveland Amory
Alan Arkin
Bea Arthur
Isaac Asimov
Burt Bacharach
Joan Baez
Anne Bancroft
Rona Barrett
Alan Bates

Saul Bellow
John Belushi
Richard Benjamin
George Benson
Leonard Bernstein
Joey Bishop
Shirley Temple Black
Robert Blake
David Brinkley
Charles Bronson
Mel Brooks
Jerry Brown

134

Anita Bryant
Carol Burnett
Ellen Burstyn
Glen Campbell
David Carradine
Diahann Carroll
Johnny Cash
Dick Cavett
Wilt Chamberlain
Ray Charles
Cher
Julia Child
Dick Clark
Natalie Cole
Sean Connery
Jimmy Connors
Rita Coolidge
Bill Cosby
Howard Cosell
Sammy Davis, Jr.
Olivia De Havilland
Catherine Deneuve
Robert De Niro
Angie Dickinson
Richard Dreyfuss
Peter Duchin
Faye Dunaway
Bob Dylan
Julius Erving
Lola Falana
Peter Falk
Sally Field
Carrie Fisher
Roberta Flack
Redd Foxx
Aretha Franklin
James Garner
Andy Gibb
Eydie Gorme
Elliott Gould
Cary Grant
Merv Griffin

Alex Haley
Dorothy Hamill
Marvin Hamlisch
Valerie Harper
Patty Hearst
Hugh Hefner
Lillian Hellman
Audrey Hepburn
Charlton Heston
Dustin Hoffman
Lena Horne
Rock Hudson
Engelbert Humperdinck
Lauren Hutton
Glenda Jackson
Rev. Jesse Jackson
Kate Jackson
Michael Jackson
Reggie Jackson
Bianca Jagger
Billy Joel
Elton John
James Earl Jones
Tom Jones
Louis Jourdan
Madeline Kahn
Gabe Kaplan
Gene Kelly
Henry Kissinger
Earth Kitt
Calvin Klein
Jack Klugman
Gladys Knight
Steve Lawrence
Jerry Lewis
Liberace
Hal Linden
Rich Little
Chris Evert Lloyd
Sophia Loren
Paul McCartney
Ali MacGraw

Melissa Manchester
Chuck Mangione
Barry Manilow
Dean Martin
Marcello Mastroianni
Johnny Mathis
Walter Matthau
Melina Mercouri
Liza Minnelli
Mary Tyler Moore
Jim Nabors
Ralph Nader
Ile Nastase
Wayne Newton
Richard Nixon
Laurence Olivier
Christina Onassis
Christina Onassis
Jacqueline Onassis
Tony Orlando
Donny Osmond
Marie Osmond
Al Pacino
Gregory Peck
Anthony Perkins
Sidney Poitier
Richard Pryor
Anthony Quinn
Gilda Radner
Tony Randall
Dan Rather

Lou Rawls
Nancy Reagan
Burt Reynolds
Joan Rivers
Jason Robards, Jr.
Linda Ronstadt
Diana Ross
Telly Savalas
Tom Seaver
Neil Sedaka
Omar Sharif
Dinah Shore
Paul Simon
Tom Snyder
Bruce Springsteen
Sylvester Stallone
Rod Steiger
Gloria Steinem
Donna Summer
James Taylor
Marlo Thomas
Lily Tomlin
Peter Ustinov
Mike Wallace
Raquel Welch
Orson Welles
Barry White
Flip Wilson
Stevie Wonder
Tammy Wynette

## HAZEL EYES

Jane Alexander
Brigitte Bardot
Carol Burnett
George Carlin
Johnny Carson
Shaun Cassidy
Ben Gazzara
Arlo Guthrie

Emmylou Harris
Ron Howard
Bruce Jenner
Jessica Lange
Peggy Lee
Ed McMahon
Robert Mitchum
Robert Morley

Patricia Neal
Rod Stewart

Barbara Walters
Henry Winkler

## GREEN EYES

Lauren Bacall
Marisa Berenson
Alice Cooper
Neil Diamond
Farrah Fawcett
Diane Keaton
Penny Marshall

Helen Reddy
Rex Reed
Jaclyn Smith
Sissy Spacck
Jean Stapleton
Shelley Winters
Joanne Woodward

## GRAY EYES

Tony Bennett
Mike Douglas

Rudy Vallee

## BLUE-GREEN EYES

Warren Beatty

Dick Cavett

## BLUE-GRAY EYES

Rudolf Nureyev
Anthony Newley

Nicol Williamson

## GREEN-GRAY EYES

James Coburn
Cloris Leachman

Romy Schneider

## LAVENDER EYES

Elizabeth Taylor

# CELEBRITY PHOBIAS

|  | **Fear(s)** |
|---|---|
| Ray Bradbury | Airplanes |
| Graham Greene | Blood; birds; bats |
| Alfred Hitchcock | Policemen |
| Howard Hughes | Germs |
| Evel Knievel | Airplanes |
| Dean Martin | Elevators |
| Robert Mitchum | Crowds |
| Gene Shalit | Airplanes |
| Maureen Stapleton | Airplanes |
| David Steinberg | Snakes |
| Joanne Woodward | Airplanes |

# CELEBRITY LEFTIES

About 15% of the U.S. population is left-handed, and the celebrity world certainly has its rightful share of lefties. In fact, lefties seem to be well represented in certain fields. There is, for example, a surprisingly large number of comedians who are left-handed, not to mention certain athletes.

Here is a representative list of celebrity lefties:

Eddie Albert (actor)
June Allyson (actress)
Earl Anthony (bowler)
Dan Aykroyd (comedian)
F. Lee Bailey (lawyer)
Robert Blake (actor)
Bill Bradley (U.S. senator)
Lenny Bruce (comedian)
McGeorge Bundy (presidential advisor)
Carol Burnett (comedienne)
George Burns (comedian)
George Bush (U.S. vice-president)
Ruth Buzzi (comedienne)
Brendan Byrne (ex-governor of NJ)
Sid Caesar (comedian)
Vicki Carr (singer)
Jack Carter (comedian)
Peggy Cass (comedienne)
Charlie Chaplin (comedian)

Prince Charles (heir to British throne)
Natalie Cole (singer)
Chuck Connors (actor)
Jimmy Connors (tennis player)
Hans Conreid (actor)
Angel Cordero (jockey)
Olivia De Havilland (actress)
Albert De Salvo (Boston Strangler)
John Dillinger (bank robber)
Robert Dole (U.S. senator)
Richard Dreyfuss (actor)
Bob Dylan (singer, composer)
Albert Einstein (physicist)
Queen Elizabeth (the Queen mother)
W. C. Fields (comedian)
Peter Fonda (actor)
Gerald Ford (38th president of U.S.)
Henry Ford, II (auto executive)
Allen Funt (TV personality)
Judy Garland (singer)
Errol Garner (pianist)
Uri Geller (parapsychologist)
Euell Gibbons (naturalist)
Paul Michael Glaser (actor)
George Gobel (comedian)
Betty Grable (actress)
Cary Grant (actor)
Peter Graves (actor)
Dorothy Hamill (ice skater)
Rex Harrison (actor)
Huntington Hartford (A&P heir)
Goldie Hawn (actress)
Isaac Hayes (composer)
Joey Heatherton (actress)
Jimi Hendrix (musician)
Ben Hogan (golfer) (played righty)
Rock Hudson (actor)
Daniel Inouye (U.S. senator)
Kate Jackson (actress)
Bruce Jenner (Olympic decathlon medalist)
Hamilton Jordan (presidential aide)
Gabe Kaplan (comedian)
Danny Kaye (comedian)

Caroline Kennedy (U.S. president's daughter)
Graham Kerr (TV chef)
Phyllis Kirk (actress)
Michael Landon (actor)
Hope Lange (actress)
Peter Lawford (actor)
Cloris Leachman (actress)
Hal Linden (actor)
Cleavon Little (actor)
Paul McCartney (singer, composer)
John McEnroe (tennis player)
Robert McNamara (presidential aide)
Kristy McNichol (actress)
Steve McQueen (actor)
Marcel Marceau (mime)
Harpo Marx (comedian)
Marsha Mason (actress)
Bill Mauldin (cartoonist)
Anne Meara (comedienne)
James Michener (author)
Ray Milland (actor)
Johnny Miller (golfer) (plays righty)
Marilyn Monroe (actress)
Barry Morse (actor)
Robert Morse (actor)
Edward R. Murrow (correspondent)
LeRoy Neiman (artist)
Anthony Newley (actor)
Kim Novak (actress)
Ryan O'Neal (actor)
Estelle Parsons (actress)
Pélé (soccer player)
Pablo Picasso (artist)
Cole Porter (composer, lyricist)
Robert Preston (actor)
Richard Pryor (comedian)
Robert Redford (actor)
Don Rickles (comedian)
Nelson Rockefeller (U.S. vice-president)
Bobby Rydell (singer)
Eva Marie Saint (actress)
Wally Schirra (astronaut)
Hugh Scott (U.S. senator)

Jean Seberg (actress)
Shields and Yarnell (mime team)
Dick Smothers (comedian)
Mark Spitz (Olympic swimmer)
Ringo Starr (drummer)
Rod Steiger (actor)
Casey Stengel (baseball manager)
Roscoe Tanner (tennis player)
Terry-Thomas (comedian)
Tiny Tim (ukelele player)
Rip Torn (actor)
Brenda Vaccaro (actress)
Karen Valentine (actress)
Rudy Vallee (singer)
Dick Van Dyke (comedian)
Andy Varipapa (bowler)
Guillermo Vilas (tennis player)
John Weitz (fashion designer)
Jessamyn West (author)
James Whitmore (actor)
Paul Williams (singer, songwriter)
Joanne Woodward (actress)
Keenan Wynn (actor)

## AILMENTS AND HANDICAPS OVERCOME

| | |
|---|---|
| Kaye Ballard | Deaf in one ear |
| Walter Brennan | No teeth |
| Bing Crosby | Color-blind |
| Sammy Davis, Jr. | Blind in one eye |
| Sandy Duncan | Blind in one eye |
| Deanna Durbin | Withered arm |
| Peter Falk | Blind in one eye |
| John Ford | Blind in one eye |
| Rex Harrison | Blind in one eye |
| Stacy Keach | Harelip |
| Alan Jay Lerner | Blind in one eye |
| Harold Lloyd | Missing two fingers on right hand |
| Paul Newman | Color-blind |
| Harold Russell | Missing both hands |
| Norma Shearer | Cross-eyed |
| Raoul Walsh | Blind in one eye |

# FAMOUS HEMORRHOID SUFFERERS

Hemorrhoids are very common in adults, with an estimated 50% of the population having the problem to some degree. It is reasonable to assume that celebrities are by no means immune to the ailment, but they don't exactly have their public relations people broadcast the fact. However, here are a few of the famous people who have suffered from the problem:

George Brett
Jimmy Carter
Gerald Ford
Billy Martin

Marilyn Monroe
Elizabeth Taylor
Earl Warren

# WOUNDED IN THE ARMED FORCES

| | |
|---|---|
| James Arness | World War II |
| Art Carney | World War II |
| Clint Eastwood | post-World War II |
| Blake Edwards | World War II |
| Lee Marvin | World War II |
| Jack Palance | World War II |
| Jean Renoir | World War II |
| William Wellman | World War I |

## THE WIT AND WISDOM OF...

Certain celebrities (or their writers) have a knack for coming up with memorable lines on and off the screen.

Among those eminently quotable luminaries are Groucho Marx, W. C. Fields, Mae West, Tallulah Bankhead, and Samuel Goldwyn.

To follow are samplers of the wit and wisdom (and occasional cynicism) of these quotable quoters:

### ...GROUCHO MARX

"Politics doesn't make strange bedfellows—marriage does."

"It looks as if Hollywood brides keep the bouquets and throw away the grooms."

"In America you can go on the air and kid the politicians, and the politicians can go on the air and kid the people."

"My mother loved children—she would have given anything if I had been one."

"I don't care to belong to a club that accepts people like me as members."

"I was so long writing my review that I never got around to reading the book."

"She's afraid that if she leaves, she'll become the life of the party."

"There's one way to find out if a man is honest: ask him; if he says yes, you know he is crooked."

"I didn't like the play, but then I saw it under adverse conditions—the curtain was up."

"I never forget a face, but in your case I'll make an exception."

"I'd horsewhip you if I had a horse."

"The husband who wants a happy marriage should learn to keep his mouth shut and his checkbook open."

"If you've heard this story before, don't stop me, because I'd like to hear it again."

"I'm 42 around the chest, 42 around the waist, 96 around the golf course, and a nuisance around the house."

"I never make a move without first ignoring my press agent."

"She got her good looks from her father—he's a plastic surgeon."

"Wives are people who feel that they don't dance enough."

## ... W. C. FIELDS

"Once during Prohibition, I was forced to live for days on nothing but food and water."

"Show me a great actor and I'll show you a lousy husband; show me a great actress and you've seen the devil."

"When some comedians are on the air, I find it hard to breathe."

"I gargle with whiskey several times a day and I haven't had a cold in years."

"Horse sense is what a horse has that keeps him from betting on people."

144

"The best cure for insomnia is to get a lot of sleep."

"I never worry about being driven to drink; I just worry about being driven home."

"What contemptible scoundrel stole the cork from my lunch?"

"The cost of living has gone up another dollar a quart."

"My illness is due to my doctor's insistence that I drink milk, a whitish fluid they force down helpless babies."

"After two days in the hospital, I took a turn for the nurse."

"If at first you don't succeed, try, try again; then quit—there's no use being a damn fool about it."

"I never drink water—I'm afraid it will become habit-forming."

"The world is getting to be such a dangerous place, a man is lucky to get out of it alive."


### ... MAE WEST

"I do all my writing in bed; everybody knows I do my best work there."

"Few men know how to kiss well; fortunately, I've always had time to teach them."

"Save a boyfriend for a rainy day, and another in case it doesn't rain."

"To err is human, but it feels divine."

"It's not the men in my life that counts—it's the life in my men."

"When I'm good, I'm very good. But when I'm bad, I'm better."

"It isn't what I do but how I do it. It isn't what I say but how I say it. And how I look when I do it."

"I'm the finest woman who walked the streets."

"Why don't you come sometime and see me. I'm home every evening. . . . Come up, I'll tell your fortune."

## . . . TALLULAH BANKHEAD

"It's the good girls who keep diaries; the bad girls never have the time."

"I'm as pure as the driven slush."

"There's only one man in the theater that can count on steady work—the night watchman."

"If you want to help the American theater, don't be an actress—be an audience."

## . . . SAMUEL GOLDWYN

"Include me out." (Said at a party thrown by Elsa Maxwell, after the guests were asked to write their own epitaphs.)

"I don't care if my pictures don't make a dime, so long as everyone comes to see them."

"Never mind about the cost. If it's a good picture, we'll make it." (Said in response to a director's complaining that a script was too *caustic!*)

"I had a monumental idea this morning, but I didn't like it."

"In this business it's dog eat dog, and nobody's going to eat me."

"Anyone who goes to a psychiatrist should have his head examined."

"A verbal contract isn't worth the paper it's written on."

"In two words: im possible!"

"We have all passed a lot of water since then."

"Tell me, how did you love the picture?"

"A producer shouldn't get ulcers, he should give them."

"I was always an independent, even when I had partners."

"It rolls off my back like a duck."

"You've got to take the bull by the teeth."

"I read part of it all the way through."

"We can get all the Indians we need at the reservoir."

"I was on the brink of a great abscess." (Regarding an illness.)

"What will they think of next?" (After seeing a 14th-century sundial.)

"I'm overpaying him, but he's worth it." (About Fredric March.)

"I wouldn't pay that much to a *first* baseman." (After hearing how much a particular third baseman was being paid.)

"Oh, Charlie MacArthur. The little dummy." (Referring to Edgar Bergen's dummy but confusing him with Ben Hecht's writing partner.)

"It's a goddamn sight easier to climb up a greased pole than to *stay* there."

"She was wonderful—that Lynn Fontaine. The best I ever saw." (After seeing Margot Fonteyn in the ballet *Giselle* at the Metropolitan Opera House in New York City.)

"Goldwynisms! Don't talk to me about Goldwynisms, f'Chrissake. You want to hear some Goldwynisms go talk to Jesse Lasky."

"Modern dancing is so old-fashioned!"

Not to be outdone by "highfalutin" Hollywood actors, sports figures occasionally come up with a good line or keen observation. In some cases (e.g., Yogi Berra and Casey Stengel) the observations often defy the rules of logic and grammar, but nevertheless they have become classics:

**Henry Aaron:** "It took me seventeen years to get three thousand hits in baseball. I did it in one afternoon on the golf course."

**Muhammad Ali:** "Charlton Heston, John Wayne, Steve McQueen, and Paul Newman—they're all in trouble with me around."

**Dick Allen:** "If horses won't eat it, I don't want to play on it." (Re Astroturf.)

**Yogi Berra:** "We made too many wrong mistakes." (After losing the World Series.)

"Nobody goes there anymore; it's too crowded." (About a Minneapolis restaurant.)

"You can observe a lot by watching."

"If people don't want to come to the ballpark, how are you going to stop them?"

"I usually take a two-hour nap, from one o'clock to four."

**Jim Bouton:** "The older they get, the better they were when they were younger."

**Howard Cosell:** "Let us reflect nostalgically on the past."

"They didn't give me looks but they gave me an absolute monopoly on brains and talent."

**Dizzy Dean:** "Some people who don't say ain't, ain't eating."

**Leo Durocher:** "You don't save a pitcher for tomorrow. Tomorrow it may rain."

**Bill Fitch:** "Last year wasn't all that bad. We led the league in flu shots."

**George Foreman:** "The question isn't at what age I want to retire, it's at what income."

**Lou Holtz:** "The only place you can start at the top is digging a hole."

**Gordie Howe:** "All pro athletes are bilingual. They speak English and profanity."

**Reggie Jackson:** "Why can't they understand the cold logic of it? I'm the straw that stirs the drink."

**Bruce Jenner:** "The only time sex has smothered me is when I do it during the competition."

**Wee Willie Keeler:** "Hit 'em where they ain't."

**Don King:** "Even God needed promoters. He had 12 disciples. . . ."

**Sandy Koufax:** "Pitching is . . . the art of instilling fear."

**Bob Lemon:** "They gave me an office I couldn't refuse."

**Vince Lombardi:** "A school without football is in danger of deteriorating into a medieval study hall."

**Ron Luciano:** "Umpires never win."

**Billy Martin:** "Out of 25 guys there should be 15 who would run through a wall for you, two or three who don't like you at all, five who are indifferent and maybe three undecided. My job is to keep the last two groups from going the wrong way."

**Mark McCormack:** "I'm not an agent. I'm an engineer of careers."

**Al McGuire:** "I think everyone should go to college and get a degree and then spend six months as a bartender and six months as a cab driver. Then they would really be educated."

"A team should be an extension of the coach's personality. My teams were arrogant and obnoxious."

**Calvin Murphy:** "The worst prejudice in sports isn't skin color, it is size."

**Joe Namath:** "When you win, nothing hurts."

**Walter O'Malley:** "Only half the lies they tell about the Irish are true."

**Willie Pep:** "First the legs go, then the reflexes go, then your friends go."

**Richard Petty:** "Cheat neat!"

**Dr. Renée Richards:** "No one would undergo a sex change for a reason as shallow as playing tennis."

**Bobby Riggs:** "A woman's place is in the bedroom and the kitchen, in that order."

"Women can't play a lick. I'll prove that. I'll set women's tennis back twenty years."

**Sugar Ray Robinson:** "Hurting people is my business."

**Babe Ruth:** "The greatest cure for a batting slump ever invented." (On scallions.)

**Casey Stengel:** "Going to bed with a woman never hurt a ballplayer. It's staying up all night looking for them that does you in."

"I'll never make the mistake of bein' seventy again."

"Ability is the art of getting credit for all the home runs somebody else hits."

"The Mets has come along slow, but fast!"

"The British are very consistent. They were just as calm about my arrival tonight as they were back in 1924."

<table>
<tr><td><h1>Party Time</h1></td><td><h1>10.</h1></td></tr>
</table>

## TRUMAN CAPOTE'S MASKED BALL AT THE PLAZA HOTEL

### THE PARTY OF THE DECADE

Author Truman Capote was a cherubic forty-two years old when he staged his famous "Black and White" masked ball in honor of publisher Kay Graham at the Plaza Hotel. The date was November 18, 1966, and Capote was riding on the crest of fame from the success of his nonfiction novel *In Cold Blood*. According to Charlotte Curtis, society editor of the *New York Times*, Capote was "stunned by the number of prominent people who begged him to invite them." The guest list was truly impressive. Five hundred people who dripped of success, if not money—from Charles Addams, the cartoonist, to Darryl Zanuck, the movie mogul. Sinatra was in attendance with his then wife Mia Farrow. Arthur Schlesinger, Jr. and William F. Buckley, Jr. were there, dancing with taller women, noted Miss Curtis. Mr. Capote called it his "little masked ball for Kay Graham and all my friends," but by most accounts it was the party of the decade. The following is a partial guest list of the glitterati who were invited to the event:

Charles Addams
Mr. and Mrs. Gianni Agnelli
Edward Albee
Mr. and Mrs. Joseph Alsop
Mr. and Mrs. Stewart Alsop
Cleveland Amory
Mr. and Mrs. Richard Avedon
Mr. and Mrs. George Axelrod
Mr. and Mrs. Harold Arlen

Billy Baldwin
James Baldwin
Tallulah Bankhead
Cecil Beaton
Mr. and Mrs. Harry Belafonte
Candice Bergen
Mr. and Mrs. Irving Berlin
Mr. and Mrs. Leonard
  Bernstein

Mr. and Mrs. Benjamin Bradlee
Donald Brooks
Mr. and Richard Brooks
Mr. and Mrs. William F. Buckley, Jr.
Dr. and Mrs. Ralph Bunche
Mr. and Mrs. McGeorge Bundy
Mr. and Mrs. Carter Burden
Mr. and Mrs. Abe Burrows
Mr. and Mrs. Richard Burton
Sir Noel Coward
Mr. and Mrs. Gardner Cowles
Charlotte Curtis
Mr. and Mrs. John Daly
Mr. and Mrs. Sammy Davis, Jr.
Oscar De La Renta
Marlene Dietrich
Mr. and Mrs. Douglas Dillon
Mrs. Peter Duchin
Mr. and Mrs. Robert Dunphy
Mr. and Mrs. Ralph Ellison
Douglas Fairbanks, Jr.
Mr. and Mrs. Mel Ferrer
Janet Flanner
Mr. and Mrs. Henry Fonda
Mr. and Mrs. Martin Gabel
Mr. and Mrs. J. Kenneth Galbraith
Greta Garbo
Mr. and Mrs. Brendan Gill
Mr. and Mrs. Arthur Goldberg
Mr. and Mrs. Samuel Goldwyn
Henry Golightly
Mr. & Mrs. Winston Guest
Mr. and Mrs. W. Averill Harriman
Mr. and Mrs. Leland Hayward
Mr. and Mrs. William Randolph Hearst, Jr.
Mr. and Mrs. John Hersey
Christopher Isherwood
Sen. and Mrs. Jacob Javits
Lynda Bird Johnson

Philip Johnson
Mr. and Mrs. Garson Kanin
Sen. and Mrs. Edward M. Kennedy
Mrs. John F. Kennedy
Mrs. Joseph P. Kennedy
Mr. and Mrs. Robert F. Kennedy
Mr. and Mrs. Walter Kerr
Melvin Laird
Vivien Leigh
Mr. and Mrs. Alan Jay Lerner
Mr. and Mrs. Walter Lippman
Anita Loos
Mr. and Mrs. Henry Luce
Shirley MacLaine
Mr. and Mrs. Norman Mailer
Mr. and Mrs. Joseph Mankiewicz
Marya Mannes
Mr. and Mrs. Stanley Marcus
Gian-Carlo Menotti
David Merrick
Robert Merrill
Mr. and Mrs. James Michener
Mr. and Mrs. Arthur Miller
Mr. and Mrs. Vincente Minnelli
Marianne Moore
Mike Nichols
Norman Norell
Serge Obelensky
Lord and Lady David Ogilvy
John O'Hara
Mr. and Mrs. William S. Paley
Mr. and Mrs. Gordon Parks
Mr. and Mrs. Drew Pearson
George Plimpton
Mr. and Mrs. Norman Podhoretz
Mr. and Mrs. Harold Prince
Prince and Princess Stanislaus Radziwill
Mr. and Mrs. James Reston

Mr. and Mrs. Jason Robards, Jr.
Jerome Robbins
Mr. and Mrs. Nelson Rockefeller
Mr. and Mrs. Richard Rodgers
Philip Roth
Baron and Baroness Guy de Rothschild
Mr. and Mrs. Robert Sarnoff, Jr.
Mrs. David O. Selznick
Mr. and Mrs. Irwin Shaw
Mrs. Robert E. Sherwood
Mr. and Mrs. Sargent Shriver
Mr. and Mrs. Frank Sinatra
Stephen Sondheim
Ted Sorensen
Sam Spiegel
Dr. and Mrs. Jules Stein
Mr. and Mrs. John Steinbeck
Gloria Steinem
Mr. and Mrs. George Stevens, Jr.
Mr. and Mrs. William Styron
Mr. and Mrs. Arthur Ochs Sulzberger
Penelope Tree
Mr. and Mrs. Lionel Trilling
Mr. and Mrs. Giancarlo Uzielli
Mr. and Mrs. Jack Valenti
Mr. and Mrs. William vanden Heuvel
Mr. and Mrs. Alfred Gwynne Vanderbilt
Gloria Vanderbilt
Walter Wanger
Andy Warhol
Mr. and Mrs. Robert Penn Warren
Mr. and Mrs. Anthony West
Mr. and Mrs. John Hay Whitney
Mr. and Mrs. Billy Wilder
Edward Bennett Williams
Tennessee Williams
Mr. and Mrs. Edmund Wilson
Duke and Duchess of Windsor
Darryl Zanuck

# RADICAL CHIC CELEBRITIES

## GUESTS AT LEONARD BERNSTEIN'S PARTY FOR THE BLACK PANTHERS

It probably was not the biggest party that conductor Leonard Bernstein and his wife, Felicia, ever threw but it certainly was the most memorable one.

The party was a fundraiser for the Black Panther party, a group of black revolutionaries of whom 21 members were indicted on bomb plot charges in April 1969.

Pop journalist Tom Wolfe, who attended the gathering, immortalized the party in an article he published in the June 8, 1970, issue of *New York* magazine. In the article, Wolfe accused the "egregio maes-

153

tro," as he called Bernstein, and his guests of having a flagrant case of *nostalgie de la boue*, otherwise known as "slumming." Charlotte Curtis defended the party in an article that appeared in *The New York Times* the next day. She quoted Felicia as saying that it was "not a frivolous party, but a chance for all of us to hear what's happening to them. They've really been treated very inhumanely." And the next day, a *Times* editorial appeared denouncing the party as "elegant slumming," saying that it "mocked the memory of Martin Luther King, Jr.," whose birthday was observed the day after the party.

Call it what you will, it was a remarkable party: limousine liberals and Black Panthers sharing caviar and exchanging philosophies. Here are some of the 90 people who attended:

Richard Avedon
Julie Belafonte
Schuyler Chapin
Betty Comden
Aaron Copland
Don Cox (field marshall of
   Black Panthers)
Charlotte Curtis
Peter Duchin
Lukas Foss
Adolph Green
Sheldon Harnick
Lillian Hellman
Murray Kempton
Burton Lane

Goddard Lieberson
Gail Lumet
Gian-Carlo Menotti
Phyllis Newman
Mike Nichols
Patrick O'Neal
Otto Preminger
Larry Rivers
Jason Robards, Jr.
Jerome Robbins
Stephen Sondheim
Roger Wilkins
Livingston Wingate (executive
   director of Urban League)
Tom Wolfe

## YOUTHFUL BUT OVER 40

Youth *is* fleeting but some people seem to hide it better than others. The following celebrities, most of whom are well over 40 years old, still manage to convey an aura of youth, in spite of their real ages:

|  | **Date of Birth** |
|---|---|
| Tab Hunter | July 11, 1931 |
| Edd "Kookie" Byrnes | July 30, 1933 |
| Kris Kristofferson | June 22, 1936 |
| Warren Beatty | March 30, 1937 |
| Dustin Hoffman | August 8, 1937 |
| Robert Redford | August 18, 1937 |
| Jane Fonda | December 21, 1937 |
| Mary Tyler Moore | December 29, 1937 |
| Troy Donahue | January 27, 1938 |
| Connie Francis | December 12, 1938 |
| Roberta Flack | February 10, 1939 |
| Ringo Starr | July 7, 1940 |
| Frankie Avalon | September 8, 1940 |
| Paul Simon | November 5, 1941 |
| John Davidson | December 13, 1941 |
| Mike Farrell | February 6, 1942 |
| Michael York | March 27, 1942 |
| Paul McCartney | June 18, 1942 |
| Karen Black | July 1, 1942 |
| Genevieve Bujold | July 1, 1942 |
| Raquel Welch | September 5, 1942 |

Annette Funicello        October 22, 1942
Herve Villechaize       April 23, 1943
Mick Jagger           July 26, 1943
Marlo Thomas         November 21, 1943

# MISS AMERICA

Miss America and runners-up are selected every year on the basis of beauty, talent, poise, and charm by a panel of celebrity judges. Contestants represent each of the 50 states, the District of Columbia, and U.S. Territories. The winner receives a $20,000 scholarship, various other prizes, and a one-year contract to make publicity appearances.

Among those winners to later achieve some fame are Bess Myerson, Lee Meriwether, Mary Ann Mobley, and Phyllis George.

1921 Margaret Gorman, Washington, DC
1922 Mary Campbell, Columbus, OH
1923 (No pageant)
1924 Ruth Malcolmson, Philadelphia, PA
1925 Fay Lanphier, Oakland, CA
1926 Norma Smallwood, Tulsa, OK
1927 Lois Delaner, Joliet, IL
1928–32 (No pageants)
1933 Marion Bergeron, West Haven, CT
1934 (No pageant)
1935 Henrietta Leaver, Pittsburgh, PA
1936 Rose Coyle, Philadelphia, PA
1937 Bette Cooper, Bertrand Island, NJ
1938 Marilyn Meseke, Marion, OH
1939 Patricia Donnelly, Detroit, MI
1940 Frances Marie Burke, Philadelphia, PA
1941 Rosemary LaPlanche, Los Angeles, CA
1942 Jo-Carroll Dennison, Tyler, TX
1943 Jean Bartel, Los Angeles, CA
1944 Venus Ramey, Washington, DC
1945 Bess Myerson, New York, NY
1946 Marilyn Buferd, Los Angeles, Ca
1947 Barbara Walker, Memphis, TN
1948 BeBe Shopp, Hopkins, MN
1949 Jacque Mercer, Litchfield, AZ

1950 (No pageant)
1951 Yolande Betbeze, Mobile, AL
1952 Coreen Kay Hutchins, Salt Lake City, UT
1953 Neva Jane Langley, Macon, GA
1954 Evelyn Margaret Ay, Ephrata, PA
1955 Lee Meriwether, San Francisco, CA
1956 Sharon Ritchie, Denver, CO
1957 Marian McKnight, Manning, SC
1958 Marilyn Van Derbur, Denver, CO
1959 Mary Ann Mobley, Brandon, MS
1960 Lynda Lee Mead, Natchez, MS
1961 Nancy Fleming, Montague, MI
1962 Maria Fletcher, Asheville, NC
1963 Jacquelyn Mayer, Sandusky, OH
1964 Donna Axum, El Dorado, AR
1965 Vonda Kay Van Dyke, Phoenix, AZ
1966 Deborah Irene Bryant, Overland Park, KS
1967 Jane Anne Jayroe, Laverne, OK
1968 Debra Dene Barnes, Moran, KS
1969 Judith Anne Ford, Belvidere, IL
1970 Pamela Anne Eldred, Birmingham, MI
1971 Phyllis Ann George, Denton, TX
1972 Laurie Lea Schaefer, Columbus, OH
1973 Terre Anne Meeuwsen, De Pere, WI
1974 Rebecca Ann King, Denver, CO
1975 Shirley Cothran, Fort Worth, TX
1976 Tawny Elaine Godin, Yonkers, NY
1977 Dorothy Kathleen Benham, Edina, MN
1978 Susan Perkins, Columbus, OH
1979 Kylene Barker, Roanoke, VA
1980 Cheryl Prewitt, Ackerman, MS
1981 Susan Powell, Elk City, OK
1982 Elizabeth Ward, Russelville, AR
1983 Debra Sue Maffett, Anaheim, CA
1984 Vanessa Williams, Millwood, NY

# PLAYMATE OF THE YEAR: CELEBRITY SKIN

*Playboy* magazine editors have the burdensome task of poring over each year's twelve centerfold Playmates of the Month in order to select the Playmate of the Year. The winning Playmate not only gets

157

a $10,000 cash award and other prizes, but also gets extensive media coverage (uncoverage), plus an opportunity to mingle in Hugh Hefner's Hollywood crowd, which often leads to TV and movie appearances.

Other than having magnificent bodies, the only things the Playmates seem to have in common is a lack of moles and skin blemishes and a profound interest in Proust and Flaubert:

|      | Playmate of the Year |
|------|----------------------|
| 1960 | Ellen Statton |
| 1961 | Linda Gamble |
| 1962 | Christa Speck |
| 1963 | June Cochran |
| 1964 | Donna Michelle |
| 1965 | Jo Collins |
| 1966 | Allison Parks |
| 1967 | Lisa Baker |
| 1968 | Angela Dorian |
| 1969 | Connie Kreski |
| 1970 | Claudia Jennings |
| 1971 | Sharon Clark |
| 1972 | Liv Lindeland |
| 1973 | Marilyn Cole |
| 1974 | Cyndi Wood |
| 1975 | Marilyn Lange |
| 1976 | Lillian Muller |
| 1977 | Patti McGuire |
| 1978 | Debra Jo Fondren |
| 1979 | Monique St. Pierre |
| 1980 | Dorothy Stratten |
| 1981 | Terri Wells |
| 1982 | Shannon Tweed |
| 1983 | Marianne Gravatte |

# WARREN BEATTY'S GIRL FRIENDS

Handsome actor-producer Warren Beatty is quite a lady's man, and it is not just a studio image thrust upon him. He's a real charmer, and scores of women can verify that. Except for an occasional negative comment (Carly Simon supposedly wrote the song "You're So Vain" with Warren in mind), he gets good reviews from his girl

158

friends. Columnist Sheilah Graham wrote that "Warren could be president of the United States if he wanted to be. He could win the votes of the ladies he has loved." The following women comprise only part of his electorate:

| | |
|---|---|
| Candice Bergen | Diane Keaton |
| Leslie Caron | Maya Plisetskaya |
| Julie Christie | Lee Radziwill |
| Joan Collins | Vanessa Redgrave |
| Barbara Harris | Carly Simon |
| Kate Jackson | Natalie Wood |

# On the Cover of... 12.

## PEOPLE WHO HAVE APPEARED MOST OFTEN ON *TIME* MAGAZINE COVERS

Since 1923, when it was first published, *Time* magazine has pictured more than twenty-five hundred people on its magazine covers. Few people appear on more than one cover, and only a few dozen people appear with regularity or did during their periods of influence. U.S. presidents and statesmen tend to be on the covers most frequently; athletes and authors are usually good for just one cover.

The following celebrated people have graced the covers of *Time* magazine at least 10 times:

| | Number of Times on Cover | | Number of Times on Cover |
|---|---|---|---|
| Richard M. Nixon | 64 | Nikita Khrushchev | 15 |
| James E. Carter | 33 | Mao Tse-tung | 13 |
| Ronald Reagan | 23 | Charles de Gaulle | 13 |
| Lyndon Baines Johnson | 23 | Hubert Humphrey | 12 |
| Gerald R. Ford | 22 | Nelson Rockefeller | 12 |
| Dwight D. Eisenhower | 21 | Anwar Sadat | 11 |
| Leonid I. Brezhnev | 18 | John F. Kennedy | 11 |
| Henry Kissinger | 17 | Spiro T. Agnew | 10 |
| Joseph Stalin | 17 | Chiang Kai-shek | 10 |
| Jesus Christ | 15 | Mary, Mother of Jesus | 10 |

# *TIME* MAGAZINE'S MAN OF THE YEAR

Every year the editors of *Time* magazine select an individual (or individuals) who have had the greatest impact on the lives of Americans, and these chosen people appear as "Man of the Year" in early January of each year. The presence of people like Adolf Hitler and the Ayatollah Khomeini makes it clear that the person does not necessarily have a *positive* effect on history:

1927 Charles Lindbergh
1928 Walter P. Chrysler
1929 Owen D. Young
1930 Mahatma Gandhi
1931 Pierre Laval
1932 Franklin Delano Roosevelt
1933 Hugh S. Johnson
1934 Franklin Delano Roosevelt
1935 Haile Selassie
1936 Wallis Warfield Simpson
1937 General and Mme. Chiang Kai-shek
1938 Adolf Hitler
1939 Joseph Stalin
1940 Winston Churchill
1941 Franklin Delano Roosevelt
1942 Joseph Stalin
1943 George C. Marshall
1944 Dwight D. Eisenhower
1945 Harry Truman
1946 James F. Byrnes
1947 George C. Marshall
1948 Harry Truman
1949 Winston Churchill
1950 American Fighting Man
1951 Mohammed Mossadegh
1952 Queen Elizabeth II
1953 Konrad Adenauer
1954 John Foster Dulles
1955 Harlow Curtice

1956 Hungarian Freedom Fighter
1957 Nikita Khrushchev
1958 Charles de Gaulle
1959 Dwight D. Eisenhower
1960 15 U.S. Scientists (John F. Ender, Willard F. Libby, Linus C. Pauling, Isidor I. Rabi, Edward Teller, Joshua Lederberg, Donald A. Glaser, Robert B. Woodward, Charles Draper, William Shockley, Emilio G. Segre, Charles Townes, George W. Beadle, James A. Van Allen, and Edward Purcell)
1961 John F. Kennedy
1962 Pope John XXIII
1963 Martin Luther King, Jr.
1964 Lyndon B. Johnson
1965 General William Westmoreland
1966 Youth (Americans 25 and under)
1967 Lyndon B. Johnson
1968 Apollo 8 Astronauts (William Anders, Frank Borman, and James Lovell)
1969 The Middle Americans

1970 Willy Brandt
1971 Richard Nixon
1972 Richard M. Nixon &
     Henry Kissinger
1973 Judge John J. Sirica
1974 King Faisal of
     Saudi Arabia
1975 12 U.S. Women
     (Alison Cheek, Billie Jean
     King, Carla Hills, Jill
     Conway, Betty Ford,
     Susie Sharp, Barbara
     Jordan, Ella Grasso,
     Addie Wyatt, Susan
     Brownmiller, Carol
     Sutton, and Kathleen
     Byerly)

1976 Jimmy Carter
1977 Anwar Sadat
1978 Teng Hsiao-p'ing
1979 Ayatollah Khomeini
1980 Ronald Reagan
1981 Lech Walesa
1982 Computer (Machine
     of the Year)

# CELEBRITIES WHO HAVE APPEARED ON THE COVER OF *TV GUIDE* 10 OR MORE TIMES*

Since *TV Guide*'s first issue was published (April 3, 1953), only thirteen television personalities have appeared on the cover ten or more times. Curiously, only two of the personalities are women, but one woman, lovable Lucy, holds the record:

| | Number of Times on TV Guide Cover |
|---|---|
| Lucille Ball | 24 |
| Michael Landon | 17 |
| Arthur Godfrey | 16 |
| Mary Tyler Moore | 16 |
| Johnny Carson | 13 |
| Raymond Burr | 12 |
| Bob Hope | 11 |
| James Arness | 11 |
| Lawrence Welk | 11 |
| Red Skelton | 10 |
| Perry Como | 10 |
| Efrem Zimbalist, Jr. | 10 |
| Jackie Gleason | 10 |

*Source: *TV Guide* (through May 1983).

# MOST POPULAR *PEOPLE* MAGAZINE COVERS

*People* magazine sells about 2,500,000 copies a week, 74 percent of which are newsstand sales. Newsstand sales, as with all magazines, vary by issue and often depend on who appears on the magazine's cover. Here are the people who, when they appeared on the covers of *People*, sold the greatest number of newsstand copies:*

Princess Grace of Monaco
Prince Charles and Lady Diana (wedding)
The "Dallas" cast ("Who Shot J.R.?")
Farrah Fawcett
Brooke Shields
Olivia Newton-John
E.T.
Barbra Streisand and Jon Peters
Cher (with her family)
Prince Charles and Lady Diana (wedding)


*Note: The list is not in rank order.

# Jocks and Jockettes 13.

## ATHLETES WHO BECAME ACTORS

Professional athletes tend to have short careers, but they often leverage their popularity into other fields, especially ones for which the public buys tickets.

Few athletes make it in the movie business, but here are a few who successfully made the transition:

| | Sport | Movie Credits (partial) |
|---|---|---|
| Muhammad Ali | boxing | *The Greatest* (1977) |
| | | "Freedom Road" (1979) TV miniseries |
| Max Baer | boxing | *The Prizefighter and the Lady* (1933) |
| | | *The Harder They Fall* (1956) |
| Buddy Baer | boxing | *Jack and the Beanstalk* (1952) |
| | | *Snow White and the Three Stooges* (1961) |
| Bruce Bennett (Herman Brix) | discus | *The New Adventures of Tarzan* (1935) |
| | | *The Treasure of Sierra Madre* (1947) |
| Johnny Mack Brown | football | *Billy the Kid* (1933) |
| | | *Ride 'Em Cowboy* (1941) |
| Chuck Connors | baseball, basketball | *Pat and Mike* (1952) |
| | | *Pancho Villa* (1971) |
| | | "The Rifleman" (1958–63) TV series |

| | | |
|---|---|---|
| Buster Crabbe | swimming | *Tarzan the Fearless* (1933) |
| | | *Flash Gordon's Trip to Mars* (1938) |
| | | *Buck Rogers* (1939) |
| | | "Captain Gallant of the Foreign Legion" (TV series) |
| Bruce Jenner | decathlon | *Can't Stop the Music* (1980) |
| | | TV commentating |
| Alex Karras | football | *Blazing Saddles* (1974) |
| | | "Babe" (1977) TV movie |
| Canada Lee | boxing | *Lifeboat* (1943) |
| | | *Cry, the Beloved Country* (1952) |
| Joe Namath | football | *C.C. Rider & Company* (1970) |
| | | *The Last Rebel* (1971) |
| | | TV appearances; summer stock |
| Maxie Rosenbloom | boxing | *Mr. Broadway* (1933) |
| O. J. Simpson | football | "Roots" (1976) TV miniseries |
| | | *Towering Inferno* (1974) |
| Woody Strode | football | *The Ten Commandments* (1956) |
| | | *Sergeant Rutledge* (1960) |
| | | *The Professionals* (1966) |
| Johnny Weissmuller | swimming | *Tarzan the Ape Man* (1932) & other Tarzan movies through 1948 |
| | | *Swamp Fire* (1946) |
| Fred Williamson | football | *M\*A\*S\*H* (1970) |
| | | *Boss Nigger* (1975) |

# ATHLETE OF THE YEAR

Every year sports editors of the Associated Press member newspapers select the Athlete of the Year (male and female) from both professional and amateur sports.

Here are the winners and their sports:

**Male Athletes of the Year**

1931  Pepper Martin, Baseball
1932  Gene Sarazen, Golf
1933  Carl Hubbell, Baseball

1934 Dizzy Dean, Baseball
1935 Joe Louis, Boxing
1936 Jesse Owens, Track and field
1937 Don Budge, Tennis
1938 Don Budge, Tennis
1939 Nile Kinnick, Football
1940 Tommy Harmon, Football
1941 Joe DiMaggio, Baseball
1942 Frank Sinkwich, Football
1943 Gunder Haegg, Track and field
1944 Byron Nelson, Golf
1945 Byron Nelson, Golf
1946 Glenn Davis, Football
1947 Johnny Lujack, Football
1948 Lou Boudreau, Baseball
1949 Leon Hart, Football
1950 Jim Konstanty, Baseball
1951 Dick Kazmaier, Football
1952 Bob Mathias, Track and field, Football
1953 Ben Hogan, Golf
1954 Willie Mays, Baseball
1955 "Hopalong" Cassidy, Football
1956 Mickey Mantle, Baseball
1957 Ted Williams, Baseball
1958 Herb Elliott, Track and field
1959 Ingemar Johansson, Boxing
1960 Rafer Johnson, Track and field
1961 Roger Maris, Baseball
1962 Maury Wills, Baseball
1963 Sandy Koufax, Baseball
1964 Don Schollander, Swimming
1965 Sandy Koufax, Baseball
1966 Frank Robinson, Baseball
1967 Carl Yastrzemski, Baseball
1968 Denny McLain, Baseball
1969 Tom Seaver, Baseball
1970 George Blanda, Football
1971 Lee Trevino, Golf
1972 Mark Spitz, Swimming
1973 O. J. Simpson, Football
1974 Muhammad Ali, Boxing
1975 Fred Lynn, Baseball

1976 Bruce Jenner, Track and field
1977 Steve Cauthen, Horse Racing
1978 Ron Guidry, Baseball
1979 Willie Stargell, Baseball
1980 U.S. Olympic Hockey Team
1981 John McEnroe, Tennis
1982 Wayne Gretzky, Hockey

## Female Athlete of the Year

1931 Helene Madison, Swimming
1932 Babe Didrikson, Track and field
1933 Helen Jacobs, Tennis
1934 Virginia Van Wie, Golf
1935 Helen Wills Moody, Tennis
1936 Helen Stephens, Track and field
1937 Katherine Rawls, Swimming
1938 Patty Berg, Golf
1939 Alice Marble, Tennis
1940 Alice Marble, Tennis
1941 Betty Hicks Newell, Golf
1942 Gloria Callen, Swimming
1943 Patty Berg, Golf
1944 Ann Curtis, Swimming
1945 Babe Didrikson Zaharias, Golf
1946 Babe Didrikson Zaharias, Golf
1947 Babe Didrikson Zaharias. Golf
1948 Fanny Blankers-Koen, Track and field
1949 Marlene Bauer, Golf
1950 Babe Didrikson Zaharias, Golf
1951 Maureen Connolly, Tennis
1952 Maureen Connolly, Tennis
1953 Maureen Connolly, Tennis
1954 Babe Didrikson Zaharias, Golf
1955 Patty Berg, Golf
1956 Pat McCormick, Diving
1957 Althea Gibson, Tennis
1958 Althea Gibson, Tennis
1959 Maria Bueno, Tennis
1960 Wilma Rudolph, Track and field
1961 Wilma Rudolph, Track and field
1962 Dawn Fraser, Swimming

1963  Mickey Wright, Golf
1964  Mickey Wright, Golf
1965  Kathy Whitworth, Golf
1966  Kathy Whitworth, Golf
1967  Billie Jean King, Tennis
1968  Peggy Fleming, Figure Skating
1969  Debbie Meyer, Swimming
1970  Chi Cheng, Track and field
1971  Evonne Goolagong, Tennis
1972  Olga Korbut, Gymnastics
1973  Billie Jean King, Tennis
1974  Chris Evert, Tennis
1975  Chris Evert, Tennis
1976  Nadia Comaneci, Gymnastics
1977  Chris Evert, Tennis
1978  Nancy Lopez, Golf
1979  Tracy Austin, Tennis
1980  Chris Evert Lloyd, Tennis
1981  Chris Evert Lloyd, Tennis
1982  Mary Decker Tabb, Track

# HIGHLY PAID ATHLETES*

## 15 HIGHLY PAID BASEBALL PLAYERS**

| | |
|---|---|
| Gary Carter | $2,000,000 |
| George Foster | 1,600,000 |
| Dave Winfield | 1,500,000 |
| Pete Rose | 1,300,000 |
| Mike Schmidt | 1,200,000 |
| Fred Lynn | 1,200,000 |
| Eddie Murray | 1,000,000 |
| Nolan Ryan | 1,000,000 |
| Phil Niekro | 1,000,000 |
| George Brett | 1,000,000 |
| Reggie Jackson | 975,000 |
| Dave Parker | 900,000 |
| Rod Carew | 900,000 |
| Dave Concepcion | 900,000 |
| Bobby Grich | 825,000 |

*Source: *The World Almanac and Book of Facts 1983*, Newspaper Enterprise Association, New York, 1983.
**Includes annual salary and deferred payments but not income from endorsements, commercials, and so on.

# 13 HIGHLY PAID BASKETBALL PLAYERS

| | |
|---|---|
| Moses Malone | $2,000,000 |
| Kareem Abdul-Jabbar | 1,000,000 |
| Marquis Johnson | 1,000,000 |
| Otis Birdsong | 900,000 |
| Mitch Krupchak | 800,000 |
| James Edwards | 800,000 |
| Scott Wedman | 800,000 |
| Gus Williams | 750,000 |
| David Thompson | 750,000 |
| Julius Erving | 700,000 |
| Larry Bird | 650,000 |
| Magic Johnson | 600,000 |
| Bob Lanier | 450,000 |

# 11 HIGHLY PAID FOOTBALL PLAYERS

| | |
|---|---|
| Walter Payton | $600,000 |
| Archie Manning | 600,000 |
| Tom Cousineau | 500,000 |
| Terry Bradshaw | 470,000 |
| Ron Jaworski | 410,000 |
| George Rogers | 375,000 |
| Billy Sims | 350,000 |
| Randy White | 318,000 |
| Steve Bartkowski | 230,000 |
| Jack Ham | 230,000 |
| Lee Roy Selmon | 218,000 |

# 5 HIGHLY PAID HOCKEY PLAYERS

| | |
|---|---|
| Wayne Gretzky | $1,000,000 |
| Mike Bossy | 640,000 |
| Marcel Dionne | 600,000 |
| Gil Perreault | 350,000 |
| Tony Esposito | 300,000 |

# TOP 10 PROFESSIONAL TENNIS PLAYERS
## IN 1982*

## Men's Tennis

|  | Earnings |
|---|---|
| Ivan Lendl | $1,628,850 |
| Jose-Luis Clerc | 590,400 |
| Tomas Smid | 552,200 |
| Jimmy Connors | 543,850 |
| Wojtek Fibak | 533,626 |
| John McEnroe | 525,725 |
| Guillermo Vilas | 502,150 |
| Johan Kriek | 364,094 |
| Vitas Gerulaitis | 340,875 |
| Kevin Curren | 293,427 |

## Women's Tennis

|  | Earnings |
|---|---|
| Martina Navratilova | $1,475,055 |
| Chris Evert Lloyd | 689,458 |
| Andrea Jaeger | 423,315 |
| Wendy Turnbull | 371,196 |
| Pam Shriver | 354,168 |
| Barbara Potter | 270,015 |
| Bettina Bunge | 248,598 |
| Hana Mandlikova | 231,283 |
| Sylvia Hanika | 215,151 |
| Anne Smith | 212,754 |

*Source: *The New York Times*, Jan. 2, 1983.

# TOP 10 PROFESSIONAL GOLFERS IN 1982*

## PGA

|  | Earnings |
|---|---|
| Craig Stadler | $446,462 |
| Ray Floyd | 386,809 |
| Tom Kite | 341,081 |
| Calvin Peete | 317,381 |
| Tom Watson | 316,483 |
| Lanny Wadkins | 306,827 |
| Bob Gilder | 296,598 |
| Jerry Pate | 280,141 |
| Wayne Levi | 268,631 |
| Curtis Strange | 263,378 |

## LPGA

|  | Earnings |
|---|---|
| JoAnne Carner | $310,399 |
| Sandra Haynie | 245,432 |
| Sally Little | 228,941 |
| Patty Sheehan | 225,032 |
| Beth Daniel | 223,635 |
| Amy Alcott | 169,981 |
| Nancy Lopez | 166,474 |
| Hollis Stacy | 161,379 |
| Kathy Whitworth | 138,693 |
| Jan Stephenson | 133,212 |

*Source: *The New York Times,* Jan. 2, 1983.

## ALFRED HITCHCOCK'S MOVIE APPEARANCES

The late British movie director Alfred Hitchcock, the master of suspense, always made an effort to appear in his movies, usually for just one or two seconds. The public anticipation of his "cameos" became so strong that he eventually made his appearances early in the movies lest the suspense be interrupted.

The following is a list of Hitchcock's appearances in his own movies:

| Movie (Year) | Cameo |
|---|---|
| *The Lodger* (1927) | A man wearing a cap, standing next to a policeman; also at a desk in a newsroom (two appearances) |
| *Murder* (1929) | A man on a street |
| *Blackmail* (1929) | A man reading a book on a subway train, being pestered by a little boy |
| *The 39 Steps* (1935) | A man walking down the street |
| *Young and Innocent* (1937) | A photographer standing outside the courthouse |
| *The Lady Vanishes* (1938) | A man standing at a railway station |
| *Rebecca* (1940) | A man standing next to a telephone booth in which George Sanders is making a phone call |

| | |
|---|---|
| *Foreign Correspondent* (1940) | A man reading a newspaper as Joel McCrea passes by |
| *Mr. and Mrs Smith* (1941) | A man walking past Robert Montgomery |
| *Saboteur* (1942) | A man standing in front of a newsstand |
| *Shadow of a Doubt* (1943) | A man playing cards on the train (he has a full house) |
| *Lifeboat* (1944) | The man in the weight-reducing ad in the newspaper being read by William Bendix. The ad shows Hitchcock before and after, the latter being a retouched photo |
| *Spellbound* (1945) | A man carrying a violin, exiting an elevator |
| *Notorious* (1946) | A man drinking champagne at a party |
| *The Paradine Case* (1947) | A man carrying a cello |
| *Rope* (1948) | A man crossing a street, after the credits |
| *Under Capricorn* (1949) | A man listening to a speech; a man on the stairs of the government house |
| *Stage Fright* (1950) | A man who stares at Jane Wyman on the street |
| *Strangers on a Train* (1951) | A man with a bass fiddle boarding a train as Farley Granger gets off the train |
| *I Confess* (1953) | A man seen crossing the top of a staircase |
| *Dial M for Murder* (1954) | A man in the photograph of a class reunion |
| *Rear Window* (1954) | The man winding a clock |
| *To Catch a Thief* (1955) | The man seated next to Cary Grant on the bus |
| *The Trouble with Harry* (1956) | A man walking in front of John Forsythe's outdoor exhibition |
| *The Man Who Knew Too Much (1956)* | The man watching acrobats in the Moroccan marketplace, as seen from the bank |

| | |
|---|---|
| *The Wrong Man* (1957) | The narrator of the movie's prologue |
| *Vertigo* (1958) | A man crossing the street |
| *North by Northwest* (1959) | The man who misses the bus, |
| *Vertigo* (1958) | A man crossing the street |
| *North by Northwest* (1959) | The man who misses the bus, with the door slamming in his face |
| *Psycho* (1960) | The man wearing a cowboy hat, outside the realty office |
| *The Birds* (1963) | The man leading two white French poodles out of the pet shop |
| *Marnie* (1964) | A man walking down the hotel corridor |
| *Torn Curtain* (1966) | The man with a baby on his lap, waiting in the hotel lobby |
| *Topaz* (1969) | The man in a wheelchair being pushed by a nurse at the airport |
| *Frenzy* (1970) | A man in the crowd listening to the speech given near the Thames |
| *Family Plot* (1976) | The man whose shadow is seen through the door window in the office of vital statistics |

## NONACTORS WHO HAVE APPEARED IN MOVIES

| | **Movie(s) in Which They Appeared** |
|---|---|
| Julian Bond | *Greased Lightning* (1977) |
| Jimmy Breslin | *If Ever I See You Again* (1978) |
| Truman Capote | *Murder by Death* (1976) |
| Pablo Casals | *Windjammer* (1958) |
| Ty Cobb | *The Ninth Inning* (1942) |
| James J. Corbett (Gentleman Jim) | The first fight film for Thomas Edison (1894); *Man from the Golden West* (1913); *The Prince of Avenue A* (1920); *Broadway After Dark* (1924) |

175

| | |
|---|---|
| Babe Didrikson Zaharias | *Pat and Mike* (1952) |
| Dionne Quintuplets | *Reunion* (1936); *The Country Doctor* (1936); *Going on Two* (1936, short); *Five of a Kind* (1938); *Quintupland* (1938, short) |
| Everett Dirksen | *The Monitors* (1969) |
| Red Foley | *Sing a Song, for Heaven's Sake* (1966) |
| Lou Gehrig | *Rawhide* (1938); *The Ninth Inning* (1942) |
| Rube Goldberg | *He Danced Himself to Death* (1914) |
| Abel Green (editor of *Variety*) | *Copacabana* (1947) |
| Oscar Hammerstein II | *Main Street to Broadway* (1953) |
| Gabriel Heatter | *Champagne for Caesar* (1950); *The Day the Earth Stood Still* (1951) |
| Ben Hecht | *The Scoundrel* (1935) |
| Harry Houdini | *The Master Mystery* (1918, serial); *The Grim Game* (1919); *Terror Island* (1920); *The Man from Beyond* (1921); and others |
| Chet Huntley | *I Cheated the Law* (1949); *Arctic Manhunt* (1949, narrator); *The Pride of St. Louis* (1952); *Mau Mau* (1955, narrator); *Cry Terror* (1958); *Behind the Great Wall* (1959, narrator) |
| William Inge | *Splendor in the Grass* (1961) |
| Janis Joplin | *Petulia* (1968); *Big Brother* (1968); *Monterey Pop* (1969); *Woodstock* (1970) |
| Estes Kefauver | *The Captive City* (1952) |
| Dorothy Kilgallen | *Sinner Take All* (1936); *Pajama Party* (1964) |
| Jerzy Kosinski | *Reds* (1981) |
| Gus Lesnevitch | *Requiem for a Heavyweight* (1962) |
| John V. Lindsay | *Rosebud* (1975) |
| Sonny Liston | *Harlow* (1965); *Head* (1968) |

| | |
|---|---|
| Frank Loesser | *Red, Hot, and Blue* (1949) |
| Frankie Lymon | *Mister Rock and Roll* (1957) |
| Moms Mabley | *Emperor Jones* (1970); *It's Your Thing* (1970) |
| Charles MacArthur | *Crime Without Passion* (1934); *Scoundrel* (1936) |
| Norman Mailer | *Wild 90* (1967); *Maidstone* (1969) *Ragtime* (1981) |
| Bernarr Macfadden | *Building of the Health of a Nation* series (1915–1916); *The Wrongdoers* (1925) |
| Somerset Maugham | *Trio* (1950); *Quartet* (1948); *Encore* (1951) |
| Elsa Maxwell | *Hotel for Women* (1939); *Public Deb No. 1* (1940); *Stage Door Canteen* (1943) |
| Jimmy McHugh | *The Helen Morgan Story* (1957) |
| Glenn Miller | *Orchestra Wives* (1942); *Sun Valley Serenade* (1942) |
| Jim Morrison | *Machine Gun McCain* (1970) |
| Edward R. Murrow | *The Seige of Leningrad* (1943, narrator); *Around the World in 80 Days* (1956); *Satchmo the Great* (1958, narrator) |
| Alfred Newman | *They Shall Have Music* (1939) |
| Ignace Jan Paderewski | *Moonlight Sonata* (1937) |
| Westbrook Pegler | *Madison Square Garden* (1937) |
| Pablo Picasso | *La Vie Commence Demain* (1952); *Orphée; Le testament d'Orphée* (1962) |
| Wiley Post | *Air Hawks* (1935) |
| Joe Pyne | *Mother Goose a Go-Go* (1966); *The Love-Ins* (1967) |
| Jackie Robinson | *The Jackie Robinson Story* (1950) |
| Mike Romanoff | *Arch of Triumph* (1948); *Von Ryan's Express* (1965); *Tony Rome* (1967); *Lady in Cement* (1968); plus others |
| Barney Ross | *Requiem for a Heavyweight* (1962); *The Doctor and the Playgirl* (1965) |

| | |
|---|---|
| Robert Ruark | *Africa Adventure* (1954, narrator); *Target Earth* (1955) |
| Damon Runyon | *Madison Square Garden* (1932) |
| Babe Ruth | *Headin' Home* (1920); *Babe Come Home* (1927); *Speedy* (1928); *Pride of the Yankees* (1942); plus Vitaphone short in 1937 |
| Erich Segal | *Without Apparent Motive* (1972) |
| Rod Serling | *Deadly Fathoms* (1973, narrator); *The Outer Space Connection* (1975) |
| George Bernard Shaw | *Masks and Faces* (1918) |
| Casey Stengel | *Safe at Home* (1941) |
| Bill Stern | *Pride of the Yankees* (1942); *Stage Door Canteen* (1943); *Here·Come the Co-Eds* (1945); *Spirit of West Point* (1947); *Go, Man, Go* (1954) |
| Jim Thorpe | *White Eagle* (1932); *Big City* (1937); *Outlaw Trail* (1944); *Wagonmaster* (1950) |
| Mrs. Tom Thumb | *The Lilliputian's Courtship* (1915) |
| Countess Tolstoy (wife of Leo Tolstoy) | *George Robey's Day Off* (1918) |
| Trotsky, Leon | *My Official Wife* (1914) |

# NARRATORS OF MAJOR MOVIES

Narrators are rarely used in movies but when they are, they are important aspects of casting. The right voice can add texture, dimension, and drama to the film. The following is a representative list of movies and their narrators:

| | **Movie** |
|---|---|
| Lionel Barrymore | *Dragon Seed* |
| Anne Baxter | *Mother Wore Tights* |
| Jackson Beck | *Take the Money and Run* |
| Richard Boone | *The Big Knife* |
| George Burns | *The Solid Gold Cadillac* |

178

| | |
|---|---|
| Richard Burton | *Zulu* |
| Louis Calhern | *It's a Big Country* |
| Ray Collins | *The Unseen* |
| Joseph Cotten | *The Wild Heart* |
| Hume Cronyn | *The Secret Heart* |
| Peter Cushing | *The Mummy's Shroud* |
| John Dehner | *The Hallelujah Trail* |
| Cedric Hardwicke | *The Picture of Dorian Gray* |
| | *The War of the Worlds* |
| Celeste Holm | *A Letter to Three Wives* |
| Victor Jory | *MacKenna's Gold* |
| James Robertson Justice | *Those Magnificent Men in Their Flying Machines* |
| Michael MacLiammoir | *Tom Jones* |
| Walter Pidgeon | *Quo Vadis* |
| Alexander Scourby | *"Victory at Sea"* series |
| Kim Stanley | *To Kill a Mockingbird* |
| Spencer Tracy | *How the West Was Won* |
| Rudy Vallee | *The Night They Raided Minsky's* |
| Orson Welles | *Duel in the Sun* |
| | *The Swiss Family Robinson* |
| | *The Vikings* |
| James Whitmore | *The Red Badge of Courage* |

# MOVIE DEBUTS AT AN EARLY AGE

The following actors and actresses made their movie debuts at early ages. This list is representative and by no means complete:

| | Age at | Movie (Date of Release) |
|---|---|---|
| Dickie Moore | 1 | *The Beloved Rogue* (1927) |
| Jackie Coogan | 2 | *Skinner's Baby* (1917) |
| Baby LeRoy | 2 | *A Bedtime Story* (1933) |
| Gigi Perreau | 2 | *Madame Curie* (1943) |
| Scotty Becket | 3 | *Our Gang* comedies |
| Shirley Temple | 3 | Short subjects (1932) |
| Margaret O'Brien | 4 | *Babes on Broadway* (1941) |
| Mickey Rooney | 4 | *Orchids and Ermine* (1927) |
| Virginia Wiedler | 4 | *Surrender* (1931) |
| Natalie Wood | 5 | *The Happy Land* (1943) |

179

| | | |
|---|---|---|
| Robert Blake | 6 | *Our Gang* comedies (1939) |
| Jackie Cooper | 6 | *Sunny Side Up* (1929) |
| Bobby Driscoll | 6 | *Lost Angel* (1943) |
| Jackie "Butch" Jenkins | 6 | *The Human Comedy* (1943) |
| Mark Lester | 6 | *Allez France!* (1964) |
| George "Foghorn" Wilson | 6 | *Room for One More* (1952) |
| Jane Withers | 6 | *Handle with Care* (1932) |
| Peggy Ann Garner | 7 | *Little Miss Thoroughbred* (1938) |
| Darryl Hickman | 7 | *If I Were King* (1938) |
| Johnny Sheffield | 7 | *Tarzan Finds a Son!* (1939) |
| Roddy McDowall | 8 | *Murder in the Family* (1936) |
| Tommy Rettig | 8 | *Panic in the Streets* (1950) |
| "Alfalfa" Switzer | 8 | *Our Gang* comedies (1935) |
| Dean Stockwell | 9 | *The Valley of Decision* (1945) |
| Brandon de Wilde | 10 | *The Member of the Wedding* (1952) |
| Tatum O'Neal | 10 | *Paper Moon* (1973) |
| Elizabeth Taylor | 10 | *There's One Born Every Minute* (1942) |
| Freddie Bartholomew | 11 | *David Copperfield* (1935) |
| Patty McCormack | 11 | *The Bad Seed* (1956) |
| "Spanky" McFarland | 11 | *Our Gang* comedies (1939) |
| Patty Duke Astin | 12 | *The Goddess* (1958) |
| Carole Lombard | 13 | *A Perfect Crime* (1921) |
| Hayley Mills | 13 | *Tiger Bay* (1959) |
| Donald O'Connor | 13 | *Sing You Sinners* (1938) |
| Judy Garland | 14 | *Pigskin Parade* (1936) |
| Annette Funicello | 15 | *Johnny Tremain* (1957) |
| Jane Powell | 15 | *Song of the Open Road* (1944) |
| Ann Blyth | 16 | *Chip Off the Old Block* (1944) |
| Ida Lupino | 16 | *Her First Affaire* (1933) |
| Ann Miller | 17 | *The Devil on Horseback* (1936) |
| Lana Turner | 17 | *A Star Is Born* (1937) |

# MOVIE DEBUTS AT A LATE AGE

Not all actors make their screen debuts at early ages, a la Shirley Temple, Jackie Coogan, and Jackie Cooper.

Some actors either started acting later in life or they were stage actors reluctant to sell out to a new medium.

The following people are among those who made their movie debuts at a relatively late age:

180

| | Age | Movie |
|---|---|---|
| Dame May Whitty | 72 | *The Thirteenth Chair* (1937) |
| John Houseman | 71 | *The Paper Chase* (1973) (won Academy Award for Best Supporting Actor) |
| Chief Dan George | 70 | *Smith!* (1969) |
| Sydney Greenstreet | 62 | *The Maltese Falcon* (1941) |
| Charles Coburn | 58 | *Boss Tweed* (1933) |
| Edmund Gwenn | 56 | *How He Lied to Her Husband* (1931) |
| S. Z. Sakall | 55 | *It's a Date* (1940) |
| George Arliss | 53 | *The Devil* (1921) |
| Florence Bates | 52 | *Rebecca* (1940) |
| Monty Woolley | 49 | *Live, Love and Learn* (1937) |
| Margaret Rutherford | 44 | *Talk of the Devil* (1936) |
| Barry Fitzgerald | 42 | *Juno and the Paycock* (1930) |

# UNCREDITED APPEARANCES OF ACTORS AND ACTRESSES IN MOVIES

Well-known actors and actresses occasionally appear in movies without receiving credits. They may just be doing a favor for another actor or director, they may have stopped by the studio that day and were asked to make a brief appearance, or they may not want to be identified with the movie for one reason or another. Here are some actors and actresses who appeared in movies without receiving credit:

| | Movie(s) |
|---|---|
| Lauren Bacall | *Two Guys from Milwaukee* |
| Jack Benny | *Without Reservations; It's a Mad, Mad, Mad Mad World; Beau James; The Great Lover* |
| Humphrey Bogart | *Always Together; Two Guys from Milwaukee; The Love Lottery; Road to Bali* |
| Yul Brynner | *The Magic Christian* |
| Richard Burton | *What's New Pussycat?* |
| Joseph Cotten | *Touch of Evil* |
| Bing Crosby | *My Favorite Blonde; The Princess and the Pirate,* plus various Bob Hope movies; *Scared Stiff* |

181

| | |
|---|---|
| Tony Curtis | *Chamber of Horrors* |
| Sammy Davis, Jr. | *A Raisin in the Sun* |
| Marlene Dietrich | *Touch of Evil* |
| Jimmy Durante | *Beau James* |
| Peter Finch | *The First Men in the Moon* |
| Clark Gable | *Callaway Went Thataway* |
| Ava Gardner | *The Band Wagon* |
| Cary Grant | *Without Reservations* |
| Helen Hayes | *Third Man on the Mountain* |
| Bob Hope | *The Oscar; Scared Stiff* |
| Rock Hudson | *Four Girls in Town* |
| Glenda Jackson | *The Boy Friend* |
| Boris Karloff | *Bikini Beach* |
| Gene Kelly | *Love Is Better than Ever* |
| Alan Ladd | *My Favorite Brunette* |
| Jerry Lewis | *It's a Mad, Mad, Mad Mad World; Road to Bali* |
| Peter Lorre | *Meet Me in Las Vegas* |
| Myrna Loy | *The Senator Was Indiscreet* |
| Shirley MacLaine | *Ocean's Eleven* |
| Dorothy Malone | *Fate Is the Hunter* |
| Dean Martin | *Road to Bali* |
| Groucho Marx | *Will Success Spoil Rock Hunter?* |
| Ray Milland | *Miss Tatlock's Millions* |
| David Niven | *Road to Hong Kong* |
| Edmund O'Brien | *The Greatest Show on Earth* |
| Peter O'Toole | *Casino Royale* |
| Vincent Price | *Beach Party* |
| Edward G. Robinson | *Robin and the Seven Hoods* |
| Jane Russell | *Road to Bali* |
| Margaret Rutherford | *The ABC Murders* |
| Peter Sellers | *Road to Hong Kong* |
| Red Skelton | *Susan Slept Here* |
| Elizabeth Taylor | *Winter Kills; What's New Pussycat?; Anne of the Thousand Days; Scent of Mystery* |
| Robert Taylor | *I Love Melvin; Callaway Went Thataway* |
| Lana Turner | *Du Barry Was a Lady* |
| Robert Vaughn | *The Glass Bottom Boat* |
| David Warner | *Straw Dogs* |
| John Wayne | *I Married a Woman* |

# UNSUNG HEROES AND HEROINES

## STARS OF MUSICALS WHO DIDN'T REALLY SING

Many Hollywood musical stars were cast for their "box-office appeal" and not for their singing voices. Consequently their voices had to be dubbed for the song numbers. The real singers were rarely given screen credits, so for the record here the unsung heroes and heroines of select movies and musicals:

| Movie | Actor/Actress | Real Voice |
|---|---|---|
| *The Band Wagon* | Cyd Charisse | India Adams |
| *West Side Story* | Richard Beymer | Jim Bryant |
| *The Belle of New York* | Vera-Ellen | Anita Ellis |
| *The Merry Widow* | Lana Turner | Trudy Erwin |
| *Orchestra Wives* | Lynn Bari | Pat Friday |
| *With a Song in My Heart* | Susan Hayward | Jane Froman |
| *The Helen Morgan Story* | Ann Blyth | Gogi Grant |
| *Pal Joey* | Rita Hayworth | Jo Ann Greer |
| *State Fair* | Jeanne Crain | Lorraine Hogan |
| *The Jolson Story* | Larry Parks | Al Jolson |
| *Gypsy* | Rosalind Russell | Lisa Kirk |
| *The Sound of Music* | Christopher Plummer | Bill Lee |
| *The King and I* | Deborah Kerr | Marni Nixon |
| *My Fair Lady* | Audrey Hepburn | Marni Nixon |
| *West Side Story* | Natalie Wood | Marni Nixon |
| *Brigadoon* | Cyd Charisse | Carole Richards |
| *Call Me Madam* | Vera-Ellen | Carole Richards |
| *A Song Is Born* | Virginia Mayo | Muriel Smith |
| *South Pacific* | Juanita Hall | Jeri Sullivan |
| *South Pacific* | Rossano Brazzi | Giorgio Tozzi |
| *Gigi* | Leslie Caron | Betty Wand |
| *West Side Story* | Rita Moreno | Betty Wand |
| *Show Boat* | Ava Gardner | Annette Warren |
| *To Have and Have Not* | Lauren Bacall | Andy Williams(!) |
| *Cover Girl* | Rita Hayworth | Nan Wynn |
| *Gilda* | Rita Hayworth | Nan Wynn |

# ACTORS WHO HAVE DIRECTED
## AT LEAST ONE MOVIE

**Movie***

| | |
|---|---|
| Alan Arkin | *Little Murders* (1971) |
| Alan Alda | *The Four Seasons* (1981) |
| Richard Attenborough | *Oh! What a Lovely War* (1969); *Gandhi* (1982) |
| Lionel Barrymore | *Confession* (1929) |
| Marlon Brando | *One-Eyed Jacks* (1960) |
| Richard Burton | *Dr. Faustus* (1967) co-director |
| James Caan | *Hide in Plain Sight* (1980) |
| James Cagney | *Short Cut to Hell* (1958) |
| Ricardo Cortez | *City Girl* (1938) and others |
| John Derek | *Once Before I Die* (1966); *Tarzan* (1981) |
| Clint Eastwood | *Breezy* (1973) and others |
| José Ferrer | *The Shrike* (1954) |
| Mel Ferrer | *Girl of the Limberlost* (1945) |
| Albert Finney | *Charlie Bubbles* (1968) |
| Peter Fonda | *The Hired Hand* (1971) |
| Al Freeman, Jr. | *A Fable* (1971) |
| Laurence Harvey | *The Ceremony* (1963) |
| David Hemmings | *Running Scared* (1972) |
| Paul Henreid | *For Men Only* (1951) |
| Charlton Heston | *Antony and Cleopatra* (1971) |
| Dennis Hopper | *Easy Rider* (1969) and others |
| Leslie Howard | *Pygmalion* (1938) and others |
| Charles Laughton | *Night of the Hunter* (1955) |
| Jack Lemmon | *Kotch* (1971) |
| Peter Lorre | *Die Verlorene Ehre der Katharina Blum* (1950) |
| Ida Lupino | *Not Wanted* (1949); many TV movies |
| Roddy McDowall | *Tam Lin* (1970) |
| Karl Malden | *Time Limit* (1957) |
| Walter Matthau | *Gangster Story* (1960) |
| Burgess Meredith | *The Yin and the Yang* (1970) |
| Ray Milland | *A Man Alone* (1955) and others |
| John Mills | *Sky West and Crooked* (1965) |
| George Montgomery | *Samar* (1962) and others |
| Robert Montgomery | *The Lady in the Lake* (1946) and others |

184

| | |
|---|---|
| Anthony Newley | *Can Hieronymus Merkin. . . .* (1969) |
| Paul Newman | *Sometimes a Great Notion* (1971); *Rachel, Rachel* (1968) |
| Jack Nicholson | *Drive, He Said* (1970) |
| Edmund O'Brien | *Shield for Murder* (1954) codirector |
| Dennis O'Keefe | *The Diamond Wizard* (1954) |
| Laurence Olivier | *Hamlet* (1948) and others |
| Dick Powell | *Split Second* (1953) and others |
| Anthony Quinn | *The Buccaneer* (1959) |
| Robert Redford | *Ordinary People* (1980) |
| Ralph Richardson | *Home at Seven* (1952) |
| Cliff Robertson | *J. W. Coop* (1972) |
| Peter Sellers | *Mr. Topaze* (1961) |
| Frank Sinatra | *None But the Brave* (1965) |
| Peter Ustinov | *School for Secrets* (1946) and others |
| John Wayne | *The Green Berets* (1968) |
| Cornel Wilde | *Storm Fear* (1955) and others |
| Mai Zetterling | *The War Game* (1962) |

*Representative movie—list not complete

# DIRECTORS WHO HAVE APPEARED ON SCREEN

Many actors get the desire to direct movies and make at least one attempt at directing (see list of actors who have directed movies), but directors who become actors are extremely rare. John Huston is perhaps the best example of a director (and writer) who has appeared in movies as an actor, and he gave some especially good performances in *The Cardinal* (1963) and *The Bible* (1966). Orson Welles really started out as both an actor and director but has leaned toward acting in recent years. Most directors who do get on camera appear briefly and without screen credits. The following directors have also made screen appearances, usually but not always in movies which they directed:

| | **Movie(s)** |
|---|---|
| Robert Aldrich | *The Big Knife* |
| Ingmar Bergman | *Waiting Woman* |

| | |
|---|---|
| Peter Bogdanovich | *Targets* |
| Frank Borzage | *Jeanne Eagels* |
| Claude Chabrol | *Les Biches; The Road to Corinth* |
| Jean Cocteau | *Orphee; Le Testament d'Orphee* |
| Jules Dassin | *Never on Sunday* |
| Cecil B. De Mille | *Sunset Boulevard; The Buster Keaton Story; Star Spangled Girl; Son of Paleface* |
| Samuel Fuller | *House of Bamboo* |
| Joseph Losey | *The Intimate Stranger* |
| Andrew McLaglen | *Paris Underground* |
| Sydney Pollack | *Tootsie* |
| Nicholas Ray | *55 Days in Peking* |
| Jean Renoir | *Rules of the Game* |
| Tony Richardson | *Tom Jones* |
| Preston Sturges | *Sullivan's Travels; Paris Holiday* |
| François Truffaut | *The Wild Child; Close Encounters of The Third Kind* |

# FAMOUS WRITERS WHO SPENT SOME TIME IN TINSELTOWN

The great Hollywood dream machine attracts writers of all types. From hack studio writers to Algonquin Round Table wits seeking "some time in the sun" (to use writer Tom Dardis' phrase), the studios could afford to buy or "rent" almost any writer. Here are some well-respected writers, some of whom won Nobel and Pulitzer prizes, who spent some time on the studio payrolls to write scripts:

| **Writer** | **Works, Awards** | **Scripts Worked On** |
|---|---|---|
| Maxwell Anderson | *Winterset* *Both Your Houses* (Pultizer Prize—1933) *Anne of the Thousand Days* | *All Quiet on the Western Front* (1930) *Rain* (1932) *Washington Merry-Go-Round* (1932) *Joan of Arc* (1948) *The Wrong Man* (1957) *Death Takes a Holiday* (1934) |

| | | |
|---|---|---|
| Theodore Dreiser | *An American Tragedy* <br> *Sister Carrie* <br> *Jenny Gerhardt* | *An American Tragedy (1931)* <br> *Tobacco and Men* (1935) <br> *My Gal Sal* (1942) |
| William Faulkner (Nobel Prize— 1949) | *The Sound and the Fury* <br> *A Fable* (Pulitzer Prize—1955) <br> *The Reivers* (Pulitzer Prize—1963) <br> *Absalom, Absalom!* | *Today We Live* (1933) <br> *Road to Glory* (1936) <br> *To Have and Have Not* (1945) <br> *The Big Sleep* (1946) <br> *Land of the Pharaohs* (1955) |
| F. Scott Fitzgerald | *The Great Gatsby* <br> *Tender is the Night* <br> *This Side of Paradise* <br> *The Last Tycoon* | *A Yank at Oxford* (1938) <br> *Three Comrades* (1938) <br> *Gone With the Wind* (1939) <br> *The Women* (1939) <br> *Madame Curie* (1943) |
| Ernest Hemingway (Nobel Prize— 1954) | *A Farewell to Arms* <br> *For Whom the Bell Tolls* <br> *The Old Man and the Sea* (Pulitzer Prize— 1953) | *The Spanish Earth* (1937) <br> *The Old Man and the Sea* (1956) |
| James Hilton | *Goodbye, Mr. Chips* <br> *Lost Horizon* <br> *We Are Not Alone* | *Camille* (1936) <br> *We Are Not Alone* (1939) <br> *The Tuttles of Tahiti* (1942) <br> *Mrs. Miniver* (1942) (Academy Award) <br> *Forever and a Day* (1944) |
| Aldous Huxley | *Chrome Yellow* <br> *Antic Hay* <br> *Brave New World* | *Pride and Prejudice* (1940) <br> *Jane Eyre* (1944) <br> *A Woman's Vengeance* (1947) |
| William Inge | *Come Back, Little Sheba* <br> *Bus Stop* <br> *Picnic* | *Splendor in the Grass* (1961) (Academy Award) <br> *All Fall Down* (1963) <br> *The Stripper* (1964) |
| Clifford Odets | *Waiting for Lefty* <br> *Golden Boy* <br> *The Country Girl* | *The General Died at Dawn* (1936) <br> *None But the Lonely* |

| | *The Big Knife* | *Heart* (1944) |
| --- | --- | --- |
| | | *Sweet Smell of Success* (1957) |
| | | *The Story on Page One* (1960) |
| | | *Wild in the Country* (1961) |
| Ayn Rand | *The Fountainhead* | *Love Letters* (1945) |
| | *Atlas Shrugged* | *You Came Along* (1945) |
| | *We, the Living* | *The Fountainhead* (1949) |
| George Bernard Shaw (Nobel Prize— 1925) | *The Devil's Disciple* *Man and Superman* *Back to Methuselah* *Caesar and Cleopatra* | *Pygmalion* (1938) (Academy Award) *Major Barbara* (1941) *Caesar and Cleopatra* (1946) |
| John Steinbeck (Nobel Prize— 1962) | *The Grapes of Wrath* (Pulitzer Prize—1940) *Of Mice and Men* *East of Eden* *Tortilla Flat* | *The Forgotten Village* (1941) *Lifeboat* (1944) (Academy Award) *A Medal for Benny* (1945) (Academy Award) *The Pearl* (1948) *The Pony* (1949) *Viva Zapata* (1952) (Academy Award) |
| Thornton Wilder | *The Bridge at San Luis Rey* (Pulitzer Prize— 1928) *Our Town* (Pulitzer Prize—1938) *The Skin of Our Teeth* Pulitzer Prize—1943) | *The Dark Angel* (1935) *Our Town* (1940) *Shadow of a Doubt* (1943) |

Other well-known writers who worked on screenplays were Dashiell Hammett, Lillian Hellman, Raymond Chandler, Christopher Isherwood, S. J. Perelman, Nathanael West, Dorothy Parker, Ben Hecht, Charles MacArthur, and dozens of others.

# ACTORS TURNED POLITICIANS

Charles de Gaulle once remarked that politics was too serious a matter to be left to politicians, but one suspects that he did not have actors in mind as potential politicians when he made the statement. Yet, a few actors, capitalizing on their relative popularity and their ability to address audiences, have entered the field of politics with varying degrees of success. Here are the best examples of actors who turned politicians:

### Ronald Reagan

Elected governor of California, 1966–1974
Elected U.S. president, 1980–

### Shirley Temple Black

Ran for Congress in 1967. Lost to Paul McCloskey
Appointed by President Nixon as delegate to UN's 24th General Assembly
Appointed U.S ambassador to Ghana in 1974 by President Ford

### George Murphy

Elected U.S. senator in 1964. Beat Pierre Salinger
Lost reelection in 1970 to John Tunney

### Charles Farrell

Mayor of Palm Springs, California, for seven years

**John Davis Lodge**

Elected governor of Connecticut in 1950 and served one term
Ambassador to Spain (1955–1961)
Ambassador to Argentina (1969–1973)

**Helen Gahagan Douglas**

Delegate to 1940 Democratic convention
Elected congresswoman of California's 14th district
Ran for U.S. Senate in 1950. Lost to Richard M. Nixon

# THE 100 MOST INFLUENTIAL PERSONS IN HISTORY

When author Michael H. Hart set out to write *The 100: A Ranking of the Most Influential Persons in History* (Galahad, 1982), his mission was to determine the 100 persons "who had the greatest effect on history and on the course of the world," ranked in order of importance. One would expect Jesus Christ to be number one on the list but, curiously, he is number three. Muhammad is ranked number one because, according to Hart, he "had a much greater personal influence on the formulation of the Moslem religion than Jesus had on the formulation of the Christian religion." Hart points out that whereas Jesus was "responsible for the main ethical and moral precepts of Christianity (insofar as these differed from Judaism), St. Paul was the main developer of Christian theology, its principal proselytizer, and the author of a large portion of the New Testament." Hart further observed that Muhammad was a secular leader as well as a religious one, unlike Jesus, and therefore had more influence. Although the list is highly debatable, the book is fascinating, especially for history buffs and famous-people-watchers.

1. Muhammad (religious, secular leader)
2. Isaac Newton (scientist)
3. Jesus Christ (religious leader)
4. Buddha (religious leader
5. Confucius (philosopher)
6. St. Paul (Apostle)
7. Ts'ai Lun (inventor of paper)
8. Johann Gutenberg (printer)
9. Christopher Columbus (explorer)
10. Albert Einstein (scientist)

11. Karl Marx (political philosopher)
12. Louis Pasteur (chemist, biologist)
13. Galileo Galilei (astronomer)
14. Aristotle (philosopher)
15. Lenin (political leader)
16. Moses (prophet)
17. Charles Darwin (evolutionist)
18. Shih Huang Ti (emperor)
19. Augustus Caesar (emperor)
20. Mao Tse-tung (political leader)
21. Genghis Khan (conqueror)
22. Euclid (mathematician)
23. Martin Luther (religious leader)
24. Nicolaus Copernicus (astronomer)
25. James Watt (inventor)
26. Constantine the Great (emperor)
27. George Washington (U.S. president)
28. Michael Faraday (inventor)
29. James Clerk Maxwell (physicist)
30. Orville Wright and Wilbur Wright (aviators)
31. Antoine Laurent Lavoisier (scientist)
32. Sigmund Freud (psychoanalyst)
33. Alexander the Great (conqueror)
34. Napoleon Bonaparte (emperor)
35. Adolf Hitler (political dictator)
36. William Shakespeare (playwright)
37. Adam Smith (economist)
38. Thomas Edison (inventor)
39. Antony van Leeuwenhoek (scientist)
40. Plato (philosopher)
41. Guglielmo Marconi (inventor)
42. Ludwig van Beethoven (composer)
43. Werner Heisenberg (physicist)
44. Alexander Graham Bell (inventor)
45. Alexander Fleming (scientist)
46. Simón Bolívar (political liberator)
47. Oliver Cromwell (military leader)
48. John Locke (philosopher)
49. Michelangelo (artist)
50. Pope Urban II (religious leader)
51. Umar ibn al-Khattab (caliph)
52. Asoka (monarch)

53. St. Augustine (theologian)
54. Max Planck (physicist)
55. John Calvin (theologian)
56. William T. G. Morton (anesthetist)
57. William Harvey (physician)
58. Antoine Henri Becquerel (physicist)
59. Gregor Mendel (scientist)
60. Joseph Lister (surgeon)
61. Nikolaus August Otto (inventor)
62. Louis Daguerre (photographer)
63. Joseph Stalin (political dictator)
64. René Descartes (philosopher, mathematician)
65. Julius Caesar (emperor)
66. Francisco Pizarro (explorer)
67. Hernando Cortes (explorer)
68. Queen Isabella I (political leader)
69. William the Conqueror (ruler)
70. Thomas Jefferson (U.S. president)
71. Jean-Jacques Rousseau (philosopher)
72. Edward Jenner (physician)
73. Wilhelm Conrad Rontgen (scientist)
74. Johann Sebastian Bach (composer)
75. Lao Tzu (philosopher)
76. Enrico Fermi (physicist)
77. Thomas Malthus (economist)
78. Francis Bacon (political leader)
79. Voltaire (philosopher)
80. John F. Kennedy (U.S. president)
81. Gregory Pincus (biologist)
82. Sui Wen Ti (emperor)
83. Mani (prophet)
84. Vasco da Gama (explorer)
85. Charlemagne (emperor)
86. Cyrus the Great (emperor)
87. Leonhard Euler (mathematician)
88. Niccolò Machiavelli (political philosopher)
89. Zoroaster (prophet)
90. Menes (king)
91. Peter the Great (czar)
92. Mencius (philosopher)
93. John Dalton (scientist)
94. Homer (poet)

95. Queen Elizabeth I (monarch)
96. Justinian I (emperor)
97. Johannes Kepler (scientist)
98. Pablo Picasso (artist)
99. Mahavira (religious leader)
100. Niels Bohr (physicist)

**Honorable Mentions and Interesting Misses:** St. Thomas Aquinas, Archimedes, Charles Babbage, Cheops, Marie Curie, Benjamin Franklin, Gandhi, Abraham Lincoln, Ferdinand Magellan, and Leonardo da Vinci.

# CELEBRITY ANAGRAMS

An anagram is the rearranging of the letters of a word or words into other words. Here are some anagrams of the names of celebrated people of the past and present:

Spiro Agnew—Grow a penis
Truman Capote—Apt court name
Grover Cleveland—Govern, clever lad!
Dwight D. Eisenhower—Wow! He's right, indeed!
Richard Gere—Ride charger
Bob Hope—Hep boob
Lyndon Baines Johnson—No ninny, he's on job, lads
Liberace—Lice bear; bare lice
Richard M. Nixon—In hard corn mix
Theodore Roosevelt—Hero told to oversee
Gore Vidal—I love drag
Xerxes—Sex rex

# THE 103 RICHEST AMERICANS

*Forbes* magazine recently inaugurated its "Forbes Four Hundred" list: "A compilation of the Big rich—not of jetsetters or media celebrities." While many of the people are not well known, it is surprising that Daniel K. Ludwig, the richest person in the country, is virtually unknown by the public and is very rarely mentioned in the media. (If Ludwig has a press agent, the agent clearly has been hired to keep him *out of* the news.)

Of course, one expects to see du Ponts and Rockefellers well represented, but the real surprise is to see that a famous entertainer (hint:
he's a comedian) is worth $280 million.

The following people, according to *Forbes*, are worth at least $240
million, making them the 103 richest Americans. Oil, real estate, and
inheritances seem to be where it's at:

| | Age | Worth | Source of Wealth |
|---|---|---|---|
| Perry Richardson Bass | 67 | | |
| Sid Richardson Bass | 39 | $2 billion | Oil; investments |
| Roy H. Cullen | 52 | | |
| Margaret Cullen Marshall | 61 | | |
| Wilhelmina Cullen Robertson | 59 | $2 billion | Inheritance; oil |
| Isaac Arnold, Jr. | 46 | | |
| Daniel Keith Ludwig | 85 | $2 billion+ | Shipping |
| Pierre Samuel du Pont III | 71 | | |
| Mary Belin du Pont Faulkner | 75 | $1.5 billion | Inheritance |
| Esther Driver du Pont Thouron | 74 | | (du Pont) |
| Willis Harrington du Pont | 46 | | |
| Gordon Peter Getty | 48 | $1.4 billion | Inheritance |
| Cyril Wagner, Jr. | 48 | | |
| Jack Brown | 56 | $1.1 billion | Oil |
| Barbara Cox Anthony | 59 | | |
| Anne Cox Chambers | 62 | $1 billion | Inheritance |
| A. N. Pritzker | 86 | | |
| Jay Arthur Pritzker | 60 | $1 billion | Financiers; |
| Robert Alan Pritzker | 56 | | real estate |
| Robert R. Carpenter, Jr. | 67 | | |
| William K. Carpenter | 63 | $1 billion | Inheritance |
| Irene Carpenter Draper | 71 | | (du Pont) |
| Margaret Hunt Hill | 67 | $1 billion | Inheritance |
| Caroline Hunt Schoellkopf | 59 | $1 billion | Inheritance |
| Philip Anschutz | 43 | $1 billion | Oil, drilling |
| David Rockefeller | 67 | $1 billion | Inheritance; real estate |
| Walter H. Annenberg | 74 | $800 million | Publishing |

| | | | |
|---|---|---|---|
| Charles G. Koch | 46 | | |
| David H. Koch | 41 | $800 million | Oil |
| William J. Koch | 41 | | |
| Stephen D. Bechtel, Sr. | 81 | $750 million | Engineering, |
| Stephen D. Bechtel, Jr. | 57 | | construction |
| Harry B. Helmsley | 72 | $750 million | Real estate |
| Sam M. Walton | 64 | $690 million | Wal-Mart stores |
| Wiliam R. Hewlett | 69 | $650 million | Electronics |
| Samuel J. Newhouse, Jr. | 54 | $600 million | Newspaper |
| Donald Newhouse | 52 | | chain |
| H. L. Hunt III | 65 | $600 million | Inheritance |
| William W. Caruth, Jr. | 70 | $600 million | Real estate |
| Lawrence A. Tisch | 58 | $600 million | Loews Corp.; |
| Preston R. Tisch | 55 | | hotels |
| Richard M. De Vos | 56 | | |
| Jay Van Andel | 58 | $550 million | Amway Corp. |
| A. Alfred Taubman | 57 | $525 million | Shopping centers |
| Larry Fisher | Late | | |
| Zachary Fisher | 60's | $500 million | Real estate |
| Edward J. DeBartolo | 64 | $500 million | Shopping centers |
| Henry Crown | 86 | | |
| Lester Crown | 57 | $500 million | Financiers |
| Jack Rudin | 58 | | |
| Lewis Rudin | 55 | $500 million | Real estate |
| Henry Lea Hillman | 63 | $500 million | Industrialist |
| Paul Mellon | 75 | $500 million | Inheritance |
| Leonard N. Stern | 44 | $500 million | Hartz Mountain Industries |
| Richard Mellon Scaife | 49 | $500 million | Inheritance; investments |
| Robert O. Anderson | 65 | $500 million | Oil; land |

| | | | |
|---|---|---|---|
| Curtis L. Carlson | 68 | $500 million | Trading stamps; hotels |
| Jack Kent Cooke | 70 | $500 million | Publishing; cable TV, real estate; sports |
| Trammel Crow | 67 | $500 million | Real estate |
| Kenneth W. Ford | 74 | $500 million | Timber |
| Samuel J. LeFrak | 64 | $500 million | Real estate |
| J. R. Simplot | 73 | $500 million | Potatoes |
| Samuel Curtis Johnson | 54 | $500 million | Johnson Wax |
| Laurance S. Rockefeller | 72 | $450 million | Inheritance; investments |
| Edwin L. Cox | 60 | $450 million | Oil |
| Charles C. Gates | 61 | $420 million | Gates Corp. |
| Michel Fribourg | 69 | $400 million | Grain trading |
| George P. Mitchell | 63 | $400 million | Oil; real estate |
| Winthrop P. Rockefeller | 34 | $400 million | Inheritance |
| Malcolm Purcell McLean | 68 | $400 million | Trucking; shipping |
| David H. Murdock | 59 | $400 million | Real estate; acquisitions |
| Cordelia Scaife May | 54 | $400 million | Inheritance |
| Lammot du Pont Copeland | 76 | $400 million | Inheritance |
| Roger Milliken | 66 | $400 million | Textiles |
| Carlton Beal | 66 | $400 million | Oil |
| Albert B. Alkek | 71 | $350 million | Oil |
| Donald L. Bren | 48 | $350 million | Real estate |
| John L. Cox | 57 | $350 million | Oil |
| H. Ross Perot | 52 | $325 million | Computer services |

| | | | |
|---|---|---|---|
| Raymond A. Kroc | 79 | $320 million | McDonald's hamburger chain |
| Arthur M. Wirtz | 81 | $300 million | Real estate; sports |
| Leonard Marx | 76 | $300 million | Real estate |
| August A. Busch, Jr. | 83 | $300 million | Anheuser-Busch |
| Marion du Pont | 88 | $300 million | Inheritance (du Pont) |
| John T. Lupton | 56 | $300 million | Coca-Cola bottling |
| Georgia Rosenbloom Frontiere | 52 | $300 million | Inheritance |
| Bob Hope | 79 | $280 million | Entertainment; real estate |
| Leon Hess | 67 | $275 million | Oil |
| Philip H. Knight | 44 | $275 million | Nike athletic shoes |
| Clint W. Murchison, Jr. | 58 | $260 million | Oil; investments |
| Clarence Scharbauer, Jr. | 57 | $250 million | Inheritance |
| Jake Louis Hamon, Jr. | 80 | $250 million | Oil; gas |
| O. Wayne Rollins | 70 | $250 million | Rollins, Inc. |
| Walter Shorenstein | 67 | $250 million | Real estate |
| Joe Lewis Allbritton | 57 | $250 million | Newspapers; TV |
| David B. Shakarian | 68 | $250 million | Health food stores |
| Ted Arison | 57 | $250 million | Shipping |
| Arthur B. Belfer | 75 | $250 million | Oil; real estate |
| Jane Engelhard | 65 | $250 million | Inheritance |
| Edward L. Gaylord | 63 | $250 million | Newspapers; TV |

| Warren Buffett | 52 | $250 million | Stock market |
| John Jeffry Louis, Jr. | 57 | $240 million | Inheritance |
| Betsey Cushing Whitney | 74 | $250 million | Inheritance |

Source: *Forbes* magazine, September 13, 1982

## TOP 25 HIGHEST PAID EXECUTIVES IN THE U.S. (1982)*

| Chief Executive | Company | Total Compensation | | |
| --- | --- | --- | --- | --- |
| | | **Salary, Bonus, Etc** | **Stock Gains** | **Total** |
| Frederick W. Smith | Federal Express | $ 414,000 | $51,130,000 | $51,544,000 |
| Charles Lazarus | Toys 'R' Us | 1,488,000 | 42,360,000 | 43,848,000 |
| Ronald G. Assaf | Sensormatic Electronics | 291,000 | 6,995,000 | 7,286,000 |
| Steven J. Ross | Warner Communications | 3,681,000 | — | 3,681,000 |
| George L. Shinn | First Boston | 2,443,000 | 1,090,000 | 3,533,000 |
| Richard K. Eamer | National Medical Enterprises | 792,000 | 2,653,000 | 3,445,000 |
| John P. Laborde | Tidewater | 745,000 | 2,469,000 | 3,214,000 |
| David J. Mahoney | Norton Simon | 1,851,000 | 1,145,000 | 2,996,000 |
| Thomas V. Jones | Northrop | 2,911,000 | — | 2,911,000 |
| Harrington Drake | Dun & Bradstreet | 845,000 | 1,701,000 | 2,546,000 |
| Richard L. Gelb | Bristol-Myers | 1,000,000 | 1,406,000 | 2,406,000 |
| J. Paul Sticht | R. J. Reynolds | 1,139,000 | 1,194,000 | 2,333,000 |
| John W. Dixon | E-Systems | 2,178,000 | 110,000 | 2,288,000 |
| Donald H. Runsfeld | G. D. Searle | 728,000 | 1,527,000 | 2,255,000 |
| J. Robert Fluor | Fluor | 1,513,000 | 733,000 | 2,246,000 |
| W. Paul Thayer | LTV | 1,154,000 | 944,000 | 2,098,000 |
| George T. Scharffenberger | City Investing | 1,323,000 | 766,000 | 2,089,000 |

*Source: *Forbes* magazine, June 6, 1983.

| | | | | |
|---|---|---:|---:|---:|
| William A. Marquand | American Standard | 1,096,000 | 957,000 | 2,053,000 |
| David S. Lewis | General Dynamics | 526,000 | 1,421,000 | 1,947,000 |
| Maurice Segall | Zayre | 1,074,000 | 851,000 | 1,925,000 |
| Robert Cizik | Cooper Industries | 305,000 | 1,509,000 | 1,814,000 |
| Arthur J. Santry, Jr. | Combustion Engineering | 1,355,000 | 446,000 | 1,801,000 |
| Thornton A. Wilson | Boeing | 1,220,000 | 577,000 | 1,797,000 |
| Robert E. Kirby | Westinghouse Electric | 1,043,000 | 747,000 | 1,790,000 |
| Robert A. Schoellhorn | Abbott Laboratories | 769,000 | 1,014,000 | 1,783,000 |

# 21 WELL-PAID WOMEN SPEAKERS

The lecture circuit has become a lucrative venture for many celebrities. The following women are booked as speakers (by Ross Associates) for meetings, conventions, and symposia for the indicated fees:

| | Fee per Lecture |
|---|---|
| Barbara Walters (TV personality) | $20,000 |
| Ann Landers (columnist) | 8–10,000 |
| Diane Sawyer (TV journalist) | 8,500 |
| Polly Bergen (actress) | 7,000–8,000 |
| Jane Bryant Quinn (financial columnist) | 7,000–8,000 |
| Pearl Bailey (singer) | 7,000 |
| Mary E. Cunningham (business executive) | 7,000 |
| Jane Cahill Pfeiffer (ex-NBC executive) | 6,000 |
| Bess Myerson (ex-Miss America) | 5,000–6,000 |
| Shana Alexander (journalist) | 5,000–6,000 |
| Cicely Tyson (actress) | 5,000–6,000 |
| Celeste Holm (actress) | 5,000 |
| Jane Pauley (TV personality) | 4,000–5,000 |
| Arlene Dahl (actress) | 4,000–5,000 |
| Nancy Dickerson (TV personality) | 4,000–5,000 |

| | |
|---|---|
| Letitia Baldridge (etiquette expert) | 4,000–5,000 |
| Dr. Joyce Brothers (pop psychologist) | 4,000–5,000 |
| Virginia Graham (TV personality) | 3,000–4,000 |
| Joan Fontaine (actress) | 3,000–4,000 |
| Barbara Howar (journalist) | 3,000–4,000 |
| Eleanor Smeal (ex-president of NOW) | 3,000–4,000 |

# ACADEMY AWARDS

### Best Actor

| | |
|---|---|
| 1928 | Emil Jannings, *The Way of All Flesh; The Last Command* |
| 1929 | Warner Baxter, *In Old Arizona* |
| 1930 | George Arliss, *Disraeli* |
| 1931 | Lionel Barrymore, *A Free Soul* |
| 1932 | Fredric March, *Dr. Jekyll and Mr. Hyde* |
| | Wallace Beery, *The Champ* |
| 1933 | Charles Laughton, *The Private Life of Henry VIII* |
| 1934 | Clark Gable, *It Happened One Night* |
| 1935 | Victor McLaglen, *The Informer* |
| 1936 | Paul Muni, *The Story of Louis Pasteur* |
| 1937 | Spencer Tracy, *Captains Courageous* |
| 1938 | Spencer Tracy, *Boys Town* |
| 1939 | Robert Donat, *Goodbye, Mr. Chips* |
| 1940 | James Stewart, *The Philadelphia Story* |
| 1941 | Gary Cooper, *Sergeant York* |
| 1942 | James Cagney, *Yankee Doodle Dandy* |
| 1943 | Paul Lukas, *Watch on the Rhine* |
| 1944 | Bing Crosby, *Going My Way* |
| 1945 | Ray Milland, *The Lost Weekend* |
| 1946 | Fredric March, *The Best Years of Our Lives* |
| 1947 | Ronald Colman, *A Double Life* |
| 1948 | Laurence Olivier, *Hamlet* |
| 1949 | Broderick Crawford, *All the King's Men* |
| 1950 | José Ferrer, *Cyrano de Bergerac* |
| 1951 | Humphrey Bogart, *The African Queen* |
| 1952 | Gary Cooper, *High Noon* |
| 1953 | William Holden, *Stalag 17* |
| 1954 | Marlon Brando, *On the Waterfront* |
| 1955 | Ernest Borgnine, *Marty* |
| 1956 | Yul Brynner, *The King and I* |

| 1957 | Alec Guinness, *The Bridge on the River Kwai* |
| 1958 | David Niven, *Separate Tables* |
| 1959 | Charlton Heston, *Ben-Hur* |
| 1960 | Burt Lancaster, *Elmer Gantry* |
| 1961 | Maximilian Schell, *Judgment at Nuremberg* |
| 1962 | Gregory Peck, *To Kill a Mockingbird* |
| 1963 | Sidney Poitier, *Lilies of the Field* |
| 1964 | Rex Harrison, *My Fair Lady* |
| 1965 | Lee Marvin, *Cat Ballou* |
| 1966 | Paul Scofield, *A Man for All Seasons* |
| 1967 | Rod Steiger, *In the Heat of the Night* |
| 1968 | Cliff Robertson,*Charly* |
| 1969 | John Wayne, *True Grit* |
| 1970 | George C. Scott, *Patton* |
| 1971 | Gene Hackman, *The French Connection* |
| 1972 | Marlon Brando, *The Godfather* |
| 1973 | Jack Lemmon, *Save the Tiger* |
| 1974 | Art Carney, *Harry and Tonto* |
| 1975 | Jack Nicholson, *One Flew over the Cuckoo's Nest* |
| 1976 | Peter Finch, *Network* |
| 1977 | Richard Dreyfuss, *The Goodbye Girl* |
| 1978 | Jon Voight, *Coming Home* |
| 1979 | Dustin Hoffman, *Kramer vs. Kramer* |
| 1980 | Robert De Niro, *Raging Bull* |
| 1981 | Henry Fonda, *On Golden Pond* |
| 1982 | Ben Kingsley, *Gandhi* |

## Best Actress

| 1928 | Janet Gaynor, *Seventh Heaven; Street Angel; Sunrise* |
| 1929 | Mary Pickford, *Coquette* |
| 1930 | Norma Shearer, *The Divorce* |
| 1931 | Marie Dressler, *Min and Bill* |
| 1932 | Helen Hayes, *The Sin of Madelon Claudet* |
| 1933 | Katharine Hepburn, *Morning Glory* |
| 1934 | Claudette Colbert, *It Happened One Night* |
| 1935 | Bette Davis, *Dangerous* |
| 1936 | Luise Rainer, *The Great Ziegfeld* |
| 1937 | Luise Rainer, *The Good Earth* |
| 1938 | Bette Davis, *Jezebel* |
| 1939 | Vivien Leigh, *Gone With the Wind* |
| 1940 | Ginger Rogers, *Kitty Foyle* |

| | |
|---|---|
| 1941 | Joan Fontaine, *Suspicion* |
| 1942 | Greer Garson, *Mrs. Miniver* |
| 1943 | Jennifer Jones, *The Song of Bernadette* |
| 1944 | Ingrid Bergman, *Gaslight* |
| 1945 | Joan Crawford, *Mildred Pierce* |
| 1946 | Olivia De Havilland, *To Each His Own* |
| 1947 | Loretta Young, *The Farmer's Daughter* |
| 1948 | Jane Wyman, *Johnny Belinda* |
| 1949 | Olivia De Havilland, *The Heiress* |
| 1950 | Judy Holliday, *Born Yesterday* |
| 1951 | Vivien Leigh, *A Streetcar Named Desire* |
| 1952 | Shirley Booth, *Come Back, Little Sheba* |
| 1953 | Audrey Hepburn, *Roman Holiday* |
| 1954 | Grace Kelly, *The Country Girl* |
| 1955 | Anna Magnani, *The Rose Tattoo* |
| 1956 | Ingrid Bergman, *Anastasia* |
| 1957 | Joanne Woodward, *The Three Faces of Eve* |
| 1958 | Susan Hayward, *I Want to Live!* |
| 1959 | Simone Signoret, *Room at the Top* |
| 1960 | Elizabeth Taylor, *Butterfield 8* |
| 1961 | Sophia Loren, *Two Women* |
| 1962 | Anne Bancroft, *The Miracle Worker* |
| 1963 | Patricia Neal, *Hud* |
| 1964 | Julie Andrews, *Mary Poppins* |
| 1965 | Julie Christie, *Darling* |
| 1966 | Elizabeth Taylor, *Who's Afraid of Virginia Woolf?* |
| 1967 | Katharine Hepburn, *Guess Who's Coming to Dinner* |
| 1968 | Katharine Hepburn, *The Lion in Winter* |
| | Barbra Streisand, *Funny Girl* |
| 1969 | Maggie Smith, *The Prime of Miss Jean Brodie* |
| 1970 | Glenda Jackson, *Women in Love* |
| 1971 | Jane Fonda, *Klute* |
| 1972 | Liza Minnelli, *Cabaret* |
| 1973 | Glenda Jackson, *A Touch of Class* |
| 1974 | Ellen Burstyn, *Alice Doesn't Live Here Anymore* |
| 1975 | Louise Fletcher, *One Flew over the Cuckoo's Nest* |
| 1976 | Faye Dunaway, *Network* |
| 1977 | Diane Keaton, *Annie Hall* |
| 1978 | Jane Fonda, *Coming Home* |
| 1979 | Sally Field, *Norma Rae* |
| 1980 | Sissy Spacek, *Coal Miner's Daughter* |
| 1981 | Katharine Hepburn, *On Golden Pond* |

1982    Meryl Streep, *Sophie's Choice*

## Best Supporting Actor

1936    Walter Brennan, *Come and Get It*
1937    Joseph Schildkraut, *The Life of Emile Zola*
1938    Walter Brennan, *Kentucky*
1939    Thomas Mitchell, *Stagecoach*
1940    Walter Brennan, *The Westerner*
1941    Donald Crisp, *How Green Was My Valley*
1942    Van Heflin, *Johnny Eager*
1943    Charles Coburn, *The More the Merrier*
1944    Barry Fitzgerald, *Going My Way*
1945    James Dunn, *A Tree Grows in Brooklyn*
1946    Harold Russell, *The Best Years of Our Lives*
1947    Edmund Gwenn, *Miracle on 34th Street*
1948    Walter Huston, *The Treasure of the Sierra Madre*
1949    Dean Jagger, *Twelve O'Clock High*
1950    George Sanders, *All About Eve*
1951    Karl Malden, *A Streetcar Named Desire*
1952    Anthony Quinn, *Viva Zapata!*
1953    Frank Sinatra, *From Here to Eternity*
1954    Edmund O'Brien, *The Barefoot Contessa*
1955    Jack Lemmon *Mister Roberts*
1956    Anthony Quinn, *Lust for Life*
1957    Red Buttons, *Sayonara*
1958    Burl Ives, *The Big Country*
1959    Hugh Griffith, *Ben-Hur*
1960    Peter Ustinov, *Spartacus*
1961    George Chakiris, *West Side Story*
1962    Ed Begley, *Sweet Bird of Youth*
1963    Melvyn Douglas, *Hud*
1964    Peter Ustinov, *Topkapi*
1965    Martin Balsam, *A Thousand Clowns*
1966    Walter Matthau, *The Fortune Cookie*
1967    George Kennedy, *Cool Hand Luke*
1968    Jack Albertson, *The Subject Was Roses*
1969    Gig Young, *They Shoot Horses, Don't They?*
1970    John Mills, *Ryan's Daughter*
1971    Ben Johnson, *The Last Picture Show*
1972    Joel Grey, *Cabaret*
1973    John Houseman, *The Paper Chase*

| 1974 | Robert De Niro, *The Godfather, Part II* |
| 1975 | George Burns, *The Sunshine Boys* |
| 1976 | Jason Robards, Jr., *All the President's Men* |
| 1977 | Jason Robards, Jr., *Julia* |
| 1978 | Christopher Walken, *The Deer Hunter* |
| 1980 | Timothy Hutton, *Ordinary People* |
| 1981 | Sir John Gielgud, *Arthur* |
| 1982 | Louis Gossett, Jr., *An Officer and a Gentleman* |

## Best Supporting Actress

| 1936 | Gale Sondergaard, *Anthony Adverse* |
| 1937 | Alice Brady, *In Old Chicago* |
| 1938 | Fay Bainter, *Jezebel* |
| 1939 | Hattie McDaniel, *Gone With the Wind* |
| 1940 | Jane Darwell, *The Grapes of Wrath* |
| 1941 | Mary Astor, *The Great Lie* |
| 1942 | Teresa Wright, *Mrs. Miniver* |
| 1943 | Katina Paxinou, *For Whom the Bell Tolls* |
| 1944 | Ethel Barrymore, *None But the Lonely Heart* |
| 1945 | Anne Revere, *National Velvet* |
| 1946 | Anne Baxter, *The Razor's Edge* |
| 1947 | Celeste Holm, *Gentleman's Agreement* |
| 1948 | Claire Trevor, *Key Largo* |
| 1949 | Mercedes McCambridge, *All the King's Men* |
| 1950 | Josephine Hull, *Harvey* |
| 1951 | Kim Hunter, *A Streetcar Named Desire* |
| 1952 | Gloria Grahame, *The Bad and the Beautiful* |
| 1953 | Donna Reed, *From Here to Eternity* |
| 1954 | Eva Marie Saint, *On the Waterfront* |
| 1955 | Jo Van Fleet, *East of Eden* |
| 1956 | Dorothy Malone, *Written on the Wind* |
| 1957 | Miyoshi Umeki, *Sayonara* |
| 1958 | Wendy Hiller, *Separate Tables* |
| 1959 | Shelley Winters, *The Diary of Anne Frank* |
| 1960 | Shirley Jones, *Elmer Gantry* |
| 1961 | Rita Moreno, *West Side Story* |
| 1962 | Patty Duke Astin, *The Miracle Worker* |
| 1963 | Margaret Rutherford, *The V.I.P.s* |
| 1964 | Lila Kedrova, *Zorba the Greek* |
| 1965 | Shelley Winters, *A Patch of Blue* |
| 1966 | Sandy Dennis, *Who's Afraid of Virginia Woolf?* |

| 1967 | Estelle Parsons, *Bonnie and Clyde* |
| 1968 | Ruth Gordon, *Rosemary's Baby* |
| 1969 | Goldie Hawn, *Cactus Flower* |
| 1970 | Helen Hayes, *Airport* |
| 1971 | Cloris Leachman, *The Last Picture Show* |
| 1972 | Eileen Heckart, *Butterflies Are Free* |
| 1973 | Tatum O'Neal, *Paper Moon* |
| 1974 | Ingrid Bergman, *Murder on the Orient Express* |
| 1975 | Lee Grant, *Shampoo* |
| 1976 | Beatrice Straight, *Network* |
| 1977 | Vanessa Redgrave, *Julia* |
| 1978 | Maggie Smith, *California Suite* |
| 1979 | Meryl Streep, *Kramer vs. Kramer* |
| 1980 | Mary Steenburgen, *Melvin and Howard* |
| 1981 | Maureen Stapleton, *Reds* |
| 1982 | Jessica Lange, *Tootsie* |

# TONY AWARDS

### Best Actor (Dramatic Role)

| 1947 | Jose Ferrer, *Cyrano de Bergerac* |
| | Fredric March, *Years Ago* |
| 1948 | Henry Fonda, *Mister Roberts* |
| | Paul Kelly, *Command Decision* |
| | Basil Rathbone, *The Heiress* |
| 1949 | Rex Harrison, *Anne of the Thousand Days* |
| 1950 | Sidney Blackmer, *Come Back, Little Sheba* |
| 1951 | Claude Rains, *Darkness at Noon* |
| 1952 | José Ferrer, *The Shrike* |
| 1953 | Tom Ewell, *The Seven Year Itch* |
| 1954 | David Wayne, *The Teahouse of the August Moon* |
| 1955 | Alfred Lunt, *Quadrille* |
| 1956 | Paul Muni, *Inherit the Wind* |
| 1957 | Fredric March, *Long Day's Journey into Night* |
| 1958 | Ralph Bellamy, *Sunrise at Campobello* |
| 1959 | Jason Robards, Jr., *The Disenchanted* |
| 1960 | Melvyn Douglas, *The Best Man* |
| 1961 | Zero Mostel, *Rhinoceros* |
| 1962 | Paul Scofield, *A Man for All Seasons* |
| 1963 | Arthur Hill, *Who's Afraid of Virginia Woolf?* |

| 1964 | Alec Guinness, *Dylan* |
| 1965 | Walter Matthau, *The Odd Couple* |
| 1966 | Hal Holbrook, *Mark Twain Tonight* |
| 1967 | Paul Rogers, *The Homecoming* |
| 1968 | Martin Balsam, *You Know I Can't Hear You When the Water's Running* |
| 1969 | James Earl Jones, *The Great White Hope* |
| 1970 | Fritz Weaver, *Child's Play* |
| 1971 | Brian Bedford, *The School for Wives* |
| 1972 | Cliff Gorman, *Lenny* |
| 1973 | Alan Bates, *Butley* |
| 1974 | Michael Moriarty, *Find Your Way Home* |
| 1975 | Mohn Kani, *Sizwe Banzi* |
|      | Winston Ntshona, *The Island* |
| 1976 | John Wood, *Travesties* |
| 1977 | Al Pacino, *The Basic Training of Pavlo Hummel* |
| 1978 | Barnard Hughes, *Da* |
| 1979 | Tom Conti, *Whose Life Is It Anyway?* |
| 1980 | John Rubinstein, *Children of a Lesser God* |
| 1981 | Ian McKellen, *Amadeus* |
| 1982 | Roger Rees, *The Life and Adventures of Nicholas Nickleby* |
| 1983 | Harvey Fierstein, *Torch Song Trilogy* |

**Best Actress (Dramatic Role)**

| 1947 | Ingrid Bergman, *Joan of Lorraine* |
|      | Helen Hayes, *Happy Birthday* |
| 1948 | Judith Anderson, *Medea* |
|      | Katherine Cornell, *Antony and Cleopatra* |
|      | Jessica Tandy, *A Streetcar Named Desire* |
| 1949 | Martitia Hunt, *The Madwoman of Chaillot* |
| 1950 | Shirley Booth, *Come Back, Little Sheba* |
| 1951 | Uta Hagen, *The Country Girl* |
| 1952 | Julie Harris, *I Am a Camera* |
| 1953 | Shirley Booth, *Time of the Cuckoo* |
| 1954 | Audrey Hepburn, *Ondine* |
| 1955 | Nancy Kelly, *The Bad Seed* |
| 1956 | Julie Harris, *The Lark* |
| 1957 | Margaret Leighton, *Separate Tables* |
| 1958 | Helen Hayes, *Time Remembered* |
| 1959 | Gertrude Berg, *A Majority of One* |
| 1960 | Anne Bancroft, *The Miracle Worker* |

| 1961 | Joan Plowright, *A Taste of Honey* |
| 1962 | Margaret Leighton, *Night of the Iguana* |
| 1963 | Uta Hagen, *Who's Afraid of Virginia Woolf?* |
| 1964 | Sandy Dennis, *Any Wednesday* |
| 1965 | Irene Worth, *Tiny Alice* |
| 1966 | Rosemary Harris, *The Lion in Winter* |
| 1967 | Beryl Reid, *The Killing of Sister George* |
| 1968 | Zoe Caldwell, *The Prime of Miss Jean Brodie* |
| 1969 | Julie Harris, *Forty Carats* |
| 1970 | Tammy Grimes, *Private Lives* |
| 1971 | Maureen Stapleton, *Gingerbread Lady* |
| 1972 | Sada Thompson, *Twigs* |
| 1973 | Julie Harris, *The Last of Mrs. Lincoln* |
| 1974 | Colleen Dewhurst, *A Moon for the Misbegotten* |
| 1975 | Ellen Burstyn, *Same Time, Next Year* |
| 1976 | Irene Worth, *Sweet Bird of Youth* |
| 1977 | Julie Harris, *The Belle of Amherst* |
| 1978 | Jessica Tandy, *The Gin Game* |
| 1979 | Constance Cummings, *Wings* |
| | Carole Shelley, *The Elephant Man* |
| 1980 | Phyllis Frelich, *Children of a Lesser God* |
| 1981 | Jane Lapotaire, *Piaf* |
| 1982 | Zoe Caldwell, *Medea* |
| 1983 | Jessica Tandy, *Foxfire* |

## Best Actor (Musical)

| 1948 | Paul Hartman, *Angel in the Wings* |
| 1949 | Ray Bolger, *Where's Charley?* |
| 1950 | Ezio Pinza, *South Pacific* |
| 1951 | Robert Alda, *Guys and Dolls* |
| 1952 | Phil Silvers, *Top Banana* |
| 1953 | Thomas Mitchell, *Hazel Flagg* |
| 1954 | Alfred Drake, *Kismet* |
| 1955 | Walter Slezak, *Fanny* |
| 1956 | Ray Walston, *Damn Yankees* |
| 1957 | Rex Harrison, *My Fair Lady* |
| 1958 | Robert Preston, *The Music Man* |
| 1959 | Richard Kiley, *Redhead* |
| 1960 | Jackie Gleason, *Take Me Along* |
| 1961 | Richard Burton, *Camelot* |

| 1962 | Robert Morse, *How to Succeed in Business Without Really Trying* |
|---|---|
| 1963 | Zero Mostel, *A Funny Thing Happened on the Way to the Forum* |
| 1964 | Bert Lahr, *Foxy* |
| 1965 | Zero Mostel, *Fiddler on the Roof* |
| 1966 | Richard Kiley, *Man of La Mancha* |
| 1967 | Robert Preston, *I Do! I Do!* |
| 1968 | Robert Goulet, *The Happy Time* |
| 1969 | Jerry Orbach, *Promises, Promises* |
| 1970 | Cleavon Little, *Purlie* |
| 1971 | Hal Linden, *The Rothschilds* |
| 1972 | Phil Silvers, *A Funny Thing Happened on the Way to the Forum* |
| 1973 | Ben Vereen, *Pippin* |
| 1974 | Christopher Plummer, *Cyrano* |
| 1975 | John Cullum, *Shenandoah* |
| 1976 | George Rose, *My Fair Lady* |
| 1977 | Barry Bostwick, *The Robber Bridegroom* |
| 1978 | John Cullum, *On the Twentieth Century* |
| 1979 | Len Cariou, *Sweeney Todd* |
| 1980 | Jim Dale, *Barnum* |
| 1981 | Kevin Kline, *The Pirates of Penzance* |
| 1982 | Ben Harney, *Dreamgirls* |
| 1983 | Tommy Tune, *My One and Only* |

### Best Actress (Musical)

| 1948 | Grace Hartman, *Angel with Wings* |
|---|---|
| 1949 | Nanette Fabray, *Love Life* |
| 1950 | Mary Martin, *South Pacific* |
| 1951 | Ethel Merman, *Call Me Madam* |
| 1952 | Gertrude Lawrence, *The King and I* |
| 1953 | Rosalind Russell, *Wonderful Town* |
| 1954 | Dolores Gray, *Carnival in Flanders* |
| 1955 | Mary Martin, *Peter Pan* |
| 1956 | Gwen Verdon, *Damn Yankees* |
| 1957 | Judy Holliday, *Bells Are Ringing* |
| 1958 | Thelma Ritter, *New Girl in Town* |
|  | Gwen Verdon, *New Girl in Town* |
| 1959 | Gwen Verdon, *Red Head* |
| 1960 | Mary Martin, *The Sound of Music* |

| 1961 | Elizabeth Seal, *Irma La Douce* |
| 1962 | Anna Maria Alberghetti, *Carnival* |
| | Diahann Carroll, *No Strings* |
| 1963 | Vivien Leigh, *Tovarich* |
| 1964 | Carol Channing, *Hello, Dolly!* |
| 1965 | Liza Minnelli, *Flora, the Red Menace* |
| 1966 | Angela Lansbury, *Mame* |
| 1967 | Barbara Harris, *The Apple Tree* |
| 1968 | Patricia Routledge, *Darling of the Day* |
| | Leslie Uggams, *Hallelujah, Baby!* |
| 1969 | Angela Lansbury, *Dear World* |
| 1970 | Lauren Bacall, *Applause* |
| 1971 | Helen Gallagher, *No, No, Nanette* |
| 1972 | Alexis Smith, *Follies* |
| 1973 | Glynis Johns, *A Little Night Music* |
| 1974 | Virginia Capers, *Raisin* |
| 1975 | Angela Lansbury, *Gypsy* |
| 1976 | Donna McKechnie, *A Chorus Line* |
| 1977 | Dorothy Loudon, *Annie* |
| 1978 | Liza Minnelli, *The Act* |
| 1979 | Angela Lansbury, *Sweeney Todd* |
| 1980 | Patti Lupone, *Evita* |
| 1981 | Lauren Bacall, *Woman of the Year* |
| 1982 | Jennifer Holliday, *Dreamgirls* |
| 1983 | Natalia Makarova, *On Your Toes* |

## Best Supporting or Featured Actress (Dramatic)

| 1947 | Patricia Neal, *Another Part of the Forest* |
| 1948 | No award |
| 1949 | Shirley Booth, *Goodbye, My Fancy* |
| 1950 | No award |
| 1951 | Maureen Stapleton, *The Rose Tattoo* |
| 1952 | Marian Winters, *I Am a Camera* |
| 1953 | Beatrice Straight, *The Crucible* |
| 1954 | Jo Van Fleet, *The Trip to Bountiful* |
| 1955 | Patricia Jessel, *Witness for the Prosecution* |
| 1956 | Una Merkel, *The Ponder Heart* |
| 1957 | Peggy Cass, *Auntie Mame* |
| 1958 | Anne Bancroft, *Two for the Seesaw* |
| 1959 | Julie Newmar, *The Marriage-Go-Round* |
| 1960 | Anne Revere, *Toys in the Attic* |

1961    Colleen Dewhurst, *All the Way Home*
1962    Elizabeth Ashley, *Take Her, She's Mine*
1963    Sandy Dennis, *A Thousand Clowns*
1964    Barbara Loden, *After the Fall*
1965    Alice Ghostley, *The Sign in Sidney Brustein's Window*
1966    Zoe Caldwell, *Slapstick Tragedy*
1967    Marian Seldes, *A Delicate Balance*
1968    Zena Walker, *Joe Egg*
1969    Jane Alexander, *The Great White Hope*
1970    Blythe Danner, *Butterflies Are Free*
1971    Rae Allen, *And Miss Reardon Drinks a Little*
1972    Elizabeth Wilson, *Sticks and Bones*
1973    Leora Dana, *The Last of Mrs. Lincoln*
1974    Frances Sternhagen, *The Good Doctor*
1975    Rita Moreno, *The Ritz*
1976    Shirley Knight, *Kennedy's Children*
1977    Trazana Beverley, *For Colored Girls Who Have Considered Suicide. . . .*
1978    Ann Wedgeworth, *Chapter Two*
1979    Joan Hickson, *Bedroom Farce*
1980    Dinah Manoff, *I Ought to Be in Pictures*
1981    Swoosie Kurtz, *Fifth of July*
1982    Amanda Plummer, *Agnes of God*
1983    Judith Ivey, *Steaming*

### Best Supporting or Featured Actor (Dramatic)

1949    Arthur Kennedy, *Death of a Salesman*
1950    No award
1951    Eli Wallach, *The Rose Tattoo*
1952    John Cromwell, *Point of No Return*
1953    John Williams, *Dial M for Murder*
1954    John Kerr, *Tea and Sympathy*
1955    Francis L. Sullivan, *Witness for the Prosecution*
1956    Ed Begley, *Inherit the Wind*
1957    Frank Conroy, *The Potting Shed*
1958    Henry Jones, *Sunrise at Campobello*
1959    Charlie Ruggles, *The Pleasure of His Company*
1960    Roddy McDowall, *The Fighting Cock*
1961    Martin Gabel, *Big Fish, Little Fish*
1962    Walter Matthau, *A Shot in the Dark*
1963    Alan Arkin, *Enter Laughing*

| 1964 | Hume Cronyn, *Hamlet* |
| 1965 | Jack Albertson, *The Subject Was Roses* |
| 1966 | Patrick Magee, *Marat/Sade* |
| 1967 | Ian Holm, *The Homecoming* |
| 1968 | James Patterson, *The Birthday Party* |
| 1969 | Al Pacino, *Does a Tiger Wear a Necktie?* |
| 1970 | Ken Howard, *Child's Play* |
| 1971 | Paul Sand, *Story Theatre* |
| 1972 | Vincent Gardenia, *The Prisoner of Second Avenue* |
| 1973 | John Lithgow, *The Changing Room* |
| 1974 | Ed Flanders, *A Moon for the Misbegotten* |
| 1975 | Frank Langella, *Seascape* |
| 1976 | Edward Herrmann, *Mrs. Warren's Profession* |
| 1977 | Jonathan Price, *Comedians* |
| 1978 | Lester Rawlins, *Da* |
| 1979 | Michael Gough, *Bedroom Farce* |
| 1980 | David Rounds, *Mornings at Seven* |
| 1981 | Brian Backer, *The Floating Light Bulb* |
| 1982 | Zakes Mokae, *Master Harold . . . and the Boys* |
| 1983 | Matthew Broderick, *Brighton Beach Memoirs* |

## Best Supporting or Featured Actress (Musical)

| 1950 | Juanita Hall, *South Pacific* |
| 1951 | Isabel Bigley, *Guys and Dolls* |
| 1952 | Helen Gallagher, *Pal Joey* |
| 1953 | Sheila Bond, *Wish You Were Here* |
| 1954 | Gwen Verdon, *Can-Can* |
| 1955 | Carol Haney, *The Pajama Game* |
| 1956 | Lotte Lenya, *The Threepenny Opera* |
| 1957 | Edie Adams, *Li'l Abner* |
| 1958 | Barbara Cook, *The Music Man* |
| 1959 | Pat Stanley, *Goldilocks* |
|      | Cast, *La Plume de Ma Tante* |
| 1960 | Patricia Neway, *The Sound of Music* |
| 1961 | Tammy Grimes, *The Unsinkable Molly Brown* |
| 1962 | Phyllis Newman, *Subways Are for Sleeping* |
| 1963 | Anna Quayle, *Stop the World, I Want to Get Off* |
| 1964 | Tessie O'Shea, *The Girl Who Came to Supper* |
| 1965 | Maria Karnilova, *Fiddler on the Roof* |
| 1966 | Beatrice Arthur, *Mame* |

211

| 1967 | Peg Murray, *Cabaret* |
| 1968 | Lillian Hayman, *Hallelujah, Baby!* |
| 1969 | Marian Mercer, *Promises, Promises* |
| 1970 | Melba Moore, *Purlie* |
| 1971 | Patsy Kelly, *No, No Nanette* |
| 1972 | Linda Hopkins, *Inner City* |
| 1973 | Patricia Elliot, *A Little Night Music* |
| 1974 | Janie Sell, *Over Here!* |
| 1975 | Dee Dee Bridgewater, *The Wiz* |
| 1976 | Carole Bishop, *A Chorus Line* |
| 1977 | Delores Hall, *Your Arm's Too Short to Box with God* |
| 1978 | Nell Carter, *Ain't Misbehavin'* |
| 1979 | Carlin Glynn, *The Best Little Whorehouse in Texas* |
| 1980 | Priscilla Lopez, *A Day in Hollywood/A Night in the Ukraine* |
| 1981 | Marilyn Cooper, *Woman of the Year* |
| 1982 | Liliane Montevecchi, *Nine* |
| 1983 | Betty Buckley, *Cats* |

## Best Supporting or Featured Actor (Musical)

| 1947 | David Wayne, *Finian's Rainbow* |
| 1948 | No award |
| 1949 | No award |
| 1950 | Myron McCormick, *South Pacific* |
| 1951 | Russell Nype, *Call Me Madam* |
| 1952 | Yul Brynner, *The King and I* |
| 1953 | Hiram Sherman, *Two's Company* |
| 1954 | Harry Belafonte, *John Murray Anderson's almanac* |
| 1955 | Cyril Ritchard, *Peter Pan* |
| 1956 | Russ Brown, *Damn Yankees* |
| 1957 | Sydney Chaplin, *Bells Are Ringing* |
| 1958 | David Burns, *The Music Man* |
| 1959 | Russell Nype, *Goldilocks* |
|      | Cast, *La Plume de Ma Tante* |
| 1960 | Tom Bosley, *Fiorello!* |
| 1961 | Dick Van Dyke, *Bye, Bye, Birdie* |
| 1962 | Charles Nelson Reilly, *How to Succeed in Business Without Really Trying* |
| 1963 | David Burns, *A Funny Thing Happened on the Way to the Forum* |
| 1964 | Jack Cassidy, *She Loves Me* |

| | | |
|---|---|---|
| 1965 | Victor Spinetti, *Oh, What a Lovely War* | |
| 1966 | Frankie Michaels, *Mame* | |
| 1967 | Joel Grey, *Cabaret* | |
| 1968 | Hiram Sherman, *How Now, Dow Jones* | |
| 1969 | Ronald Holgate, *1776* | |
| 1970 | Rene Auberjonois, *Coco* | |
| 1971 | Keene Curtis, *The Rothschilds* | |
| 1972 | Larry Blyden, *A Funny Thing Happened on the Way to the Forum* | |
| 1973 | George S. Irving, *Irene* | |
| 1974 | Tommy Tune, *Seesaw* | |
| 1975 | Ted Rose, *The Wiz* | |
| 1976 | Sammy Williams, *A Chorus Line* | |
| 1977 | Lenny Baker, *I Love My Wife* | |
| 1978 | Kevin Kline, *On the Twentieth Century* | |
| 1979 | Henderson Forsythe, *The Best Little Whorehouse in Texas* | |
| 1980 | Mandy Patinkin, *Evita* | |
| 1981 | Hinton Battle, *Sophisticated Ladies* | |
| 1982 | Cleavant Derricks, *Dreamgirls* | |
| 1983 | Charles "Honi" Coles, *My One and Only* | |

# ACTORS STUDIO AWARD RECIPIENTS

The Actors Studio on West 44th Street in New York City is the training ground for many aspiring actors who often become accomplished actors and directors—and "household words." In 1980 the Studio gave out "once-in-a-lifetime" awards to some of its graduates who had made significant contributions to the theatre arts. All of the recipients, it should be noted, have been nominated for, or won, Oscar, Emmy, or Tony Awards:

| | | |
|---|---|---|
| Lee Allen | Marlon Brando | Bradford Dillman |
| Lou Antonio | Roscoe Lee Brown | Mildred Dunnock |
| Beatrice Arthur | Ellen Burstyn | Robert Duvall |
| Barbara Bain | Zoe Caldwell | Joan Ellis |
| Carroll Baker | Pat Carroll | Tom Ewell |
| Martin Balsam | Jill Clayburgh | Norman Fell |
| Anne Bancroft | Gabriel Dell | Sally Field |
| Martine Bartlett | Robert De Niro | Gail Fisher |
| Barbara Baxley | Sandy Dennis | Jane Fonda |
| Richard Boone | Bruce Dern | John Forsythe |

| | | |
|---|---|---|
| Anthony Franciosa | Nan Martin | Jerome Robbins |
| Al Freeman, Jr. | Peter Masterson | Cliff Robertson |
| George Furth | Walter Matthau | Eva Marie Saint |
| Vincent Gardenia | Kevin McCarthy | Gene Saks |
| Ben Gazzara | Steve McQueen | Alan Schneider |
| Michael V. Gazzo | Burgess Meredith | Kim Stanley |
| Carlin Glynn | Joanna Miles | Maureen Stapleton |
| Lee Grant | Sylvia Miles | Rod Steiger |
| William Greaves | Terry Moore | Jan Sterling |
| Barbara Harris | Michael Moriarty | Beatrice Straight |
| Julie Harris | Rosemary Murphy | Lee Strasberg |
| June Havoc | Patricia Neal | Susan Strasberg |
| Gerald Hiken | Lois Nettleton | Shepperd Strudwick |
| Dustin Hoffman | Paul Newman | Inga Swenson |
| Celeste Holm | Julie Newmar | Vic Tayback |
| Kim Hunter | Jack Nicholson | Rip Torn |
| Earle Hyman | Kathleen Nolan | Joan Van Ark |
| Anne Jackson | Carroll O'Connor | Jo Van Fleet |
| Elia Kazan | Al Pacino | Ralph Waite |
| Sally Kellerman | Geraldine Page | Robert Walden |
| Shirley Knight | Estelle Parsons | Christopher Walken |
| Diane Ladd | Albert Paulsen | Eli Wallach |
| Martin Landau | Arthur Penn | Ray Walston |
| Cloris Leachman | Anthony Perkins | David Wayne |
| Ron Liebman | Eleanor Perry | Dennis Weaver |
| Viveca Lindfors | Frank Perry | Ann Wedgeworth |
| Barbara Loden | Sidney Poitier | James Whitmore |
| Sidney Lumet | Sydney Pollack | Gene Wilder |
| Robert Lupone | David Pressman | Paul Winfield |
| Karl Malden | Gilbert Price | Shelley Winters |
| Nancy Marchand | Robert Reed | Joanne Woodward |
| E. G. Marshall | Martin Ritt | |

# THE GOLDEN AND SOUR APPLE AWARD WINNERS

In the early 1940s, the Hollywood Women's Press Club began electing their "Most Cooperative" and "Least Cooperative" stars of the year, awarding the winners Golden and Sour Apples, respectively. (In the mid-60s they changed the title from "Most Cooperative" to "Star of the Year.") The following are the winners:

214

## "Most Cooperative" Stars of the Year

| | |
|---|---|
| 1941 | Bette Davis/Bob Hope |
| 1942 | Rosalind Russell/Cary Grant |
| 1943 | Ann Sheridan/Bob Hope |
| 1944 | Betty Hutton/Alan Ladd |
| 1945 | Joan Crawford/Gregory Peck |
| 1946 | Joan Crawford/Dana Andrews |
| 1947 | Joan Fontaine/Gregory Peck |
| 1948 | Dorothy Lamour/Glenn Ford |
| 1949 | June Haver/Kirk Douglas |
| 1950 | Loretta Young/Alan Ladd |
| 1951 | Anne Baxter/John Derek/William Holden |
| 1952 | Janet Leigh/Tony Curtis |
| 1953 | Dale Evans/Roy Rogers |
| 1954 | Debbie Reynolds/Dean Martin/Jerry Lewis |
| 1955 | Jane Russell/William Holden |
| 1956 | Deborah Kerr/Charlton Heston |
| 1957 | Kim Novak/Glenn Ford |
| 1958 | Dinah Shore/Tony Curtis |
| 1959 | Shirley MacLaine/David Niven |
| 1960 | Nanette Fabray/Janet Leigh/Jack Lemmon |
| 1961 | Barbara Stanwyck |
| 1962 | Connie Stevens/Richard Chamberlain |
| 1963 | Bette Davis/Dick Van Dyke |
| 1964 | Donna Reed/Lorne Greene |
| 1965 | Dorthy Malone/John Wayne |
| 1966 | Phyllis Diller/Bill Cosby |
| 1967 | Carol Channing/Sidney Poitier |
| 1968 | Barbra Streisand/Fred Astaire |
| 1969 | Mae West/Gregory Peck/Robert Young |
| 1970 | Carol Burnett/James Stewart/Robert Young |
| 1971 | Mary Tyler Moore/Hal Holbrook |
| 1972 | Liza Minnelli/Peter Falk |
| 1973 | Lucille Ball/Robert Redford |
| 1974 | Valerie Harper/Alan Alda |
| 1975 | Katharine Hepburn/George Burns |
| 1976 | Joanne Woodward/John Wayne |
| 1977 | Jane Fonda/Frank Sinatra |
| 1978 | Jacqueline Bisset/John Travolta |
| 1979 | Jill Clayburgh/Alan Alda |
| 1980 | Mary Tyler Moore/Richard Chamberlain |
| 1981 | Katharine Hepburn/Henry Fonda |
| 1982 | Joan Collins/Tom Selleck |

# SOUR APPLE AWARD WINNERS

## "Least Cooperative" Stars of the Year

| | |
|---|---|
| 1941 | Ginger Rogers/Fred Astaire |
| 1942 | Jean Arthur/George Sanders |
| 1943 | Joan Fontaine/Erroll Flynn |
| 1944 | Sonja Henie/Walter Pidgeon |
| 1945 | Greer Garson/Fred MacMurray |
| 1946 | Ingrid Bergman/Frank Sinatra |
| 1947 | Jennifer Jones/Gary Cooper |
| 1948 | Rita Hayworth/Erroll Flynn |
| 1949 | Hedy Lamarr/Humphrey Bogart |
| 1950 | Olivia De Havilland/Robert Mitchum |
| 1951 | Esther Williams/Frank Sinatra |
| 1952 | Rita Hayworth/Mario Lanza |
| 1953 | Esther Williams/Dale Robertson |
| 1954 | Doris Day/Edmond Purdom |
| 1955–59 | No award |
| 1960 | Debbie Reynolds/Elvis Presley |
| 1961 | Natalie Wood/Marlon Brando |
| 1962 | Doris Day/Warren Beatty |
| 1963 | Ann-Margret/James Franciscus |
| 1964 | Doris Day/Tony Curtis |
| 1965 | Ann-Margret/Vince Edwards |
| 1966 | Natalie Wood/Elvis Presley |
| 1967–69 | No award |
| 1970 | Jane Fonda |
| 1971–72 | No award |
| 1973 | Norman Mailer |
| 1974 | Frank Sinatra |
| 1975 | No award |
| 1976 | Pornographic moviemakers |
| 1977 | No award |
| 1978 | Paul Michael Glaser/David Soul |
| 1979 | Chuck Barris |
| 1980 | Erik Estrada |
| 1981 | Ryan O'Neal |
| 1982 | Pia Zadora |

# THE MOST AND LEAST POPULAR CELEBRITIES ACCORDING TO THE "PERFORMER Q" STUDY

Marketing evaluations/TV Q Inc., based in Port Washington, NY, evaluates celebrities in terms of their likability (or lack of) and familiarity. The information presumably is used by advertising agencies to assess the potential of a celebrity endorsement or by the networks to gain insights on the casting of shows. The TV "Q Score" is the key rating: the higher the score the more popular the personality. Two other criteria are used: familiarity and a negative "Q-Score." The "Q-Score" is essentially likability among the people who are familiar with the celebrity, familiarity is the percentage of the general public who are aware of the celebrity, and the negative score is the percentage of people who dislike the celebrity. Here are the most popular and least popular celebrities, according to the "Q-Scores":

| Most Popular | Q-Score | Familiarity | Neg. Q-Score |
| --- | --- | --- | --- |
| Alan Alda | 59% | 96% | 8 |
| Carol Burnett | 45 | 90 | 10 |
| Harry Morgan | 45 | 92 | 7 |
| Tristan Rogers* | 43 | 32 | 16 |
| Tom Selleck | 43 | 88 | 10 |
| Mike Farrell | 42 | 87 | 9 |
| Katharine Hepburn | 42 | 86 | 8 |
| Bob Hope | 41 | 91 | 14 |
| Paul Newman | 41 | 85 | 7 |
| George Burns | 40 | 90 | 17 |
| Clint Eastwood | 40 | 88 | 11 |
| Jamie Farr | 40 | 92 | 9 |
| Eddie Murphy | 40 | 51 | 16 |
| Kenny Rogers | 40 | 91 | 15 |
| Daniel J. Travanti | 40 | 57 | 11 |

*Soap opera star.

| Least Popular | Q-Score | Familiarity | Neg. Q-Score |
| --- | --- | --- | --- |
| Yoko Ono | 4% | 64% | 73% |
| David Frost | 4 | 67 | 46 |
| Priscilla Presley | 6 | 71 | 51 |
| Dr. Joyce Brothers | 6 | 79 | 43 |
| Howard Cosell | 6 | 82 | 70 |

| | | | |
|---|---|---|---|
| Charo | 7 | 78 | 56 |
| Susan Anton | 7 | 70 | 44 |
| Cher | 8 | 88 | 52 |
| Marie Osmond | 9 | 91 | 42 |
| Farrah Fawcett | 9 | 89 | 48 |
| Tatum O'Neal | 9 | 75 | 35 |

# HOLLYWOOD LICENSE PLATES

License plates in Hollywood are status symbols and sometimes cryptic ID cards. In seven letters (or numbers) or less, a star can creatively identify himself without overtly listing his name. Here are some of the license plate numbers you'll see on cars, mostly Rolls Royces and Mercedes Benzes, zipping down Sunset Boulevard or parked in front of the Beverly Hills Hotel:

|  | **License Plate Number** |
|---|---|
| Ernest Borgnine | BORG9 |
| Allan Carr | GREASE I |
| Johnny Carson | 360 GUY (for being an all-around guy!) |
| William Conrad | DARNOC (his last name spelled backwards) |
| Tim Conway | 11 YEARS (the number of years the Carol Burnet Show ran on TV) |
| Sally Field | BRS GRL (Burt ReynoldS' GiRL—off and on!) |
| Redd Foxx | XXOF (his last name spelled backwards) |
| Alex Haley | KINTE |
| Jack LaLanne | REDUCE |
| Dean Martin | DRUNKY |
| Valerie Perrine | RATS ("star" spelled backward) |
| Dinah Shore | GRUNK (her dog's name) |
| Richard Simmons | Y R U FATT |
| Rip Taylor | INSANE2 |
| Leslie Uggams | SMAGGU (her last name spelled backward) |
| Lyle Waggoner | MR COOL |

218

| Dennis Weaver | GURUJI (the Hindu word for "teacher") |
|---|---|
| Lawrence Welk | A1 AND A2 |
| Flip Wilson | KILLER |

# CELEBRITIES WITH PILOT LICENSES

F. Lee Bailey
Johnny Carson
Merv Griffin
Danny Kaye
Kris Kristofferson
Christopher Reeve
Cliff Robertson
James Stewart
John Travolta

# THE HOLLYWOOD TEN

If everyone in Hollywood who said that he was blacklisted had *actually* been blacklisted, virtually no movies would have been produced from 1947 to the mid-1950s. For the record, the following movie directors, producers, and screenwriters were the original "Hollywood Ten." These men refused to tell the House Un-American Activities Committee in 1947 whether or not they were Communists. They all served prison sentences, after which they were "blacklisted" within the American film industry and found it extremely difficult to find work:

Alvah Bessie (screenwriter)
Herbert Biberman (director, writer)
Lester Cole (screenwriter)
Edward Dmytryk (director)
Ring Lardner, Jr. (screenwriter)
John Howard Lawson (screenwriter)
Albert Maltz (screenwriter)
Sam Ornitz (screenwriter)
Adrian Scott (producer)
Dalton Trumbo (screenwriter)

# NOTABLES WHO SPENT SOME TIME IN JAIL OR PRISON

David Beck
Brendan Behan
Truman Capote
Johnny Cash
Billie Sol Estes
Albert Fall
Mahatma Gandhi
Harry Golden
O. Henry
Alger Hiss

Martin Luther King, Jr.
Sidney Lanier
Malcolm X
Christopher Marlowe
Carry Nation
Ryan O'Neal
Pope Pius VII
Mae West
Oscar Wilde

# THE WORST-DRESSED WOMEN

Dress designer Richard Blackwell, known as Mr. Blackwell, every year announces his Worst-Dressed List of women. These women are those celebrities who, in his estimation, have "violated fashion's prime purpose—to glorify women."

Here are the winners from the past thirteen years:

**1982**

1. Princess Diana ("Shy Di has invaded Queen Victoria's attic!")
2. Bonnie Franklin ("Not Charlie's aunt, but aunt Charlie!")
3. Victoria Principal ("A Dallas Valley Girl!")
4. Bette Midler ("Second-hand Rose after a hurricane!")
5. Charlene Tilton ("A Victorian lampshade holding her breath!")
6. Christina Onassis ("Daddy's tanker!")
7. Princess Yasmin Khan ("A preppie gypsy!")
8. Jan Stephenson ("Mrs. Miniver in a tutu!")
9. Cathy Lee Crosby ("It looks as if she bought out a rummage sale, wore it all, and . . . that's incredible!")
10. Dustin "Tootsie" Hoffman and Mayor Kathy Whitmire of Houston ("Lookalikes . . . wearing Betsy Bloomingdale's discards!")

**1981**

1. Barbara Mandrell
2. Lynn Redgrave
3. Dolly Parton

**1980**

1. Brooke Shields    2. Elizabeth Taylor    3. Suzanne Somers

**1979**

1. Bo Derek    2. Jill Clayburgh    3. Loni Anderson

**1978**

1. Dolly Parton    2. Suzanne Somers    3. Christina Onassis

**1977**

1. Farrah Fawcett-Majors    2. Linda Ronstadt    3. Charo

**1976**

1. Louise Lasser    2. Maralin Niska    3. Angie Dickinson

**1975**

1. Caroline Kennedy    2. Helen Reddy    3. Nancy Kissinger

**1974**

1. Helen Reddy    2. Princess Elizabeth of Yugoslavia    3. Fanne Fox

**1973**

1. Bette Midler    2. Princess Anne    3. Raquel Welch

**1972**

1. Raquel Welch    2. Julie Andrews    3. Mia Farrow

**1971**

1. Ali MacGraw    2. Jacqueline Onassis    3. Princess Anne

**1970**

1. Sophia Loren    2. Angie Dickinson   3. Gloria Vanderbilt

**Worst-Dressed List Hall of Fame**

Elizabeth Taylor
Barbra Streisand
Raquel Welch
Bo Derek

# CELEBRITY FAILURES

Successful and unsuccessful people have one thing in common—they all have encountered failure at some point in their lives. What is different about successful people is their ability to tolerate, overcome, and learn from failures. As Elbert Hubbard once wrote, "A failure is a man who has blundered but is not able to cash in on the experience." Here are some failures in the lives of famous people:

Playwright **Eugene O'Neill** was expelled from Princeton for throwing a beer bottle through the college president's window. The president of Princeton at the time was Woodrow Wilson, future president of the United States.

**Winston Churchill** failed the entrance examinations to Sandhurst, the British equivalent of West Point, several times before coaching, cramming, and luck enabled him to pass the tests.

After her first three stage appearances, actress **Sarah Bernhardt** became despondent and tried to commit suicide.

At Central High School in Louisville, Kentucky, boxing great **Muhammad Ali** graduated 376th in a class of 391 students, or in the bottom 5% of his class.

**Humphrey Bogart** was expelled from the exclusive preparatory school Phillips Academy (Andover) because of poor grades. Bogart flunked English, French, Solid Geometry, and Bible, and received a D in Algebra.

Sherlock Holmes' creator, **Sir Arthur Conan Doyle,** was a medical doctor by training. When he opened a practice in opthalmology, however, he failed to attract a single patient and took up writing.

Former presidential aide **Jody Powell** was dismissed from the U.S. Air Force Academy for cheating on a final exam in his senior year.

222

# LITTLE-KNOWN FACTS
## ABOUT FAMOUS PEOPLE

**Ann-Margret**
The actress lived in a funeral parlor in Wilmette, Illinois, as a youth.

**Johnny Carson**
The talk show host takes his lunch to work every day. He drives himself, unlike many other big stars who arrive in chauffeured limousines.

**Jane Fonda**
The actress learned from a movie gossip magazine that her mother, Frances Seymour Brokaw, committed suicide. (She previously had been told that her mother died of a heart attack.)

**Ralph Nader**
The consumer advocate was a cook in the U.S. Army.

**Olivia Newton-John**
"Livvie" is the granddaughter of Nobel Prize-winning German physicist Max Born.

**Richard M. Nixon**
The former U.S. president is a descendant of King Edward III of England.

**Richard Pryor**
The comedian grew up in a Peoria, Illinois, brothel where his grandmother was the proprietress.

**Robert Redford**
Early in his acting career, he admitted that he broke into Bel Aire mansions as a teenager and stole petty objects.

**Burt Reynolds**
His 180-acre Jupiter, Florida, ranch was once owned by gangster Al Capone.

**Hugh M. Hefner**
*Playboy* publisher Hugh M. Hefner was a virgin until he was 23 years old.

### Jerzy Kosinski
Author Jerzy Kosinski, when he first came to the United States, called telephone operators in the middle of the night to get definitions and spellings of English words.

### Barry Nelson
Barry Nelson was the first actor to play James Bond. He played the fictional spy in a TV broadcast of *Casino Royale* in 1951.

### Aristotle Onassis
Greek shipping tycoon Aristotle Onassis rarely wore an overcoat because he disliked having to pay hat-check tips at restaurants.

### Tony Randall
In his insomniac days, actor Tony Randall once went 600 nights without sleeping.

### Janis Joplin
Rock singer Janis Joplin sucked her thumb until she was 8 years old.

### Peter O'Toole
Actor Peter O'Toole always wears emerald green socks to bring him good luck.

### Gore Vidal
Author Gore Vidal learned to fly an airplane at the age of 10.

### Lily Tomlin
Comedienne Lily Tomlin was a home economics major in high school.

### Bill Rodgers
Marathon runner Bill Rodgers smoked a pack of cigarettes a day when he was in his early twenties.

### Jimmy Stewart
Actor Jimmy Stewart's son Ronald was one of the many U.S. servicemen killed in the Vietnam war.

### Arnold Scaasi
Designer Arnold Scaasi's real name, Isaacs, spelled backward is—Scaasi.

## Mickey Spillane
Detective novelist Mickey Spillane wrote comic books early in his career.

## Charles Schulz
In high school Charles Schulz's cartoons were turned down by the yearbook staff. Several years later Schulz applied for a job as a cartoonist with the Walt Disney studios and was not hired.

# The Written Word 16.

## SHOW BIZ AUTOBIOGRAPHIES

The autobiography has become a new art form in Hollywood and in some cases a new source of income. At best the autobiography is a record of a life and career—essential facts peppered with perceptions and anecdotes. At worst it becomes an opportunity for the person to embellish his or her past and to get even with ex-spouses and ex-lovers. The public is fascinated with these "confessions," hoping to find scandalous tidbits. Unfortunately, many of the books are not very revealing and often contain anecdotes of interest only because the people involved are well known to the public.

The following list of autobiographies represents most of the genre. Pick your favorite stars and read their autobiographies. You'll find out how glamorous show business careers really are.

| | |
|---|---|
| Brian Aherne | *A Proper Job* (1969) |
| Desi Arnaz | *A Book* (1975) |
| Elizabeth Ashley | *Actress: Postcards from the Road* (1978) |
| Fred Astaire | *Steps in Time* (1960) |
| Mary Astor | *My Story* (1959); *A Life on Film* (1971) |
| Jean-Pierre Aumont | *Sun and Shadow* (1977) |
| Lauren Bacall | *By Myself* (1979) |
| Rona Barrett | *Miss Rona* (1974) |
| Diana Barrymore | *Too Much Too Soon* (1958) |

| | |
|---|---|
| Ethel Barrymore | *Memories* (1956) |
| John Barrymore | *Confessions of an Actor* (1926) |
| Anne Baxter | *Intermission* (1976) |
| Joan Bennett | *The Bennett Playbill* (1970) with Louis Kibbee |
| Ingrid Bergman | *Ingrid Bergman: My Story* (1980) |
| Milton Berle | *Milton Berle* (1974) with Haskel Frankel |
| Charles Bickford | *Bulls, Balls, Bicycles and Actors* (1965) |
| Dirk Bogarde | *A Postillion Struck by Lightning* (1977) |
| Louise Brooks | *Lulu in Hollywood* (1982) |
| Joe E. Brown | *Laughter Is a Wonderful Thing* (1959) |
| Billie Burke | *With a Feather on My Nose* (1949); *With Powder on My Nose* (1959) |
| George Burns | *Living It Up* (1976) |
| Sid Caesar | *Where Have I Been?* (1982) with Bill Davidson |
| James Cagney | *Cagney by Cagney* (1976) |
| Sammy Cahn | *I Should Care* (1974) |
| Cab Calloway | *Of Minnie the Moocher and Me* (1976) |
| Frank Capra | *The Name Above the Title* (1971) |
| Hoagy Carmichael | *Washboard Blues* (1947) |
| Dick Cavett | *Cavett* (1974) with Christopher Porterfield |
| Charlie Chaplin | *My Trip Abroad* (1922); *My Wonderful Visit* (1930); *My Autobiography* (1964); *My Life in Pictures* (1974) |
| Cyd Charisse, | *The Two of Us* (1976) with Tony Martin |
| Maurice Chevalier | *With Love* (1960); *I Remember It Well* (1972) |
| Rosemary Clooney | *This for Remembrance* (1977) with Raymond Strait |
| Gladys Cooper | *Without Veils* (1953) |

| | |
|---|---|
| Noel Coward | *Present Indicative* (1937); *Middle East Diary* (1945); *Future Indefinite* (1954) |
| Cheryl Crawford | *One Naked Individual* (1977) |
| Christina Crawford | *Mommie Dearest* (1978) |
| Joan Crawford | *A Portrait of Joan* (1962) |
| Bing Crosby | *Call Me Lucky* (1953) |
| Marion Davies | *The Times We Had* (1975) |
| Bette Davis | *The Lonely Life* (1962) |
| Sammy Davis, Jr. | *Yes I Can* (1966) |
| Doris Day | *Doris Day: Her Own Story* (1976) with A. E. Hotchner |
| Laraine Day | *Day With the Giants* (1952) |
| Olivia De Havilland | *Every Frenchman Has One* (1960) |
| Cecil B. De Mille | *An Autobiography* (1960) |
| Phil Donahue | *Donahue* (1980) |
| Hugh Downs | *Yours Truly, Hugh Downs* (1960) |
| Marie Dressler | *My Own Story* (1934) |
| Frances Farmer | *Will There Ever Be a Morning?* (1972) |
| David Farrar | *No Royal Road* (1948) |
| Gracie Fields | *Sing As We Go* (1960) |
| W. C. Fields | *W. C. Fields by Himself* (1973) |
| Errol Flynn | *Beam Ends* (1934); *My Wicked, Wicked Ways* (1959) |
| Joan Fontaine | *No Bed of Roses* (1978) |
| Arlene Francis | *Arlene Francis* (1978) with Florence Rome |
| Joe Franklin | *A Gift for People* (1978) |
| Eva Gabor | *Orchids and Salami* (1954) |
| Zsa Zsa Gabor | *My Story* (1961) |
| William Gargan | *Why Me?* (1969) |
| Tay Garnett | *Light Your Torches and Pull Up Your Tights* (1973) with Fredda Dudley Balling |
| John Gielgud | *Early Stages* (1938); *Distinguished Company* (1972); *Gielgud: An Actor and His Time* (1980) |

229

| | |
|---|---|
| Lillian Gish | *The Movies, Mr. Griffith & Me* (1969) |
| Ruth Gordon | *Myself Among Others* (1970); *My Side* (1976) |
| Sheilah Graham | *Beloved Infidel* (1958); *A College of One* (1967); *Confessions of a Hollywood Columnist* (1968); *A State of Heat* (1972) |
| Rocky Graziano | *Somebody Up There Likes Me* (1955); *Somebody Down Here Likes Me, Too* (1981) with Ralph Corsel |
| Merv Griffin | *Merv* (1979) with Peter Barso-cchini |
| Rex Harrison | *Rex* (1975) |
| Moss Hart | *Act One* (1958) |
| June Havoc | *Early Havoc* (1960) |
| Helen Hayes | *Letters to Mary Catherine Hayes Brown* (1940); *On Reflection* (1960); *A Gift of Joy* (1965) |
| Ben Hecht | *A Child of the Century* (1954); *Gaily, Gaily* (1963) |
| Lillian Hellman | *An Unfinished Woman* (1969); *Pentimento* (1973); *Scoundrel Time* (1976) |
| Charlton Heston | *The Actor's Life* (1976) |
| Stanley Holloway | *Wiv a Little Bit of Luck* (1969) |
| Bob Hope | *Have Tux Will Travel* (1958); *I Owe Russia $2,000* (1963) |
| Hedda Hopper | *From Under My Hat* (1952); *The Whole Truth and Nothing But* (1963) |
| Lena Horne | *In Person* (1950); *Lena* (1966) with Richard Schickel |
| John Houseman | *Run-Through* (1972); *Front and Center* (1979); *Final Dress* (1983) |
| John Huston | *John Huston: An Open Book* (1980) |
| George Jessel | *So Help Me* (1943); *This Way, Miss* (1955); *The World I Live In* (1975) |

| | |
|---|---|
| Garson Kanin | *Hollywood* (1974) |
| Buster Keaton | *My Wonderful World of Slapstick* (1962) |
| Veronica Lake | *Veronica* (1968) |
| Hedy Lamarr | *Ecstasy and Me* (1967) |
| Jesse Lasky | *I Blow My Own Horn* (1958) |
| Jesse L. Lasky, Jr. | *Whatever Happened to Hollywood?* (1973) |
| Gertrude Lawrence | *A Star Danced* (1949) |
| Gypsy Rose Lee | *Gypsy* (1957) |
| Mervyn LeRoy | *Mervyn LeRoy: Take One* (1974) with Dick Kleiner |
| Oscar Levant | *A Smattering of Ignorance* (1944); *Memoirs of an Amnesiac* (1965) |
| Margaret Lockwood | *Lucky Star* (1955) |
| Josh Logan | *Josh* (1976) |
| Anita Loos | *A Girl Like I* (1966); *Kiss Hollywood Good-Bye* (1974); *A Cast of Thousands* (1977) |
| Sophia Loren | *Sophia: Living and Loving* (1979) with A. E. Hotchner |
| Mercedes McCambridge | *The Two of Us* (1961) |
| Tim McCoy | *Tim McCoy Remembers the West* (1977) with Ronald McCoy |
| Rod McKuen | *Finding My Father* (1976) |
| Shirley MacLaine | *Don't Fall Off the Mountain* (1970); *You Can Get There from Here* (1975); *Out on a Limb* (1983) |
| Ed McMahon | *Here's Ed* (1976) with Carroll Carroll |
| Groucho Marx | *Groucho and Me* (1959); *Memoirs of a Mangy Lover* (1964); *The Groucho Letters* (1967) |
| Harpo Marx | *Harpo Speaks!* (1961) |
| Raymond Massey | *When I Was Young* (1976); *A Hundred Different Lives* (1979) |
| Adolphe Menjou | *It Took Nine Talors* (1952) |
| Melina Mercouri | *I Was Born Greek* (1971) |
| Ethel Merman | *Who Could Ask for Anything More?* (1956) |

231

| | |
|---|---|
| Ray Milland | *Wide-Eyed in Babylon* (1974) |
| Ann Miller | *Miller's High Life* (1974) |
| Vincente Minnelli | *I Remember It Well* (1974) with Hector Arce |
| Marilyn Monroe | *My Story* (1974) |
| Kenneth More | *Happy Go Lucky* (1959) |
| Robert Morley | *Robert Morley: A Reluctant Autobiography* (1966) with Sewell Stokes |
| George Murphy | *Say, Didn't You Use to Be George Murphy?* (1970) |
| Hildegarde Neff | *The Gift Horse* (1971) *The Verdict* (1975) |
| Pola Negri | *Memories of a Star* (1970) |
| David Niven | *The Moon's a Balloon* (1972); *Bring on the Empty Horses* (1975) |
| Elliott Nugent | *Events Leading Up to the Comedy* (1965) |
| Pat O'Brien | *Wind at My Back* (1963) |
| Sir Laurence Olivier | *Confessions of an Actor* (1983) |
| Jack Paar | *I Kid You Not* (1959) with John Reddy; *My Saber is Bent* (1961) with John Reddy |
| Lilli Palmer | *Change Lobsters and Dance* (1975) |
| Joe Pasternak | *Easy the Hard Way* (1956) |
| Mary Pickford | *Sunshine and Shadow* (1955) |
| Otto Preminger | *Preminger: An Autobiography* (1977) |
| Anthony Quinn | *Original Sin* (1972) |
| Basil Rathbone | *In and Out of Character* (1956) |
| Ronald Reagan | *Where's the Rest of Me?* (1965) |
| Liz Renay | *My Face for the World to See* (1971) |
| Jean Renoir | *Renoir: My Life and My Films* (1974) |
| Paul Robeson | *Here I Stand* (1958) |
| Edward G. Robinson | *All My Yesterdays* (1973) |
| Mickey Rooney | *I. E.* (1965) |
| Rosalind Russell | *Life is a Banquet* (1977) with Chris Chase |

| | |
|---|---|
| Margaret Rutherford | *An Autobiography* (1972) |
| S. Z. Sakall | *The Story of Cuddles* (1953) |
| George Sanders | *Memoirs of a Professional Cad* (1960) |
| Joseph Schildkraut | *My Father and I* (1959) |
| Budd Schulberg | *Moving Pictures: Memories of a Hollywood Prince* (1981) |
| Omar Sharif | *The Eternal Male* (1976) with Marie-Therese Guinchard |
| Simone Signoret | *Nostalgia Isn't What It Used to Be* (1978) |
| Walter Slezak | *What Time's the Next Swan?* (1962) |
| Donald Ogden Stewart | *By a Stroke of Luck* (1975) |
| Gloria Swanson | *Swanson on Swanson* (1980) |
| Gene Tierney | *Self-Portrait* (1978) with Mickey Herskowitz |
| Lana Turner | *Lana: The Lady, the Legend, the Truth* (1982) |
| Liv Ullmann | *Changing* (1976) |
| Peter Ustinov | *Dear Me* (1977) |
| Rudy Vallee | *Let the Chips Fall. . . .* (1975) |
| King Vidor | *A Tree is a Tree* (1953) |
| Josef von Sternberg | *Fun in a Chinese Laundry* (1965) |
| Raoul Walsh | *Each Man in His Own Time* (1974) |
| Jack Warner | *My First Hundred Years in Hollywood* (1965) with Dean Jennings |
| Ethel Waters | *His Eye is on the Sparrow* (1953) |
| Mae West | *Goodness Had Nothing to Do with It* (1959); *Life, Sex and ESP* (1975) |
| Emlyn Williams | *George* (1927); *Emlyn* (1974) |
| Tennessee Williams | *Memoirs* (1975) |
| Walter Winchell | *Winchell Exclusive* (1975) |
| Shelley Winters | *Shelley: Also Known as Shirley* (1980) |
| Keenan Wynn | *Ed Wynn's Son* (1960) |
| Loretta Young | *The Things I Had to Learn* (1962) |

| Henny Youngman | *Take My Wife ... Please* (1973) with Carroll Carroll |
| Blanche Yurka | *Bohemian Girl* (1970) |
| Adolph Zukor | *The Public Is Never Wrong* (1945) |

# CELEBRITY AUTOGRAPHS

The autographs of living celebrities tend to be worth less than those of their dearly departed brethren, but the following famous (and infamous) people are among those whose autographs, according to autograph expert Charles Hamilton, have the greatest value:

|  | Autograph Value |
|---|---|
| Greta Garbo | $1,000 |
| Prince Charles of England | 300 |
| Idi Amin | 200 |
| Fidel Castro | 150 |
| Elizabeth II of England | 150 |
| Yuri Andropov | 150 |
| Sirhan Sirhan | 100 |
| Princess Diana | 100 |
| John Hinckley, Jr. | 75 |
| Gian-Carlo Menotti | 75 |
| Shirley Temple (as a child) | 50 |
| J. D. Salinger | 50 |
| James E. Carter | 40 |
| David Berkowitz | 35 |
| Andrew Wyeth | 30 |
| Gerald R. Ford | 25 |

## GUESTS ON THE FIRST ED SULLIVAN
## TV SHOW

Ed Sullivan was a television phenomenon. He was a man of ostensibly little talent and was not polished or charismatic, to say the least. But his network television show aired on CBS for twenty-three years, from June 20, 1948 to June 6, 1971; for many years his "The Toast of the Town" was a top-ten rated show. Fellow columnist Earl Wilson once commented that "Ed Sullivan knows what the public likes and one of these days he's going to give it to them." Comedian Fred Allen said that "Ed Sullivan will be a success as long as other people have talent." And putting it another way, comedian Alan King, a frequent guest on the show, observed, "Ed does nothing but he does it better than anyone else on television."

For the record, Ed Sullivan's guests on the first broadcast, June 20, 1948, were as follows:

Dean Martin and Jerry Lewis (comedy team)
Eugene List (pianist)
John Kokoman (singing New York fireman)
Kathryn Lee (ballerina)
Monica Lewis (singer)
Richard Rodgers and Oscar Hammerstein (composer, lyricist)
Lee Goodman and Jim Kirkwood (comedy team)
Ruby Goldstein (fight referee)

Plus six June Taylor dancers ("The Toastettes") and a 14-man orchestra led by conductor Ray Bloch.

# "THE TODAY SHOW"'S FEMALE COHOSTS

Most early morning television viewers can remember the male hosts (Dave Garroway, Hugh Downs, and others) of "The Today Show" but forget the female cohosts, especially before Barbara Walters became so closely identified with the show. The following women, for the record, have had the job:

Estelle Parsons                   Louise King
Helen O'Connell                   Maureen O'Sullivan
Betsy Palmer                      Barbara Walters
Florence Henderson                Jane Pauley
Beryl Pfizer

Note: Arline Frances occasionally substituted for Dave Garroway when he was on vacation; however, Miss Frances was never an official cohost.

# JOHNNY CARSON'S FIRST GUESTS ON "THE TONIGHT SHOW," OCTOBER 2, 1962

After Jack Paar departed from late night television, NBC used a host of hosts for "The Tonight Show," including Art Linkletter, Joey Bishop, Bob Cummings, Merv Griffin, Jack Carter, Jan Murray, Peter Lind Hayes and Mary Healy, Soupy Sales, Mort Sahl, Steve Lawrence, Jerry Lewis, Jimmy Dean, Arlene Francis, Jack E. Leonard, Hugh Downs, Groucho Marx, Hal March, and Donald O'Connor. But NBC was just biding time for six months until Johnny Carson, then a daytime quiz show host, could become available when his contract would expire with ABC.

Unlike his predecessors, zany Steve Allen and the emotional, unpredictable Paar, Johnny seduced late-night television viewers with his all-American appeal, consistency, quick wit, and naughty irreverence, and he has been doing it for more than twenty years. Among his frequent guests have been Joan Rivers, David Brenner, and Steve Martin, but the following people were Johnny's guests on his first "Tonight" show broadcast back on October 2, 1962:

Mel Brooks                        Groucho Marx
Tony Bennett                      Rudy Vallee
Joan Crawford

## THE GARDEN OF ALLAH DENIZENS

Once the country home of Alla Nazimova, the Russian-born silent-screen star, the Garden of Allah was converted into a hotel in 1926 and became the hostelry for scores of actors, actresses, and assorted intellectuals temporarily located in the movie capital. On any given day, at any given time, anything could happen. Marlene Dietrich might prance around in the nude, Errol Flynn might seduce or fight with his current love object, and Ernest Hemingway might give a speech on behalf of Loyalist Spain. Per square foot, more talent was quartered (and probably dissipated) in that celebrated sanctuary than anywhere else in the country. Here are a few of the notable people who were guests at the Garden of Allah at one time or another:

Lauren Bacall
Tallulah Bankhead
Robert Benchley
Lucius Beebe
Humphrey Bogart
Clara Bow
Fanny Brice
Louis Bromfield
Louis Calhern
John Carradine
Ruth Chatterton
Marc Connelly
Lili Damita
Marlene Dietrich

F. Scott Fitzgerald
Errol Flynn
Greta Garbo
Jackie Gleason
Ruth Gordon
Sheilah Graham
Jascha Heifetz
Ernest Hemingway
Woody Herman
Garson Kanin
Michael Kanin
George S. Kaufman
Buster Keaton
Ring Lardner

Charles Laughton
Joe E. Lewis
The Marx Brothers
Somerset Maugham
Dudley Nichols
John O'Hara
Dorothy Parker
Sergei Rachmaninoff
Artie Shaw
Frank Sinatra

Red Skelton
Donald Ogden Stewart
Leopold Stokowski
Igor Stravinsky
Hugh Walpole
Orson Welles
Paul Whiteman
Thomas Wolfe
Alexander Woollcott
Roland Young

# THE ALGONQUIN ROUND TABLE

In the 1920s the Algonquin Hotel in Manhattan became the meeting place of some of New York's most talented and witty people. They gathered at a special reserved table in the main dining room at lunchtime to exchange playful banter, insults, repartee, and general irreverence. The following men and women—mostly writers, producers, and playwrights—were the core members of this elite group, which became known as the "Vicious Circle":

Franklin P. Adams
George Backer
Joyce Barbour
Robert Benchley
Irving Berlin
Paul Hyde Bonner
Gerald Brooks
Heywood Broun
Raoul Fleischmann
Crosby Gaige

Beatrice Kaufman
George S. Kaufman
Harpo Marx
Alice Duer Miller
Henry Wise Miller
Dorothy Parker
Harold Ross
Herbert Bayard Swope
Alexander Woollcott

Other members through the years included Donald Ogden Stewart, Marc Connelly, Edna Ferber, Jascha Heifetz, Howard Dietz, Charles MacArthur, Peggy Wood, and Herman J. Mankiewicz.

# FAMOUS PEOPLE WHO LIVE (OR LIVED) AT THE DAKOTA*
### 1 West 72nd Street, New York, NY

When the Dakota was built in 1884, it was considered to be on the wrong side of town and "too far up." For many years it stood like a castle amid shanties right off Central Park. Designed by architect Henry Hardenbergh (later known for the hotels that he designed, the Plaza in New York, the Copley Plaza in Boston, and others), the Dakota's architectural style is officially called German Renaissance. The West Side of Manhattan is not quite as fashionable as the East Side; but the following celebrities live or have lived in what is probably the most fashionable building in the Big Apple:

Lauren Bacall (actress)
Leonard Bernstein (conductor)
Amanda Burden (socialite)
Rosemary Clooney (singer)
Larry Ellman (restaurateur)
José Ferrer (actor)
Roberta Flack (singer)
Ruth Ford (actress)
John Frankenheimer (director)
Betty Friedan (feminist author)
Paul Gallico (writer)
Judy Garland (actress, singer)
Judy Holliday (actress)
Fannie Hurst (novelist)
William Inge (playwright)
Boris Karloff (actor)
Sidney Kingsley (playwright)
John Lennon (singer, composer)
Warner Le Roy (restaurateur)
Jo Mielziner (set designer)
Patrick O'Neal (actor)
Yoko Ono (artist)
Jack Palance (actor)
Dotson Rader (writer)
Gregory Ratoff (director)
Rex Reed (film critic)
Jason Robards (actor)
Robert Ryan (actor)
Zachary Scott (actor)
Eugenia Sheppard (columnist)
Gwen Verdon (dancer)

# CELEBRITIES WITH A PLACE IN MALIBU

Malibu has a population of only 20,000, but the California coastline town is the retreat of more stars than MGM ever had on contract. Here are some of the celebrities who have a place in Malibu:

Herb Alpert
Julie Andrews
Anne Bancroft
Lloyd Bridges
Christie Brinkley
Mel Brooks
Genevieve Bujold
Dyan Cannon

*Source: Life at the Dakota, Stephen Birmingham (N.Y.: Random House, 1979)

Johnny Carson
Cheech
Dick Clark
Bruce Dern
Bob Dylan
Blake Edwards
Farrah Fawcett
Eydie Gorme
Lou Gosset
Lorne Greene
Larry Hagman
Goldie Hawn
Jascha Heifetz
Dustin Hoffman
John Houseman
Tim Hutton
Bruce Jenner
Billy Joel
Jennifer Jones
Stacy Keach
Billie Jean King
Jack Klugman
Kris Kristofferson
Michael Landon
Jack Lemmon

Rich Little
Ali MacGraw
Shirley MacLaine
Lee Majors
Dick Martin
Walter Matthau
Burgess Meredith
Joni Mitchell
Olivia Newton-John
Carroll O'Connor
Ryan O'Neal
Tatum O'Neal
Robert Redford
Don Rickles
Linda Ronstadt
Katharine Ross
Martin Sheen
Dinah Shore
Steven Spielberg
Rod Steiger
Rod Stewart
Barbra Streisand
Flip Wilson
Shelley Winters

## MARTHA'S VINEYARD CELEBRITIES

Martha's Vineyard is not quite Malibu, to say the least. But it does attract a fair number of well-known people, most of whom are celebrities but not of the movie-star variety. Here is a sampler of the people who can be seen kibbitzing at the Vineyard Haven Yacht Club on a lazy July afternoon or who can be seen cracking a lobster at an Edgartown restaurant:

Cleveland Amory
Dan Aykroyd
Leonard Bernstein
Robert Brustein
Art Buchwald
James Cagney
Walter Cronkite
Jules Feiffer
Ruth Gordon

Lillian Hellman
Garson Kanin
Patricia Neal
Harry Reasoner
Carly Simon
William Styron
James Taylor
Mike Wallace

## FAMOUS LAST WORDS AND EPITAPHS

**Max Baer** (died 1959)
"Oh God, here I go!"

**Phineas T. Barnum** (died 1901)
"How were the circus receipts tonight at Madison Square Garden?"

**John Barrymore** (died 1942)
To his friend Gene Fowler: "Tell me Gene, is it true that you're the illegitimate son of Buffalo Bill?"
To his brother Lionel: "You heard me, Mike."
In an interview shortly before his death: "Die? I should say not, dear fellow. No Barrymore would allow such a conventional thing to happen to him."

**Robert Benchley** (died 1945)
After reading a book entitled *Am I Thinking?*, he wrote the following comment on the title page: "No. And supposing you were?"

**Constance Bennett** (died 1965)
Her suggested epitaph, in response to a fan magazine inquiry: "Do not disturb."

**Paul Bern** (died 1932)
To his wife, Jean Harlow, he left the following suicide note: "Dearest Dear, Unfortunately this is the only way to make good the frightful wrong I have done you. And to wipe out my abject humiliation."

**Humphrey Bogart** (died 1957)
To Lauren Bacall: "Good-bye kid, hurry back."

**Clara Bow** (died 1965)
"I've been working hard for years and I need a rest. So I'm figuring on going to Europe for a year or more when my contract expires."

**Enrico Caruso** (died 1921)
"Doro, I can't get my breath!"

**Noel Coward** (died 1976)
To his friend Cole Lesley: "Goodnight my darlings, I'll see you tomorrow."

**Bing Crosby** (died 1977)
"That was a great game of golf, fellers."
When asked to write his own epitaph by a fan magazine: "He was an average guy who could carry a tune."

**James Dean** (died 1955)
"My fun days are over."

**Jeanne Eagels** (died 1944)
"I'm going to Dr. Caldwell's for one of my regular treatments."

**Douglas Fairbanks, Sr.** (died 1939)
"I've never felt better."

**W. C. Fields** (died 1946)
He kidded about using the following line on his epitaph but it was not used: "On the whole, I'd rather be in Philadelphia."

**F. Scott Fitzgerald** (died 1940)
To Sheilah Graham, who asked him if he wanted her to buy chocolate bars at Schwab's drugstore: "Good enough, they'll be fine."

**Erroll Flynn** (died 1959)
"I've had a hell of a lot of fun and I've enjoyed every minute of it."

**Clark Gable** (died 1960)
His last lines on camera, to Marilyn Monroe: "Just head for the big star straight on. The highways under it take us right home."

**Samuel Goldwyn** (died 1974)
To Richard Nixon, who awarded him the Medal of Freedom "for producing good, entertaining, exciting movies that were not dirty": "You have a lot to do these days."

**Cary Grant** (1904–    )
In response to a fan magazine request for him to write his own epitaph: "He was lucky, and he knew it."

**Harry Houdini** (died 1926)
"I am tired of fighting. I guess this thing is going to get me."

**Al Jolson** (died 1950)
"This is it. I'm going, I'm going."

**George S. Kaufman** (died 1961)
"I'm not afraid anymore."

**Carole Landis** (died 1948)
A suicide note: "Dearest Mommie. I'm sorry, really sorry to put you through this. But there is no way to avoid it. I love you darling. You have been the most wonderful Mom ever. And that applies to all our family. I love each and every one of them dearly. Everything goes to you. Look in the files and there is a will which decrees everything. Good-bye my angel. Pray for me."

**Louis B. Mayer** (died 1957)
Said about Mayer after his funeral: "The only reason so many people attended his funeral was that they wanted to make sure he was dead."

**Edward R. Murrow** (died 1965)
To his wife: "Well Jan, we were lucky at that."

**Waslaw Nijinsky** (died 1950)
"Mamsha!"

**Anna Pavlova** (died 1931)
"Get my 'Swan' costume ready."

**Dorothy Parker** (died 1967)
To Beatrice Ames: "I want you to tell the truth. Did Ernest [Hemingway] really like me?"
When asked to write her own epitaph: "Excuse my dust."

**Damon Runyon** (died 1946)
"You can keep the things of bronze and stone and give me one man to remember me just once a year."

**George Bernard Shaw** (died 1950)
To his nurse: "Sister, you're trying to keep me alive as an old curiosity. But I'm done, I'm finished. I'm going to die."

**Konstantin Stanislavski** (died 1938)
About his sister: "I've lots to say to her, not just something. But not now. I'm sure to get it all mixed up."

**Carl "Alfalfa" Switzer** (died 1959)
Just before he was shot in a bar: "I want that fifty bucks you owe me and I want it now!"

**Rudolph Valentino** (died 1926)
"Don't pull down the blinds. I feel fine. I want the sunlight to greet me!"

**Karl Wallenda** (died 1978)
"The only place I feel alive is the high wires."

**Ethel Waters** (died 1977)
In an interview just before she died: "I'm not afraid to die, honey. In fact I'm kind of looking forward to it. I know that the Lord has his arms wrapped around this big, fat sparrow."

**Florenz Ziegfeld** (died 1932)
Dying but imagining himself at an opening night: "Curtain! Fast music! Light! Ready for the last finale! Great! The show looks good, the show looks good!"

# DEATH AT AN EARLY AGE
"He whom the gods love, dies in youth."
—Ancient Roman epitaph

| | Age at Death | | |
|---|---|---|---|
| Olive Thomas | 20 | Adrienne Lecouvreur | 38 |
| Freddie Prinze | 22 | Marilyn Miller | 38 |
| James Dean | 24 | Gia Scala | 38 |
| Françoise Dorléac | 25 | Harry Chapin | 39 |
| Russ Columbo | 26 | John Garfield | 39 |
| Jean Harlow | 26 | Carol Haney | 39 |
| Bobby Harron | 26 | Sabu | 39 |
| Barbara LaMarr | 26 | Lenny Bruce | 40 |
| Bobby Driscoll | 28 | Jean Seberg | 40 |
| Carole Landis | 29 | Dorothy Dandridge | 41 |
| Brandon De Wilde | 30 | Carmen Miranda | 41 |
| Wallace Reid | 30 | Jeff Chandler | 42 |
| Thelma Todd | 30 | Judy Holliday | 42 |
| Renée Adorée | 31 | Elvis Presley | 42 |
| Alfalfa Switzer | 31 | Godfrey Cambridge | 43 |
| Rudolph Valentino | 31 | Linda Darnell | 43 |
| Carole Lombard | 32 | Natalie Wood | 43 |
| Mabel Normand | 32 | Billie Holiday | 44 |
| Kay Kendall | 33 | Tyrone Power | 44 |
| Maria Montez | 33 | Montgomery Clift | 45 |
| Alma Rubens | 33 | Laurence Harvey | 45 |
| John Belushi | 34 | Anna Held | 45 |
| Jayne Mansfield | 34 | Fatty Arbuckle | 46 |
| Jeanne Eagels | 35 | Lon Chaney | 47 |
| Marilyn Monroe | 36 | Judy Garland | 47 |
| Lupe Velez | 36 | Audie Murphy | 47 |
| Sal Mineo | 37 | Margaret Sullavan | 48 |
| Robert Walker | 37 | Jack Cassidy | 49 |
| John Gilbert | 38 | Pearl White | 49 |
| Mario Lanza | 38 | Steve McQueen | 50 |

# DIED OF CANCER

Bud Abbott
Laverne Andrews
Theda Bara
Richard Barthelmess
Clyde Beatty
Jack Benny
Humphrey Bogart
Bruce Cabot
Jack Carson
Nat King Cole
Gary Cooper
Marion Davies
Brian Donlevy
Marie Dressler
Dan Duryea
Fernandel
Hoot Gibson
Betty Grable
Laurence Harvey
Jean Hersholt
Judy Holliday
Edward Everett Horton
Emil Jannings
Buster Keaton
Charles Laughton
Harold Lloyd
Fredric March
Hattie McDaniel
Steve McQueen
Thomas Mitchell
Edward R. Murrow
Eva Peron
ZaSu Pitts
Dick Powell
Quentin Reynolds
Charles Ruggles
Damon Runyon
Rosalind Russell
Robert Ryan
Zachary Scott
Ann Sheridan
Gertrude Stein
Robert Taylor
Sidney Toler
Franchot Tone
Lurleen Wallace
John Wayne
Marie Wilson
Ed Wynn

# DEATH BY UNUSUAL CAUSES

## Suicides

Pedro Armandariz (1963)
Paul Bern (1932)
Charles Boyer (1978)
Dorothy Dandridge (1965)
Bella Darvi (1971)
Albert Dekker (1968)
Peter Duel (1971)
Jeanne Eagels (1929)
Bobby Harron (1920)
Phyllis Haver (1960)
George Hill (1934)
Carole Landis (1948)
Max Linder (1925)
Milos Milos (1966)
Marilyn Monroe (1962)
George Reeves (1959)
George Sanders (1972)
Jean Seberg (1979)
Everett Sloan (1965)
Margaret Sullavan (1960)

246

Lou Tellegen (1934)
Olive Thomas (1920)
Thelma Todd (1935)
Helen Twelvetrees (1959)

Lupe Velez (1944)
Doodles Weaver (1983)
Grant Withers (1959)
Anna May Wong (1940)

## Homicides

Bob Crane (1978)
Thomas H. Ince (1924)
Victor Killian (1982)
Sal Mineo (1976)
Ramon Novarro (1968)

Pier Paolo Pasolini (1975)
Carl "Alfalfa" Switzer (1959)
Sharon Tate (1969)
William Desmond Taylor (1922)

## Drug Overdoses (Possible Suicides)

Nick Adams (1968)
Pier Angeli (1971)
John Belushi (1982)
Lenny Bruce (1966)
Don Castle (1966)
Judy Garland (1969)

Jimi Hendrix (1970)
Janis Joplin (1970)
Chester Morris (1970)
Gia Scala (1972)
Inger Stevens (1970)
Philip Van Zandt (1958)

## Airplane Crashes

Vernon Castle (1918)
Jim Croce (1973)
Kenneth Hawks (1930)
Buddy Holly (1959)
Leslie Howard (1943)
Carole Lombard (1942)
Herbert Marshall (1966)
Glenn Miller (1944)

Audie Murphy (1971)
Otis Redding (1967)
Jim Reeves (1964)
The Big Bopper (1959)
    (Jiles Perry Richardson)
Will Rogers (1935)
Mike Todd (1958)
Richie Valens (1959)

## Car Crashes

Larry Blyden (1975)
Charles Butterworth (1946)
James Dean (1955)
Brandon De Wilde (1972)
Françoise Dorléac (1967)

Bernard Gorcey (1955)
Ernie Kovacs (1962)
Jayne Mansfield (1967)
Tom Mix (1940)
F. W. Murnau (1931)

## Other Causes

Russ Columbo (shot) (1934)
Linda Darnell (fire) (1965)
Richard Farina (motorcycle accident) (1966)
Joe Flynn (drowning) (1974)
Mark Freshette (prison accident) (1975)
William Holden (fall) (1981)

Brian Jones (drowning) (1969)
Buck Jones (fire) (1942)
Alan Ladd (?) (1964)
Billy Laughlin (scooter/truck accident) (1948)
Maria Montez (drowning) (1951)
Jessica Savitch (drowning) (1983)
Natalie Wood (drowning) (1981)

# FAMOUS PARENTS OF SUICIDES

Children of celebrities often suffer the stress of being overshadowed by their parents' success and fame. Some of the offspring cannot endure the pressure and for that or other reasons some of them have committed suicide. The following list shows a few of the casualties:

| Parent | Child (Age at Death) |
| --- | --- |
| Charles Boyer | Michael Boyer (21 years old) |
| Dan Dailey | Dan Dailey III (27 years old) |
| Robert Frost | Carol Frost (38 years old) |
| Art Linkletter | Diane Linkletter (19 years old) |
| Mary Tyler Moore | Richard Meeker (24 years old) |
| Paul Newman | Allan Scott Newman (28 years old) |
| Eugene O'Neill | Shane O'Neill (57 years old) |
| | Eugene O'Neill, Jr. (40 years old) |
| Gregory Peck | Jonathan Peck (30 years old) |

# CELEBRITY CEMETERIES: THE LAST REPORTS

In real life, celebrities tend to flock to certain "In" places like the Polo Lounge, Studio 54, and Elaine's and to exclusive resort areas like Palm Springs, Palm Beach, and Martha's Vineyard.

This flocking tendency applies not only in life but in death. There are even "In" cemeteries at which famous people are buried. Among these celebrity cemeteries are Forest Lawn Memorial Park in Glendale, California; Hollywood Memorial Park in Los Angeles; Woodlawn Cemetery in the Bronx; and Arlington National Cemetery in Arlington, Virginia.

Here are some of the well-known people buried at the above-mentioned "permanent addresses"*:

## BURIED AT FOREST LAWN MEMORIAL PARK
### 1712 Glendale Avenue
### Glendale, California

Gracie Allen
Warner Baxter
Wallace Beery
Humphrey Bogart
Gutzon Borglum
Clara Bow
Joe E. Brown
Francis X. Bushman
Godfrey Cambridge
Jack Carson
Lon Chaney
Nat King Cole
Russ Columbo
Dorothy Dandridge
Walt Disney
Theodore Dreiser
Marie Dressler
William Farnum
W. C. Fields
Errol Flynn
Rudolf Friml
Clark Gable
John Gilbert
King Camp Gillette
Samuel Goldwyn
Sydney Greenstreet

Jean Harlow
Gabby Hayes
Jean Hersholt
Gus Kahn
Buster Keaton
Ernie Kovacs
Alan Ladd
Carole Landis
Charles Laughton
Stan Laurel
Harold Lloyd
Carole Lombard
Ernst Lubitsch
Marjorie Main
Chico Marx
Harpo Marx
Victor McLaglen
Aimee Semple McPherson
Tom Mix
Alla Nazimova
Red Nichols
Jack Oakie
Clifford Odets
Mary Pickford
Dick Powell
Freddie Prinze

*The book *Permanent Addresses* (M. Evans and Company, Inc.), by Jean Arbeiter and Linda D. Cirino, contains a comprehensive listing of places where famous Americans are buried.

George Raft
Wallace Reid
Will Rogers
Ruth St. Denis
David O. Selznick
Casey Stengel
Robert Taylor
Jack Teagarden
Irving Thalberg

Lawrence Tibbett
Spencer Tracy
Ben Turpin
Jess Willard
Grant Withers
William Wrigley, Jr.
Ed Wynn
Florenz Ziegfeld

## BURIED AT WOODLAWN CEMETERY
### 233rd Street and Webster Avenue
### Bronx, New York

Edwin Howard Armstrong
Nora Bayes
Nellie Bly
Arde and Joseph Bulova
Ralph Bunche
Irene and Vernon Castle
George M. Cohan
Lotta Crabtree
Clarence Day
Duke Ellington
David G. Farragut
Frankie Frisch
Jay Gould
W. C. Handy
Victor Herbert
Charles Evans Hughes

Fritz Kreisler
Samuel Henry Kress
Fiorello La Guardia
Bat Masterson
Herman Melville
Marilyn Miller
James Cash Penney
Adam Clayton Powell, Jr.
Theodore Reik
Rudolph Jay Schaefer
Elizabeth Cady Stanton
Joseph Stella
Laurette Taylor
J. Walter Thompson
Harry Payne Whitney
Frank Winfield Woolworth

## BURIED AT ARLINGTON NATIONAL CEMETERY
### Arlington, Virginia

Constance Bennett
Hugo L. Black
Omar Bradley
William Jennings Bryan
Richard E. Byrd
Claire Chennault

William "Wild Bill' Donovan
William O. Douglas
John Foster Dulles
Medgar Evers
James Forrestal
Virgil Grissom

William F. "Bull" Halsey
Dashiell Hammett
Ira Hayes
Marguerite Higgins
Oliver Wendell Holmes
Lew Jenkins
John F. Kennedy
Robert F. Kennedy
Joe Louis
George C. Marshall
Audie Murphy

Ignace Jan Paderewski
Joseph Medill Paterson
Robert E. Peary
John J. Pershing
Walter Reed
Mary Roberts Rinehart
William Howard Taft
Earl Warren
George Westinghouse
Orde Wingate

## BURIED AT HOLLYWOOD MEMORIAL PARK
### 6000 Santa Monica Boulevard
### Los Angeles, California

Louis Calhern
Harry Cohn
Bebe Daniels
Marion Davies
Cecil B. De Mille
Nelson Eddy
Cass Elliott
Peter Finch

Peter Lorre
Adolph Menjou
Paul Muni
Tyrone Power
Bugsy Siegel
Rudolph Valentino
Clifton Webb

# SUBJECT

Sagittarius, 43–46
Salaries, 198–200
    athletes', 169–70
    executives', 198–99
    women speakers', 199–200
Scorpio, 41–43
Second generation actors and
    actresses, *see* Actors and
    actresses
Sex, 121–26
    first experience, 121–24
    quotes on, 124–26
Siblings, 48
Speakers, *see* Public speakers
Sports celebrities, 148–49, 166–72
    Athlete of the Year, 166–69
    golf pros, 172
    highly paid, 169–70
    quotes by, 148–49
    tennis pros, 171
    turned actors, 165–66
Suicides, 248

Tattoos, 128
Taurus, 27–30
Television, 235–36
Tennis players, 171
*Time* (magazine), 161–63
"Today Show, The," 236

"Tonight Show, The," 236
Tony Awards, 205–13
Toupees, 128
*TV Guide* (magazine), 163
Trivia, 91, 223–25
Twins, 55-56

United States-born celebrities, 17
Universities, *see* Colleges and
    universities

Virgo, 36–38

War wounds, 142
Wealth, *see* Richest Americans
*Who's Who in America* (book), 91
Wit and wisdom, *see* Quotes,
    celebrities'
Woodlawn Cemetery (Bronx,
    N.Y.), 250
Women, 162, 199–200, 220–22,
    236
Worst-dressed women, 220–22
Writers, 186–88, 227–34
    of autobiographies, 227–34
    of screenplays, 186–88

Zodiac, signs of, *see* specific sign,
    e.g., Leo